Value-Added
Records Management

Value-Added Records Management

Protecting Corporate Assets, Reducing Business Risks

2nd Edition, Updated and Expanded

KAREN L. SAMPSON

QUORUM BOOKS
Westport, Connecticut • London

Library of Congress Cataloging-in-Publication Data

Sampson, Karen L.
   Value-added records management : protecting corporate assets, reducing business
risks / Karen L. Sampson—2nd ed., updated and expanded.
      p.   cm.
   Includes bibliographical references and index.
   ISBN 1–56720–547–X (alk. paper)
   1. Business records—Management.   2. Information resources management.   I. Title.
HF5736.S25   2002
651.5—dc21   2002023045

British Library Cataloguing in Publication Data is available.

Library of Congress Catalog Card Number: 2002023045
ISBN: 1–56720–547–X

First published in 2002

Quorum Books, 88 Post Road West, Westport, CT 06881
An imprint of Greenwood Publishing Group, Inc.
www.quorumbooks.com

Printed in the United States of America

The paper used in this book complies with the
Permanent Paper Standard issued by the National
Information Standards Organization (Z39.48–1984).

10 9 8 7 6 5 4 3 2 1

Copyright Acknowledgments

Extracts from "High-Performance, Low-Maintenance Records Retention," *The Records &
Retrieval Report* 12(9): November 1996; pp. 1–16, used in Appendix III. Reprinted with
permission.

Contents

Preface

Every business that has employees, customers, or tax bills has record-keeping requirements. Records and information are an element of a company's infrastructure in that they support and protect the business. As the corporate memory, they trace the path of important business decisions and transactions to show evidence of compliance with laws and government regulations.

How well records and information are managed affects an enterprise and its employees, customers, and other stakeholders. We need information systems to retain and recall essential information at will, at the lowest cost possible. But an explosion of information technologies is now a crisis for top management. Today's office environment is populated with a number of independent information systems, and no single system satisfies the increasingly complex and demanding information needs of today's marketplace.

In our competitive, regulated, and litigious business environment, records and information management is a necessary cost of doing business. This business function is not unlike personnel management or accounting services. Yet not all executives know who in their organization is managing the company's information or how well it is being managed.

The records and information management concept is not new. What is new is the nature of the beast. Our information-intensive society exerts pressure on business to produce and process information faster than ever before. The perception that records and information management is about filing systems and records centers must be laid to rest. Today's records and information management function is far more sophisticated, as it encompasses multimedia formats and a wide range of related business risks and legal issues.

We continue to clog the arteries of our important information systems with excess and obsolete information. More and more information is created and retained in a variety of information storage formats. Explosive information growth and rapid changes in technologies are sending information beyond the control of even the most well-intentioned business. We have mountains of paper files and computer printouts. Rolls of microfilm and stacks of microfiche are filling boxes and cabinets. Audio and video tapes are hidden away in corners and desk drawers. Computer disks are scattered throughout offices, and tapes are consuming warehouse space.

We need a new way of thinking about our records and information. Instead of focusing our organizational resources on specific information carriers and technologies, we should focus on the content value of our records and information. Records and information are valuable corporate assets in many ways. They may also be a liability. What distinguishes between their existence as an asset and their existence as a liability is the judicious control and protection of business records and information.

Maintaining the right records for the right time and disposing of the right records at the right time is a perpetual and delicate balancing act. When that balance tips to one side or another, worst-case scenarios may be income losses or senseless losses in court proceedings. Basic records and information management practices identify the valuable and legally required records in all media to be retained and protected in order to meet legal and business obligations. Records no longer needed are destroyed to prevent them from becoming a direct drain on revenues or an unnecessary exposure to liabilities. The fewer and better records that are retained are organized and preserved in a manner that protects legal rights, improves efficiencies, reduces costs, and prevents losses.

PURPOSE OF THIS BOOK

This publication is a revised edition of the work by the same name published in 1992. Much of the original publication is timeless in that the records and information management principles presented change little over time. However, the nature of electronic records in the early 1990s was such that little could definitively be said about application of recordkeeping practices to electronic information systems. Since then, the legal status of electronic records, new and changing technologies, and the growing pervasiveness of electronic information systems have contributed to a wealth of useful and practical knowledge about electronic records and information.

The records and information management principles presented in the first edition are timeless, and they apply as much to electronic records as they do to paper and microfilm records. The dominating presence of information technologies in the workplace, the new uses of these technologies, and progress made in defining their legal status warrant this revised edition.

The purpose of this work is to raise levels of awareness regarding the various roles of records and information management in business today. We remain a long way from fully exploiting the opportunities and the benefits that records and information management has to offer. The gap between actual records and information management practice and its potential is widening, much like the gap between new technologies and worker capabilities. Contributing to this gap are new technologies that fragment the information systems of an enterprise. The lack of support from top management also contributes to the gap between actual practice and potential of records and information management.

Executives, professionals, and managers are the leaders and decision-makers who will make a difference regarding how management of our information resources affects a business. They are ultimately responsible for the design and implementation of a records and information management program—and for whether it adds value to an enterprise or becomes a liability.

Many topics touched on in this book, such as privacy, are deserving of more attention, but they are beyond the scope of this work. This book is intended for general information purposes to present an overview of the roles of records and information management in business. Discussions of issues are general in nature and must not be construed as providing legal advice. Any suggestions offered are based on a presumption of working within the law. Neither the author nor the publisher advocates illegal behavior or impropriety. The reader is encouraged to consult with an attorney concerning specific circumstances and legal questions.

INFORMATION TECHNOLOGIES

The number of pages in this book devoted to information technologies may seem inadequate given the overwhelming presence of electronic information and communications systems in business. These technologies are not the focus here primarily because they are simply business tools that create, process, maintain, and distribute business records and information. Although they are an important means to an end, they are not "the" end. The more valued asset is the content of the recorded information. Records retention, regulatory requirements, and litigation apply to all forms of records and information because they are concerned with the content of the records.

Technology is a wonderful thing. We communicate better. We make better decisions faster because we have instant access to more information. The relentless pace of technological changes presents new opportunities, but it also presents new challenges.

This book does not treat information technologies entirely in a positive light. The reasons are simple: Organizations too often embrace information technologies without consideration of short-term and long-term records and information management functions. Businesses create electronic records, they broadcast record content through e-mail and corporate intranets, and they transact business over the Internet with little thought given to recordkeeping requirements.

When records and information management principles are not applied to electronic records systems, organizations face challenges related to those records in litigation, new information security risks, and information systems and media obsolescence. Until a business gains control of its electronic records, those challenges can become a business crisis.

Being critical of information technologies is not a popular position to take in a business climate that is perpetually acquiring new and improved technologies. To satisfy current information needs through electronic information systems without a plan for future records and information needs is shortsighted. Businesses must concern themselves with preserving the organization's assets and rights, complying with the law, preventing harm to the organization, and preserving the corporate memory through a records and information management program.

CONTENT OVERVIEW

This book provides examples of how a comprehensive records and information management program adds value to a business. The foundational records and information management principles presented here are applicable to most sizes and types of business. Most of the scenarios used throughout the book to illustrate specific points are based on actual events and situations. In some scenarios fictitious company names are used to avoid embarrassing the real-world company that is the subject of the scenario. Likewise, fictitious names are used in scenarios that are fictions based in reality.

Each chapter covers different roles of records and information in various business activities. Individual records and information management principles are cited in more than one chapter because they relate to so many different business objectives and activities. Because the records and information management issues discussed in this book are interrelated or interdependent, cross-references are made to relevant chapters as appropriate. The chapter overviews provided here may assist the reader who wishes to study selected chapters.

The first two chapters illustrate the role of records and information in various business activities and situations. Chapter 1, "Guilty Until Proven Innocent," discusses a number of situations in which proper recordkeeping practices are necessary for an organization to defend itself. Chapter 2, "Preservation of Legal Rights and Business Assets," describes several conditions under which proper recordkeeping practices are necessary for a business to preserve its rights and to protect itself from harm or losses.

Chapter 3, "Threats to Sensitive and Valuable Records and Information," summarizes which records are sensitive and valuable and describes the potential threats to their security. Employers are generally on the defense regarding employee health and safety, employment actions, privacy, and employee behavior. An employer has certain rights to protect its business assets and reputation that relate to worker management. Recordkeeping practices related to both of these aspects of employment are covered in Chapter 4, "Employer Rights and Responsibilities."

Chapter 5, "A Day in Court," examines more specifically a company's rights and obligations regarding its records in litigation proceedings. There may be serious consequences for a company with too many records, too few records, or records not considered trustworthy. This chapter offers litigation management and support strategies.

Responsive information systems enable a business to respond quickly to changing business conditions and expectations of a wide range of constituents. Chapter 6, "The Roles of Records in Corporate Change," discusses various roles of records and information in new business ventures, ownership changes, and other business changes. Related information security requirements are described.

As much as 50 percent of a company's records may be true liabilities in that they have no financial, operational, or legal value. Keeping valueless records is an unnecessary burden and a senseless exposure to potential liabilities. Indiscriminate disposal of records may have even more serious consequences, however. Chapter 7, "Retention and Disposition," explores a number of business and legal considerations that support records retention decisions.

Computer and microform information systems are increasingly used to speed retrieval and consolidate growing volumes of business records. Guidelines for selecting the most appropriate information carrier are offered in Chapter 8, "Integrating Media Choices for the Ultimate Information System." This chapter also discusses achievement of the highest return on investments in records and information systems through appropriate design and integration of those systems.

The three new chapters in this edition are about electronic records and information and related communications technologies. Technologies that support and document business activities create business records in electronic form. Many of the records and information management principles that apply to paper and microfilm records must also be applied to electronic records. Chapter 9, "Electronic Records and Information," frankly describes the good, the bad, and the ugly aspects of electronic records and information. Records and information management responses to information technologies challenges are proposed.

Chapter 10, "The Internet," looks at employee access to the Internet and the challenges to document web site contents and business transactions completed over the Internet. Internet-related issues of privacy, intellectual properties, and security will remain unsettled for the next few years.

Chapter 11, "E-Mail," discusses today's status of e-mail systems use and the resulting business risks. Recordkeeping challenges and litigation risks related to e-mail systems are described in this chapter, along with proposed business responses to those risks.

How well—or how poorly—a business manages its records and information has an impact on the bottom line. Chapter 12, "The Bottom Line," suggests ways that a well-designed, comprehensive records and information management program adds value to the organization.

A comprehensive records and information program necessitates interactions among a number of different business functions and organizational structures. Chapter 13, "Organization and Staffing for Records and Information Management," describes the elements of a records and information management program and suggests how a program may be managed within an organization to optimize the benefits of the program.

Chapter 14, "The Challenges Ahead," summarizes records and information management faced by business today and into the future. Few businesses had smoothly functioning paper and microfilm information systems in place before they turned to electronic information technologies. New perspectives, expertise, and tools are necessary to fully exploit the capabilities of records and information management functions.

The components of a vital records program are outlined in Appendix I, "A Vital Records Program." This Appendix lists the records that should be protected as vital to a business and presents methods to protect them from a catastrophic event.

Appendix II, "Records and Information Security Program," suggests methods to prevent or reduce business risks and losses resulting from unauthorized access to or loss of sensitive and valuable records and information.

Appendix III, "High-Performance, Low-Maintenance Records Retention," condenses and updates an issue of *The Records & Retrieval Report* by the same name. It promotes the functional records retention schedule methodology and offers guidelines for development of a records retention program.

Appendix IV, "Records and Information Management Best Practices," is intended for use by individual employees who are responsible for records and information in their personal work areas. The basic records and information management practices support improved productivity and compliance with an organization's records retention program.

LOOKING AHEAD

It is the wise executive who recognizes the roles of records and information management in protecting a business and improving organizational effectiveness. Sometimes only a crisis of crippling litigation, overcrowded facilities, or a devastating fire can make the importance of effective records and information management painfully obvious. To manage records and information as an asset and a resource, rather than a burden, all employees must organize and control all records and information from the time of their origination to their ultimate disposition.

Most companies have some sort of records and information management program for their paper and microfilm documents. Too many companies, though, have not adopted those policies and principles to their electronic records.

Needed for the long term is an enterprise-wide records and information system that is easy to use, easy to manage, and easy to change. Top management, corporate counsel, and the managers of all existing and future information systems must endorse a unified records and information system. No enterprise has developed the perfect records and information management program on the first attempt, although a handful of companies have come close to doing so. The transformation from today's fragmented information systems into a comprehensive records and information management program will evolve over time.

Records and information management today is both simple and complex. An informed and commonsense approach makes the job a little easier. The same foresight and commitment necessary to build a successful business will be necessary to build a records and information program that supports and protects the enterprise. It could make the difference between mere survival and prosperity.

1

Guilty Until Proven Innocent

No matter how diligently a business tries to identify, understand, and comply with the law, inevitably it will experience some type of government investigation or litigation during its lifetime. In today's litigating society, attorneys are kept busy filing claims and defending their clients against claims involving other businesses, the government, and individuals.

After the explosion of lawsuits, the costs of insuring against them are skyrocketing, along with the jury awards. The expenses and losses related to litigation and government investigation have traditionally been viewed as a cost of doing business. Many businesses settle disputes out of court—even when innocent of the charges—to avoid the high litigation time and expense and to reduce the risks of damaged reputation or adverse ruling.

Criminal penalties and the prospect of imprisonment are relatively new incentives to anticipate the need for a proper defense against any criminal charges. Under Federal Sentencing Guidelines, lesser fines will apply if a firm establishes and enforces procedures aimed at being in compliance with federal laws. So it behooves a corporation to implement a crime prevention program. Documentation of such a program can be used to support a defense.

Government interest in business is expressed through statutes, regulations, and various rules and procedures established to protect the public interest and to assess taxes. Government requirements to routinely report information are an effort to monitor business activities for compliance with the law. The Internal Revenue Service (IRS), Environmental Protection Agency (EPA), and Occupational Health and Safety Administration (OSHA) are among the numerous government agencies intent on monitoring business in the areas of

- environment
- health and safety
- securities
- financial services
- consumer protection

Proper recordkeeping is one of many ways for a business to work within the law to protect itself. Recordkeeping can achieve compliance with the law, demonstrate that compliance, and enable a company to avoid unnecessary charges. Failure to generate and retain required records could lead to government fines and sanctions.

Not every business today is fully aware of the role of records in various business conduct issues or its legal responsibilities and rights regarding records and information. As a result, most businesses do not do much in terms of records management until they are hit with a major lawsuit or government investigation. By then, it may be too costly and time-consuming to correct past neglect—and it is often too late for protection in that particular instance.

The Federal Aviation Administration (FAA) cannot afford to have inspectors for every plane, so it is incumbent upon air carriers to demonstrate through records what aircraft inspections and maintenance activities are performed. When one discount airline did not have its maintenance records readily available for FAA inspection, the airline's fleet was grounded until the company could catch up on its paperwork. The airline never recovered from the grounding and had to shut down for good.

Any business is vulnerable to claims or charges, even when they have no validity. Current and accurate documentation can minimize the expense and burden of a defense. Regardless of whether a government requirement exists to create and maintain certain records, a business should maintain records in order to show compliance with a law and to help prevent unnecessary charges and claims against the business.

As the world prepared to avoid possible chaos from computer systems failures on January 1, 2000, massive amounts of time and expense went into Year 2000 (Y2K) projects. Businesses documented their risk and impact analyses, Y2K project efforts, and system tests. In the event that something did go wrong with a system, this documentation was retained to defend against any claims filed by contracting organizations, shareholders, regulators, customers, or others.

ENVIRONMENTAL ISSUES

Business conduct issues that are of sensitivity to the public, such as claims of environmental violations, often place a company in a position of being guilty until proven innocent. As in cases involving the word of one person against another, proper recordkeeping may be critical in this uphill battle.

Environmental affairs have traditionally been a priority for manufacturers. Today, environmental issues must be considered in product development, packaging, and marketing throughout many other industries.

Any business that uses chemicals or discharges contaminated water and air into the environment is vulnerable to charges of environmental violations. Toxic substances are common in cleaning agents, copy machines, refrigeration equipment, batteries, insulating materials, and more. The toxic substances list from various environmental regulations includes more than 200 pollutants.

The regulations are not always clear, and the knowledge regarding hazardous and toxic materials is not always adequate. In response, government recordkeeping requirements are proliferating in an attempt to develop appropriate controls through more data.

In addition to recordkeeping requirements are information disclosure requirements regarding hazardous materials and environmental problems, including the following:

• OSHA's Hazard Communication Standard and the states' workers-right-to-know laws require that workers be informed of hazardous materials.
• The Securities and Exchange Commission (SEC) requires public companies to disclose any potential and quantifiable financial liabilities regarding environmental obligations.

Individuals found to willingly and knowingly pollute are held personally responsible for environmental damages, and criminal charges may result in fines and prison sentences.

Liability for hazardous waste cleanup can fall on both past and present landowners.

In a landmark Maryland case, a bank foreclosed on a property worth $350,000. Before all was said and done, the bank eventually had to pay $550,000 for an environmental cleanup of the property.

The Comprehensive Environmental Response, Compensation, and Liability Act (CERCLA), commonly known as Superfund, is a program to clean up hazardous-waste sites. Under the program's joint and several liability system, parties who have, in the past or in the present, dumped waste at the site may be liable for the cleanup costs.

One corporation used its records to limit its financial obligations for cleanup of a Superfund site. Those records showed that it disposed of only a small fraction of what was found at the site.

Ignorance of the law or ignorance of contamination is no excuse.

The House of Good Intentions hired a painting contractor to sandblast old paint from a two-story tank. Neither the contractor nor the contracting company tested the old paint to see if it contained lead—which, in fact, it did. The contractor disposed of a large volume of the waste in a nonhazardous-waste dump, and failed to clean up all the paint chips at the site. Eventually contaminants leached into the soil and into ground water. Although the contracting company is liable for the cleanup, the firm is relying on the terms of its agreement with the contractor to force the contractor to share responsibility for dumping the toxic waste at the landfill.

Lenders, insurance companies, and others now demand environmental assessments. The environmental services industry has grown dramatically in response to demands for environmental audits. The resulting data and records of an environmental assessment attest to a company's efforts and good faith. The Department of Justice has attempted to reassure companies that they will not be criminally prosecuted if a violation revealed in an audit is reported to the proper regulatory authorities and is corrected in a reasonable time period.

In addition to maintaining environmental assessment records, companies must record or report to regulatory agencies information about hazardous substances, such as:

- logs of toxic materials
- monitoring of air emissions and ground and surface water quality
- compliance with air, water, and waste permits
- accident prevention procedures
- incident reports
- efforts to eliminate or reduce emissions
- remediation and reclamation activities

Accurate and complete environmental recordkeeping is no guarantee against charges of violations. Records of good faith efforts are, however, better than no records at all.

PRODUCT LIABILITY AND PERSONAL INJURY

As new laws, regulations, and court decisions favor the consumer, the scope of consumer responsibility narrows and corporate liability broadens. Headlines about successful claims contribute to the growing number of claims initiated by individuals against business. It is lucrative to sue when an impersonal corporation or insurance company with deep pockets can be compelled to pay.

Although appeals courts tend to reduce large jury awards, the large number of multimillion-dollar jury verdicts is a sign of a rising tide against business. Plaintiffs are asking not only for damages to compensate for losses but also for punitive damages.

Most cases are settled out of court to avoid suffering losses in a trial and the expense of an appeal. The fear of civil liability also has high costs to the U.S. economy. Innovation and research may be stifled, and foreign competitiveness may be reduced along with the workforce. Products are withdrawn from the market because of prohibitive insurance costs or because insurance cannot be bought at any price. Prices are raised to cover the cost to modify production methods and materials.

There are no clear standards for well-intentioned companies to follow and thus be assured they will not be sued—no matter how exemplary their behavior. A company in compliance with government standards has no guarantee against adverse judgments and jury awards.

One couple sued a major retailer and several suppliers for injuries suffered when they used an outdoor cooking grill indoors. They claimed that the warnings on the grill against the product's use indoors should have been written in larger letters. Rather than go through the expense of court and risks of a jury sympathetic to the injured plaintiffs, the defendants settled for $4.8 million.

A new strategy of plaintiff attorneys is to file claims against multiple defendants. After a plane crash, the airline and its manufacturer and suppliers may become defendants. Or when a driver kills someone in an auto accident, the auto manufacturer, auto parts suppliers, city maintenance department, and others may be dragged into the suit as defendants. Litigators often rely on these secondary defendants to settle more quickly than the primary target and to offer up damning evidence against the primary target.

The Food and Drug Administration (FDA) and the Federal Trade Commission (FTC) have numerous regulations intended to protect the consumer. When a manufacturer makes claims about its product, such as "low cholesterol" or "environmentally safe," it must be prepared to show through research, testing, and other documentation that those claims are true. Before a new drug may be sold to the public, drug manufacturers must have documentation from research and development and clinical trials to prove that the drug is safe for consumption.

The FDA also has an interest in tracking controlled substances. Drug distribution records are necessary for recalls, such as when Tylenol capsules were recalled after some were found to be contaminated.

In one court settlement, a drug company agreed to pay a fine of $600,000 as a result of its poor recordkeeping on the delivery of product samples to physicians. Sales personnel who delivered the controlled substances in question failed to record accurately and completely the registration numbers of samples distributed. Because the company had already paid fines for other recordkeeping violations during the previous decade, the government ordered the company to stop the practice of sales representatives' hand-delivering the samples. In the event of further violations, the company will be ordered to pay an additional $500,000.

In addition to records required by government agencies, other records may be necessary in a defense against product liability or personal injury claims. These records may include

- product and material testing results
- production quality control documentation
- equipment and vehicle inspections and maintenance records
- corporate policies and compliance audits

In recent years victims of workplace violence are suing property owners—and winning. Although there is pressure to settle to avoid a trial, an organization may prevail when it has a security program and sound documentation of that program. Among security program documentation records are

- policy and guidelines
- compliance audits
- employee hiring and disciplinary practices
- security inspections
- accurate and complete incident reports created as soon as possible after the incident

As with environmental issues, records of good faith efforts may be better than no records at all for product liability and personal injury claims. However, older documents may be taken out of context, misinterpreted, and used against a defendant.

Manville Corporation, formerly Johns Manville, manufactured asbestos products. After many years of meeting heavy demands for fire-retarding materials in public and government facilities, Manville was the target of liability claims totaling billions of dollars as people developed asbestosis, a lung disease caused by exposure to asbestos.

Over the years, the company failed to implement its records retention program, so older documents that could legally have been destroyed years before the lawsuits began had not been destroyed. Sources close to the case note that many of the records involved in the court proceedings—records dating back to the 1930s—were used by opposing parties to create an impression that Manville knew or should have known that asbestos was hazardous.

To avoid complete ruin of the business, the manufacturer filed Chapter 11 bankruptcy to protect itself from creditors until the claims could be resolved. (The company emerged from reorganization in 1988 as Manville Corporation.) Under the court settlement, Manville initially paid $2.5 billion into a trust fund to cover the claims of current and future victims, and it now operates a warehouse of 16 million pages of documents open for inspection by future claimants.

(Chapters 5, "A Day in Court," and 7, "Retention and Disposition," provide more detail on how records retention and destruction practices affect litigation.)

Release of proprietary information during the discovery process or court proceedings may also be hazardous to the health of a company. Once proprietary information becomes a part of the public record, the company forfeits future protection of the information as a trade secret. In addition, that information will be readily available to any future claimants.

A business has a right to request nondisclosure or limited disclosure of its trade secrets and other confidential information. However, there is a strong presumption of the public's right to know about potential hazards in product liability and environmental claims, so court records are generally made public. When such a disclosure would be too costly to even the most innocent of companies, that defendant may settle the lawsuit out of court.

In the first of many product liability lawsuits expected to go to trial, a defendant company requested that its product development records be protected from public view by sealing the court documents. The request was denied. Rather than risk public disclosure of as many as 8,000 pages of proprietary information, the manufacturer offered a settlement the plaintiff could not refuse. Other than the plaintiff's agreement not to disclose any of the thousands of documents exchanged by the parties, the terms of the settlement were undisclosed. The company thus retains the confidentiality of its proprietary information, and the risk and costs of similar suits in the future are reduced.

(See Chapter 5, "A Day in Court," and Appendix II, "Records and Information Security Program," for more information on the discovery process and protective orders.)

BUSINESS ORGANIZATION AND FINANCE MANAGEMENT

Recordkeeping regarding financial and other transactions is a necessity for good business management. Laws and regulations applicable to specific industries and business transactions also necessitate good recordkeeping.

Accounting records and financial statements primarily serve business management functions. They are also needed for audits for information disclosure or review by

- federal contract compliance managers
- tax and other government agencies
- regulatory commissions
- shareholders
- lending institutions and other creditors

The records to be reviewed in a financial audit may vary from one type of audit to another. Auditors may request anything from invoices and shipping receipts to sales journals and general ledgers. In order to identify any future obligations or debt restrictions, they may also request legal documents that affect the transactions being examined.

Publicly traded companies must provide audited financial statements and other information to the SEC. The SEC regulations and state securities laws are aimed at providing the public with accurate and full disclosure about securities through registration statements, prospectuses, and other information disclosures. Foreign branches of Wall Street firms are not exempt from securities laws. They must set up their recordkeeping to comply with laws of the United States and other countries.

Industries with a history of inaccurate records have become targets for government reforms. The credit-reporting industry, for example, came under fire for sloppy recordkeeping practices that lead to errors in consumer credit files.

Information accuracy requirements also exist in the area of taxes. Generally, an organization is guilty until proven innocent as far as the IRS and other tax authorities are concerned. But complete and accurate records are what proved one manufacturer innocent.

A worldwide heavy equipment manufacturer faced claims by the IRS that it owed additional taxes for an eight-year period. Because the company's retention requirement for those records had not yet expired, the company had records for those years. The records demonstrated not only that the company did not owe taxes but also that it was, in fact, due a refund of $350 million. The company is now going back to fifty states to recover additional tax refunds.

The taxpayer has the burden of proof that the claims made on the return are accurate. The IRS and other tax agencies do not generally define which records must be maintained to support the information reported on tax returns. Supporting documentation for federal and state income tax returns may, however, include

- employee payments and tax-withholding records
- proof of tax payments
- 1099 forms and support documentation
- fixed asset records
- product inventory records
- sales transactions, journals, and tax payments
- check registers

Many other regulatory agencies do not always state that certain records must be created or maintained. Nonetheless, the absence of those records may result in a loss of rights, such as the right to a defense.

The FTC has established time requirements for shipment of mail-order merchandise to buyers. When the seller has no records that show compliance with the regulation, the FTC may presume failure to comply with the time requirement.

When the Justice Department investigates companies for possible price-fixing, the following records are often needed for the investigation:

- pricing documents of recent years
- expense account documents
- telephone records
- e-mail messages
- sales representative and executive diaries and calendars
- market studies

Detailed records may also be necessary in the event of antitrust investigations. The Department of Justice or the FTC reviews potential mergers, acquisitions, or strategic alliances for possible antitrust violations. SEC requirements may also be applicable if securities or stock transactions are involved. Antitrust violations, not to be taken lightly, may result in any of the following:

- liability for treble damages
- fines or prison sentences

- court or government supervision of operations
- divestiture of stock or assets or other business relationships

Once a charge is made, the target company will rely heavily on its records to show its innocence.

Important decisions that may affect competitive relationships, agreements with suppliers or distributors, and proposed acquisitions or mergers must be documented. Such documentation may include

- contacts with competitors, customers, and distributors
- participation in specific events
- formal agreements
- rationale for an acquisition, merger, or strategic alliance
- explanation of how injury to competition is avoided

It is best to make a record of compliance before—not after—being sued or investigated.

RECORDKEEPING NECESSITIES

Organizations create and maintain records primarily to meet their own business needs, but litigation risks and government regulations also compel creation of complete and accurate records. Laws and regulations have a greater impact on business today than they did twenty years ago, and they are in a constant state of change. Regulations tend to grow fastest in newly regulated industries and in activities that may affect the public welfare or individual rights.

Thousands of federal, state, and local recordkeeping requirements are stated in laws and regulations. Which of those requirements apply to an organization depends on the type of industry and the jurisdictions in which the business operates. The consequences of failure to comply with the law can be serious indeed.

Most statutes and regulations stipulate or imply recordkeeping requirements. Certain records are created and maintained in order to comply with a law or regulation to do so. Other records are created to document a company's compliance with a law or regulation.

Stated or implied recordkeeping requirements may address

- record creation
- acceptable media form(s) of a record
- storage conditions
- record preservation

- information reporting or disclosure
- information security
- retention and destruction

Mandating good recordkeeping are litigation, stricter enforcement of laws, and hefty fines, penalties, and prison sentences. Regulated businesses and those businesses more likely to be involved in litigation will have more extensive recordkeeping requirements than do other businesses. But any organization may need to make its records available for congressional hearings on a product, service, or business practice; review, audit, or investigation by regulatory agencies; and civil or criminal proceedings.

Accurate and timely recordkeeping provides a trail of evidence showing regular patterns of activities to support a company's case. The following general business and recordkeeping practices may help reduce the risk of being sued or help persuade a plaintiff to drop a lawsuit:

- creating contemporaneous notes on meetings and phone calls
- confirming agreements in writing
- documenting internal audits of compliance with regulations and corporate policy
- writing only what you are willing to read aloud in court or to see blown up as a trial exhibit.

Also an important means to compliance with laws and regulations are corporate policies and procedures, developed in consultation with legal counsel. Policies and their documentation may be especially useful in showing good-faith efforts and compliance with various laws.

To avoid violations of software copyright law, The House of Good Intentions has a corporate policy regarding compliance with software licensing agreements. Audits of software on computers and networks are conducted at regular intervals to ensure enforcement of this corporate policy.

Corporate policies on privacy of employee and customer private information are the object of more attention today as lawsuits filed against companies for invasion of privacy are increasing. It is estimated that companies paid more than $60 million to settle privacy violation lawsuits in the 1990s. Privacy policies regarding employee and customer information must be recorded and distributed, and the efforts to enforce those policies must be documented to support a defense.

A records and information management policy and standard practices also contribute to compliance with the law.

If an employee commits a crime using a company's computer network, the employer may be subject to charges under Federal Sentencing Guidelines. Evidence of an employee Internet access policy and an electronic communications security program will be needed to demonstrate efforts to prevent criminal actions by employees. (See Chapter 10, "The Internet," for more on risks related to the security of computer networks.)

Records and information management program documentation may also prove beneficial in a court proceeding when the opposing party demands evidence of a formal records management program. (See Chapter 5, "A Day in Court," and Chapter 7, "Retention and Disposition," for more on the potential consequences when such evidence is nonexistent.)

The legal consequences of not having an adequate records and information management program are becoming more costly, and an increasing number of government agencies require a program in some form.

A business has an obligation to its shareholders, employees, and other stakeholders to support and defend its claims in civil or criminal proceedings. Proper recordkeeping may prevent or minimize the risk of losses in court proceedings or government investigation. When a business does not maintain and protect the right records, the result may be the loss of the right to a proper defense, as discussed in this chapter, or the loss of the right to file a claim, as discussed in the next chapter, "Preservation of Legal Rights and Business Assets."

2

Preservation of Legal Rights and Business Assets

Business records and information are valuable corporate assets to be guarded much like cash and property. They are tools to achieve business objectives and to prevent losses. Indeed, every business has both a right and a responsibility to preserve and protect its legal rights and business assets.

As discussed in Chapter 1, a business must maintain and preserve records necessary to defend itself. An organization will also want to create and protect records in order to

- protect revenues and future income
- analyze business risks
- reduce or eliminate exposure to risk
- file a claim or prosecute criminal actions

An enterprise relies on its own and others' records and information to analyze, reduce, and eliminate business risks that may relate to new ventures, business alliances, losses in court proceedings, or a loss of business to a competitor or a disaster. Records also help protect assets and revenues, as well as the legal right to file a claim or to prosecute another party.

LEGAL RIGHTS AND OBLIGATIONS

The security of records and information may be necessary to comply with statutes, regulations, and contract or licensing agreements. These legal remedies serve to protect the rights of the information owners by defining the obligations of those in possession of certain records and information. An information owner's failure to make a reasonable effort to protect the information not only will jeopardize the secrecy of the information but also may result in a loss of rights to protection under the law. The information owner may find itself unable to prosecute violations or to collect damages from those violations. In addition, those in possession of others' information must safeguard that information in compliance with contracts and licensing agreements.

Laws and Regulations

A number of laws and regulations protect the rights of information owners, define information security requirements, and spell out the obligations of those who possess others' intellectual properties and sensitive information.

The SEC and other regulatory bodies, such as those governing public utilities and financial institutions, require organizations under their jurisdiction to have a business continuity plan, which should include protection of records from disaster.

Computer security statutes, the attorney-client privilege, and SEC regulations relate to the unauthorized disclosure of information. Specific to intellectual properties are trademark, trade secret, patent, copyright, and similar laws.

Trademark registration and trademark laws protect a company's right to a trademark; but even with a trademark registration, a company may jeopardize its rights to that trademark if it does not use it or fails to defend it.

Harley-Davidson Inc. took a motorcycle repair shop to court, claiming trademark infringement by calling itself "Hog Farm" and for pushing "hog" products. The court found in favor of Harley-Davidson, but an appeals court ruled otherwise. The court found the term "hog" was widely used to refer to big motorcycles long before Harley-Davidson tried to cash in on it, and a company is not entitled to protection under trademark law for common descriptive words. In fact, Harley-Davidson had for years tried to disassociate itself from the word in an attempt to avoid any connection with groups such as Hell's Angels, who use the term "hog" for Harley-Davidson motorcycles.

Companies may want to further protect their trademarks by registering them as Internet domain names—the address for an Internet web site. The Cybersquatting Consumer Protection Act of 1999 provides for civil liabilities when a person registers a domain name that is a trademark owned by another or that is "confusingly similar to" another's trademark. In addition, the policy of the nonprofit body responsible for administering the Internet, the Internet Corporation for Assigned Names and Numbers (ICANN), requires registrants to agree not to infringe upon or otherwise violate the rights of a third party and to resolve disputes through arbitration. Of the 3,094 cases decided by this review from 1999 through mid-2001, 81 percent were decided in favor of the trademark holder who brought the complaint.

A trade secret is information that provides a distinct advantage in the marketplace over a competitor who does not know it or use it. Usually developed at considerable expense of time, effort, and dollars, trade secrets may include product and marketing plans, research results (both good and bad), and data on suppliers, customers, financials, and employees. To retain the right to protection under trade secret laws, the information owner must take reasonable and appropriate measures to prevent the secret from becoming available to others without prior authorization.

Patent law and international treaties protect certain intellectual properties. A patent is the exclusive right to make, use, and sell a new and useful design, process, machine, manufactured item, or other composition. The U.S. seventeen-year patent is now the twenty-year standard recognized by the rest of the world. Every major industrialized country is party to the Patent Cooperation Treaty (PCT). An organization must file a PCT application within one year of filing a U.S. patent to begin the process to obtain rights in every member country.

Copyright law protects copyrighted property, including print materials and books, web pages, software, records, tapes, films, and videos. As a general rule, the author owns all exclusive rights to a software program or other work by virtue of creating it. The "work for hire" exception allows that works made by an employee within the course and scope of employment are generally the property of the employer. Contractual agreements are the best way to clarify who owns the copyright on works created by employees or contractors.

A business uses copyright to protect its own work products, and it has an obligation to observe copyright protection of others' copyrighted property. Copyright violations may exist when approval or special arrangement with the owner is not obtained to duplicate another party's materials for use in training programs, to distribute copies of software for use on a number of desktop computers, or to allow copies to be taken home for personal use.

To protect their investments, software developers turn to patent, copyright, and trade secret laws, as well as to licensing agreements and contracts. A software buyer is licensed to use the software under the manufacturer's terms and conditions, which usually prohibit modification, copying, and transfer of the program. Licensing agreements regarding installation of a software package on desktops and networks vary, as do agreements on the number of installations allowed. The law makes no distinction between copying for sale or copying for free distribution, and software copyright owners now have the right to prohibit rental, lending, or leasing of their software.

Privacy Rights and Obligations

Federal, state, and international laws and regulations control the collection, maintenance, use, and dissemination of private customer and employee information. Unauthorized disclosure of such information may violate a law, and it may lead to loss of reputation or business. If someone suffers damages as a result of information disclosure, there is a risk of civil liability.

Records of a closed school were left in the building, which was later sold. The new owner began building renovations and tossed the school's records into trash bins. The school board is now being sued after the records found their way into the hands of the public. The find set off a flurry of gossip, humiliation, harassment, and intimidation because the documents included IQ scores, probation notices, names of families on welfare, and identification of students who were passed to the next grade because of age rather than academic record.

Some regulations dictate how to dispose of private information. A Wisconsin state law, for instance, requires that records containing personal information, such as Social Security number or credit card number, must be shredded or otherwise altered to render the personal data unreadable before final disposal.

Privacy laws, various statutes applicable to proprietary information, and certain industry-specific government recordkeeping regulations may protect the privacy of customer or student information. The Gramm-Leach-Bliley Act of 1999 requires financial institutions to notify customers of their privacy policies and to allow customers to "opt out" of practices in which the companies disclose certain financial details to other companies. This law affects banks, mortgage lenders, insurance companies, credit card companies, brokerage services, and more.

United States' firms with international operations face stricter privacy rules than do domestic operations. The European Union (EU) has a number of regulations to control private information in the business sector. Of interest to U.S. businesses is that personal information databases must be registered and personal data cannot be transferred from EU countries without adequate data protection. By 2004 Canada's Personal Information Protection and Electronic Documents Act will affect all Canadian businesses as well as U.S. companies that exchange personally identifiable information with Canadian firms. The act requires businesses to offer Canadian citizens guarantees regarding the collection and use of personal information.

Collective bargaining agreements and federal and state laws may determine employee recordkeeping, access, and disclosure requirements. (See Chapter 4, "Employer Rights and Responsibilities," for more on employee privacy and employer rights.)

Contract law also applies to employment agreements about e-mail and other employee monitoring, and affects privacy policy notices sent to customers or posted on web pages for customers and site visitors.

Contracts and Licensing Agreements

Contracts and agreements with other parties serve to protect the rights of the information owner and to determine the obligations of those who hold or have access to that information. Indeed, contracts are essential in certain situations to clarify ownership of information, such as when an employee or contractor develops intellectual properties.

Government contractors must comply with employment, privacy, and classified information laws and procedures. Any federal contractor is subject to a large number of requirements regarding record creation, record media, and related technical requirements, records retention, and information access. A firm doing business with the Pentagon, the Department of Agriculture, or the FCC is most likely to encounter government classified information to be restricted to those with both a need to know and the proper government clearance.

Contracts with an outside party for services or a product may contain a confidentiality clause to prevent indiscriminate disclosure of certain information. Separate nondisclosure or confidentiality agreements are frequently used for employees, contractors, and suppliers.

As organizations continue to outsource individual business functions, several records and information management issues are raised. Some recordkeeping issues to consider when outsourcing include

When a firm is hired to design a building or perform an environmental site remediation, who owns what records and for how long?

When a service bureau is hired to image paper documents to optical disk, who is responsible for quality control?

When one company processes worker compensation claims for another, who is responsible for maintaining those records for the time period specified in the contracting organization's retention schedule?

If a service provider receives a subpoena to produce the contracting organization's records, what procedure will be followed?

Are adequate security controls in place for data transmission and storage at Internet service providers (ISPs), application service providers (ASPs), or electronic data transmission and storage providers?

What happens to records and data if a service provider goes out of business?

To avoid a number of problems down the road, contracting organizations and service providers must clarify in their service agreement each other's rights and obligations regarding recordkeeping requirements.

Computer auction houses resell computers and servers from companies that have upgraded their systems and from companies that have gone bankrupt. If the seller does not permanently erase the data on the computers, the contract with the auction house or liquidation company must specify who is responsible for that important task. Purchasers of used computer equipment are finding licensed software, employee private data, customer lists, strategic plans, intellectual properties, and more on their bargain equipment. In addition to the loss of intellectual properties, lawsuits are possible if the equipment owner's privacy policy has been violated.

PROTECTION OF THE SENSITIVE AND VALUABLE

Sensitive and valuable records and information, as defined in the next chapter, need to be protected from damage, loss, and unauthorized disclosure in order to protect the business and its assets. Safeguarding sensitive and valuable information enables a company to

- earn income
- collect monies due
- preserve rights under the law
- prevent loss of business
- fulfill legal obligations
- resume business after a disaster

Failure to take measures to prevent information loss or unauthorized access to records could affect the well-being of a company. When valuable and sensitive records are inadequately protected, a business could find itself the subject of any number of newspaper headlines:

- "Obsolete checks found at dump are cashed"
- "Businesses fold in tornado's aftermath"
- "Strikers quote financials"
- "Customers' class-action suit seeks millions for invasion of privacy"
- "Lax security bars company from future government contracts"

In recent years the Federal Bureau of Investigation (FBI) and other government agencies made headlines when it was discovered they sold used computers that still had data on them.

One used computer broker bought two truckloads of used government computer equipment. Discovered later was that the computer tech who prepared the machines for sale had failed to scramble all the files because he used a magnet that was too weak. Among the data remaining on those hard drives were lists of confidential informants and names of people in the federal witness protection program. A frantic call from a U.S. Attorney's office was too late because the broker had already resold the computers. When asked if he read the secret names, the broker said, "I had the equipment for a month. What do you think?"

(For more on threats to records and information security, see Chapter 3, "Threats to Sensitive and Valuable Records and Information.")

Records and Information Vital to a Business

Every business has records that are essential to its operations and to its very existence. The importance of protecting those records is most fully understood and appreciated by those who have experienced losses from a flood, tornado, earthquake, or computer disaster.

The ultimate purpose of a business continuity plan is to ensure that the business, its employees, and its assets will survive a disastrous event. It is good business sense to have a plan that includes protection of records that document legal identity, rights, and obligations.

There are ethical and legal obligations to maintain the viability of a business. Pressure from shareholders, regulatory agencies, insurance carriers, and accounting firms may compel development of a business continuity plan. Insurance companies may offer breaks in insurance premiums to companies that have such a plan.

As businesses grow more dependent on information, those that lose vital electronic and paper records to a catastrophe may be forced out of business if they have not taken proper precautions.

A fire breaks out in a janitor's closet on the top floor of an office building. All floors suffer some kind of damage or loss from heat, smoke, flames, water, and debris. The ForwardThink Corporation's paper files are waterlogged and covered with soot and other debris. Its mainframe computer, which contains customer lists and accounting records, needs extensive repair. To resume operations as quickly as possible, ForwardThink leases computer hardware from a local vendor, as per a previously established agreement. Copies of the accounting and customer accounts software and backup data are recalled from the company's off-site records center for installation on the leased hardware. Damaged paper files are removed to the center for salvage procedures. For their convenience, employees receive a list of affected paper files and the locations of duplicate copies for use in the interim.

Meanwhile, on another floor, the office of Quick 'n' Dirty suffered only minor smoke damage and a power outage. However, the outage and the tremendous surge after power was restored caused serious damage to the company's own computer system as well as to its network server, affecting hundreds of customers. Now several employees are frantically making calls to find new computer equipment, software, and an army of temporaries to create a new database. The owner has been unable to locate the company's insurance records to determine if there is insurance coverage for disruption of business operations or coverage for the damaged computer equipment.

A business continuity plan is much like an insurance policy—one hopes it never has to be used, but it is there when needed.

The business continuity plan of a Charles Schwab & Co. office came to its rescue during the 1989 San Francisco earthquake. The plan identified the airports likely to be open and where to send its computer tapes for processing. The plan also outlined alternatives for phone lines and electronic mail, and it established where to locate emergency headquarters.

From natural and man-made disasters to terrorist attacks, business is at risk.

A terrorist bomb in New York's World Trade Center in 1993 disrupted many businesses and destroyed others. Five commodity exchanges in one of the trade center's buildings lost more than $1 billion in business after the explosion because they had not planned for a temporary facility from which to continue doing business in the event of a disaster. Of the businesses that did not return to the World Trade Center to resume doing business from there, 20 percent failed to open their doors again.

One investment firm, though, was among many other World Trade Center tenants who had planned for a disaster. By the Monday following the explosion, 400 of the firm's 500 employees were back at work in backup office space in New Jersey. Many companies had arrangements with companies in the city, in Denver, and in other locales for backup electronic data and computers, as well as for temporary facilities.

Tragically, terrorists attacked the Word Trade Center again in 2001. As happened after the 1993 attack, plans in place to respond to computer catastrophes came to the rescue of many businesses. Data backup services that automatically duplicate information from one computer to another contributed to the quick reopening of U.S. financial markets.

The loss of human life in this last attack on the World Trade Center was devastating. Even when no one survives to implement a business continuity plan, as so many businesses were able to do in 1993, business records are needed by the courts to dissolve a company. The business's assets must be liquidated to satisfy financial obligations to employee beneficiaries, shareholders, customers, suppliers, and tax agencies.

A business may be affected when disaster hits another organization that is a customer or a supplier. From cut fiber optic cables or scheduled (or unscheduled) power blackouts to a computer virus or other computer failures, thousands of businesses can be directly and indirectly affected. Small retailers and restaurants that depended on World Trade Center business were certainly hurt by the tragedies. The various mutations of the Code Red worm that invaded network servers in 2001 rendered many networks unavailable, causing businesses to lose revenues and the trust of their customers. (Worldwide damage resulting from the Code Red worm is in excess of $2 billion and growing at the time of this writing.) California's power blackouts during an energy crisis disrupted business operations.

In very simple terms, records vital to a business are those records necessary during the emergency conditions and those records required to fulfill its obligations, to retain its rights, and to continue or resume business activities as quickly as possible and at the lowest degree of financial loss and inconvenience. Vital records identify the rights and obligations of the company, employees and their dependents, shareholders and their heirs, customers, creditors, suppliers, bondholders, the government, and the general public.

Hurricanes on the East Coast destroy many businesses. Among the destruction by one hurricane was the computer system for a popular fast food restaurant chain. Despite hurricane warnings, the company did not have a backup information system or backup data readily available after the storm hit. Consequently, the chain was unable to pay its employees or its suppliers for weeks after the storm went back to sea.

Most organizations have some kind of insurance coverage for potential disasters. Insurance helps replace buildings and equipment, but it cannot always replace the loss of records and information. Replacement of lost information may be prohibitively expensive, or it may not even be possible. Despite insurance for the loss of a computer and its software, data replacement may not be possible in the absence of appropriate data backup procedures. Insurance cannot fix the permanent loss of proprietary information or the loss of records that preserve a company's rights—including the right to file insurance claims.

Because insurance is not always a quick fix for the loss of records and information, the safeguarding of certain records becomes a major consideration.

One railroad used an abandoned bomb shelter to store thousands of its legal documents dating back to the nineteenth century. When the area flooded during heavy rains, the ink signatures were washed away from litigation, mineral rights, and rights-of-way documents, destroying their estimated value of millions of dollars. The corporation may discover it has lost certain rights in future legal actions that require production and authentication of any of these documents.

(Appendix I, "A Vital Records Program," includes more information on identification and protection of records and information vital to a business.)

Revenue-Producing Intellectual Properties

Fired by heavy losses worldwide and by increasingly complex technologies, intellectual property matters continue to move up on the list of work handled by corporate law firms. Attorneys are conducting more intellectual property audits, providing more counseling, and filing more lawsuits.

Employees are the most dangerous threat to intellectual properties because as insiders they have access to valuable corporate information, much of which is now in electronic form and as such is more portable without detection. Disgruntled and former employees pose an even greater information security risk.

The FBI arrested one former employee of a communications software company for fraudulently transferring 200 computer files worth $1.5 million. The files were a product of years of research and included critical source code for the firm's copyrighted software program. The former employee then sold the proprietary information to a network of Chinese government and state-owned company officials. Company representatives are unsure if the employee's motive was greed or sabotage for twice being denied a promotion.

Unfortunately, this theft occurred years before implementation of the Economic Espionage Act, which specifically bars theft of intellectual property for a foreign entity. Difficulties fitting the crime into existing wire fraud and computer fraud statutes contributed to the FBI's decision to drop the charges. The company was forced into bankruptcy when financial troubles developed as a result of this intellectual property theft.

Information losses are not always reported to enforcement agencies, and the true value of certain information cannot always be determined. Millions of dollars and years of effort invested in product development can be lost when technical information falls into the hands of a competitor.

The Pharmaceutical Research and Manufacturers of America estimates that the cost to discover a new drug is around $600 million. Pharmaceutical firm research and development expenditures are projected to be more than $30.5 billion in 2001.

The Congressional Research Service estimates that U.S. companies lose $1 to global patent piracy for every $3 worth of products shipped overseas. When a competitor brings a drug to market before or soon after its developer, without having to invest in its research and development, the original developer faces a tough litigation battle while watching hard-earned revenues go into the pocket of a thieving competitor.

The U.S. International Trade Commission can halt importation of products that violate U.S. patent laws, but profits lost to overseas sales are more difficult to fight. Hardest hit by the theft of ideas and inventions in the international market are the entertainment, computer software, and pharmaceutical industries.

Efforts to protect intellectual properties are just good business sense. Failure to take adequate precautions to guard a trade secret may result in loss of the right to protection under the law, in addition to loss of property and future revenues.

The Quick 'n' Dirty Company discovered that a competitor was contacting its customers and offering the competitor's products at just below its own prices. Furious that the competitor had stolen its customer and pricing lists, believed to be trade secrets, Quick 'n' Dirty sought legal counsel.

After reviewing the situation, the attorney advised against pursuing the case because the firm had not taken measures to protect its trade secrets or to prevent disclosure of its customer and pricing information. Records of a recent promotional literature mailing indicate the competitor was on the potential customer mailing list. The promotional literature sent to the competitor included not only prices but also a list of Quick 'n' Dirty's "satisfied customers."

Even when a business secures its development documentation and properly files for patent protection of a product or invention, the company may be called upon to defend its patent rights. Patent documentation, such as notarized notes and sketches of concepts in their development, is critical in the costly and time-consuming defense against any patent challenge. Patent disputes may continue for a number of years, and the legal fees may mount to tens of thousands or even millions of dollars.

Critics of a trend in patent disputes claim that a business with the most litigation clout and staying power can essentially litigate competitors into early settlement or bankruptcy in order to obtain rights to a product.

One small company that depended on two successful products was in the process of implementing a major expansion plan. Another firm filed a temporary injunction to halt production of one of the products until a pending patent infringement suit was settled. Absent income from that product's sales, the company was forced to halt its expansion, default on debts, lay off workers, and face a mountain of legal expenses.

To retain rights to protection under trademark law, a business must

- file a use statement
- use the trademark consistently and continuously
- report trademark infringements
- file protests against any similar mark in a pending patent application
- file affidavits at the appropriate time(s)
- register ownership changes
- renew the registration before its expiration after ten years

The Business Software Alliance (BSA) estimates nearly $12 billion lost in 2000 to illegal software copying worldwide. When the BSA receives a tip about software piracy, the suspect company can expect a visit from armed federal marshals and BSA representatives, who will sniff out illegally copied software.

One university's software applications training center was charged with making unauthorized copies of programs and training manuals. In this first suit against a public university, the university agreed to pay $130,000 to the Software Publishers' Association and to host a national conference on copyright law and software use.

In a separate pursuit of violators, two federal marshals and ten lawyers raided a Chicago engineering firm. After three hours of examining 125 personal computers and finding illegal copies of software, the firm paid $300,000 to settle the issue with the software makers.

(Appendix II, "Records and Information Security Program," provides additional information on protection of intellectual properties.)

Collection of Receivables and Other Monies Due

Proper recordkeeping accelerates and ensures recovery of receivables. A company may suffer business and financial losses from legal actions or the inability to collect monies due when certain records are prematurely lost or destroyed:

- customer and receivables records
- sales agreements and purchasing contracts
- other contracts

As more companies transact business over the Internet, transaction data must be maintained as any other customer transaction records are maintained. Without such records, the company may have difficulties collecting all receivables due.

Contracts and sales agreements spell out the rights and responsibilities of the parties in a business transaction. These legal documents and the records documenting the related sales transactions are critical when a business has difficulty collecting funds owed to the company for its products or services.

Over a period of two years, a small advertising agency supplied a telecommunications giant with marketing materials to promote a satellite dish service. The telecommunications company accumulated $5 million in bills, forcing the advertising agency to lay off employees. The agency hired forensic auditors to locate every file and backup receipt pertaining to its dealings with the client. The more than 30,000 pages in documentation included backup receipts for more than 900 billings.

The agency's attorney is now preparing a breach-of-contract lawsuit that also incorporates a charge of copyright infringement. Evidence of that new misdeed: After the business relationship ended, order forms mistakenly sent to the advertising agency indicated the telecommunications company continued to copy and distribute copyrighted materials.

Agreements and other documentation may also be required when an organization chooses to file a claim against another party for failure to perform as specified in a contract.

The House of Good Intentions contracted out renovation work on one of its facilities. Careless contract employees caused extensive damage to existing carpeting and finished wood trim, and they demolished a sculpture valued at $100,000. The contract stipulated the contractor would be liable for any property damage that occurred as a result of its actions. The House of Good Intentions had records documenting the value of the damaged sculpture and other furnishings, and the contractor eventually paid The House of Good Intentions $200,000 to cover the losses.

Certain business records must be maintained for long periods to continue protecting a company's rights and future income.

A private marine-exploration company invested $50 million and 12 years to recover the largest sunken treasure in U.S. history: thousands of mint-condition gold coins and rare gold bars valued at up to $1 billion. The treasure was found in a ship that sank more than a century ago. Eight insurance companies went to court to gain ownership of the find because they had paid property loss claims after the ship sank.

A U.S. district judge rejected their arguments, however, and ruled that the exploration group could keep the treasure. The judge determined the insurance companies abandoned their rights to any recovery when they destroyed the records related to the ship's demise and when they made no effort to salvage the property. The companies did not retain insurance policies, invoices for shipments, or other records to establish a claim for the gold. The only existing documentation of claims paid after the disaster was in newspaper accounts that contained too many discrepancies to be considered reliable proof.

On appeal, the court found the insurance companies did not fully abandon their right to a claim because the insurers have no written statement to that effect. The insurance companies are entitled to a small portion of the riches. As of this writing, litigation costs continue to mount for both sides.

Records dating back to the 1800s that declare mineral rights and rights-of-way hold significant value today for mining companies, railroads, and other businesses. The longer records are to be maintained, the more likely the need for special measures to preserve the documents.

The ForwardThink Corporation has a number of property deeds dated from 1920 to 1940. Those documents may be required to prove land ownership well into the next century. Because of the extremely poor quality of paper produced in the first half of the twentieth century, ForwardThink microfilmed the deeds and de-acidified the paper documents. The original and microfilmed deeds are stored in separate facilities with environmental and security controls.

INFORMATION DISCLOSURE RIGHTS AND RESPONSIBILITIES

Occasionally a business must disclose sensitive or valuable information to an outside party.

In some situations, such as in a joint venture, it may be appropriate, even desirable, to reveal trade secrets to another party.

The TechTrack firm is developing a peripheral to be marketed in conjunction with a personal computer system. Both TechTrack and the computer manufacturer must share proprietary information and other trade secrets, such as marketing plans, so the peripheral's design will be compatible with the computer system and will be readily available to consumers. To ensure appropriate use of the information and to prevent disclosure beyond the joint partnership, both companies sign nondisclosure agreements, and they carefully mark valuable and sensitive information for easy identification by both parties.

Certain external demands for information disclosure may place that information into the hands of others or in the public domain:

- subpoena and the discovery process in litigation
- court proceedings and government investigations
- government reporting and disclosure requirements

A few owners of proprietary information are reluctant to do business with the federal government because of its information disclosure requirements. When doing business with the government, a company must consider whether the information disclosed to the agency will be subject to the Freedom of Information Act (FOIA). With certain exceptions, the public has a right to request valuable business data that is on file with federal agencies.

In the pursuit for competitor intelligence, businesses not only submit requests for information under FOIA but also take advantage of the right to request information about who is requesting information under FOIA. As a result, a cottage industry has sprung up to provide information about other people seeking information. A handful of companies and individuals have standing requests for the FDA log of FOIA requests. Companies use these services to disguise the source of the request, or they ask an employee to file a request from a private address.

The TechTrack firm frequently files FOIA requests for FOIA queries filed by others for information about its competition because the firm wants to know who else is interested in the competition. TechTrack also files similar requests for FOIA queries about itself to learn what the competition knows about the firm.

Unless specific information falls into an FOIA exemption category, a company may seek to block the release of proprietary information through a reverse-FOIA lawsuit. Exempted categories of information include

- classified documents related to national defense and foreign policy
- information exempt under other laws, such as income tax returns
- confidential business information, such as trade secrets or commercial and financial data
- personal or private information, such as employee and medical files

(See Appendix II, "Records and Information Security Program," for more on information releases to others.)

3

Threats to Sensitive and Valuable Records and Information

Gordon Gekko, portrayed by actor Michael Douglas in the film *Wall Street*, declared that the most valuable commodity is information. Although he was referring specifically to insider information, records and information are valuable commodities to a business in a number of ways. Some of those records, under certain circumstances, may also become a liability.

A business owns sensitive and valuable records and information in need of protection from damage, loss, and unauthorized disclosure. Safeguarding such records can preserve rights under the law, fulfill legal and other obligations, and prevent losses. When certain business records are not properly protected, any loss or damage could result in legal actions, inability to rightfully collect money due, loss of competitive advantages, or other consequences.

This chapter outlines the types of records and information that are valuable or sensitive, and it presents a variety of potential threats to information security. (Appendix II, "Records and Information Security Program," provides specific guidelines for the protection of sensitive and valuable records and information.)

WHAT TO PROTECT

At the heart of business records are those with real or potential financial, administrative, operational, or legal impact on the business. Business records may also have historical importance. In the normal course of business, a company might be in possession of another party's records and information, which must be treated in much the same way as the company's own records.

Some records have more value than others, and disclosing certain sensitive records to the wrong parties may cause harm. Valuable records are those that affect income and profit or those that represent a tangible asset. Sensitive records are those that must not be disclosed indiscriminately to others within or outside of the organization.

A method to classify business records helps identify the various levels of sensitivity and value. Clearly stated guidelines for each classification then prescribe how those records should be protected. A record can be both sensitive and valuable, and its classification within these two categories may change as circumstances change or after a designated time period.

Unfortunately, the terminology used to describe sensitive and valuable records and information is not standardized within the business community. "Confidential" may be used by some businesses to describe sensitive records dubbed "private" by others, and "private" is sometimes used to include "proprietary" information. "Proprietary information," "intellectual property," and "trade secret" are frequently used interchangeably, although in the true meaning of the word, proprietary is a broader category that encompasses intellectual properties such as trade secrets.

Until standards exist, the needs and preferences of an individual organization—along with consideration of privacy, security, and secrecy issues—best determine how the categories of value and sensitivity are defined. For purposes of discussion in this book, classifications of sensitive and valuable records are described in the next sections.

Proprietary Information

Proprietary information is the broad term used to encompass various types of information that have value to the owner. Unauthorized or unrestricted disclosure of proprietary information can destroy its value or give advantage to others. Classified as proprietary information are

- information that is not generally known,
- information that gives the proprietor an advantage over others, and
- information for which reasonable efforts are made to protect its secrecy.

Proprietary information can be information, records, software, and other work products developed on behalf of a company or by using the company's resources. It is information that is difficult or costly to develop or that has intrinsic value. Records and information that may be considered proprietary include

- building plans and blueprints
- business plans
- customer lists
- designs, drawings, and models
- financial and cost data
- manufacturing and production reports
- marketing plans and methods
- patents
- policies and procedures
- pricing information
- software and code
- training materials

Protection for certain types of proprietary information—intellectual properties, for instance—is provided under trade secret, patent, copyright, trademark, and other statutes and regulations. (See Chapter 2, "Preservation of Legal Rights and Business Assets," for more on the preservation of legal rights to protection of intellectual properties under the law.)

As businesses slowly entered the era of e-commerce (electronic commerce), they discovered that Internet domain names are very much a corporate asset in that they help customers walk through a company's virtual front door. In the early 1990s, individuals rushed to register domain names that were trademarks or trade names of other companies so they could later sell the registration to the rightful owner when that owner attempted to establish a presence on the Internet. The trend to do this was not slowed by any domain name registration oversight at the time. Domain names are now bought and sold for as much as millions of dollars.

An online wine dealer reportedly paid $3.3 million for the domain name wine.com, and business.com sold for $7.5 million. The typical cost of buying a domain name is several thousand dollars.

One small manufacturing firm, upon discovering that its trade name was registered to the national sales manager of a big competitor, charged trademark infringement and unfair competition. It is difficult to measure the lost opportunities or damage to the small manufacturer when browsers accessing the site saw the message "Under construction."

In another situation, when an Internet browser entered a slight variation of the

name of one worldwide hydropower company, the browser was taken directly
to the web page of the company's largest competitor.

Slowly case law began to recognize that use of a trademark as a domain name by another is trademark infringement or, in some cases, unfair competition or even fraud. New domain name registration rules and
the Cybersquatting Consumer Protection Act now offer protection in the
use of trademarks and trade names as domain names. (See Chapter 2,
"Preservation of Legal Rights and Business Assets," for more on trademark protection under the law.)

Private Records and Information

Private records and information contain sensitive data and should not
be disclosed indiscriminately within or outside the organization. Employee and customer information is typical of records in this classification. Customer records and data may be subject not only to privacy law
but also to proprietary information restrictions and regulations.

A number of federal, state, and local recordkeeping requirements exist
regarding employee and customer private records and information. They
specify the types of records to be maintained, the length of time they are
to be held, and the proper use of and access to these records. Recently,
the financial services industry instituted new regulations about the privacy of their customer information. In addition, companies doing business in other countries must comply with privacy protection rules that
are more restrictive than those in the United States.

Businesses today maintain large databases of employee and customer
information, and some of that information comes from their web sites.

Amazon.com's customer information is a significant corporate asset—23 million
registered customer names, credit card information, and purchasing records. But
how that asset is managed can turn it into a liability when the privacy of customer data is not properly protected and customer preferences are not respected.
Late in 2000, the company did not make any new friends with privacy advocates
when it announced it could give its customer information to a third party if
acquired by another company or if it sells some of its businesses. Nor were the
FTC and plaintiffs in a class-action suit happy with the company's privacy policy
when they believed Amazon.com claims about keeping personally identifiable
information on web-usage patterns private were probably not true. The company
settled the civil suits for around $2 million.

Cookies, browser-tracking software that places tags on your computer
by web sites you visit, are another example of technology's adding value,
but also resulting in a new problem. Marketers use these data to track a
browser's personal preferences and often use the results to create targeted

advertising in the form of banner ads. Many privacy advocates, however, do not want others to know what they buy and what web sites they visit.

In this new age of e-commerce, privacy advocates are concerned about what data are being collected about consumers and how that data will be used. At the time of this writing, privacy safeguards for data collected over the Internet through web sites are voluntary efforts by site operators. Owners of most Internet web sites are instituting and posting privacy policies on their web sites. It is in their best interests to earn the confidence of consumers about protection of customer information; otherwise, they may suffer loss of reputation or business or risk defending themselves in litigation. Federal and state legislators continue to address the issue as public outcries place pressure on them. Privacy issues will also be discussed in a new context in the aftermath of the terrorist attack on the United States in 2001.

A separate concern about customer and employee private data is the question of ownership. Who owns the information collected about individuals? If customers and employees own it, how a business collects, uses, and distributes that information may differ from how privacy laws treat the information. That discussion will be ongoing in future years.

Information Belonging to Others

In the normal course of business, a company may come into the possession of records that are the property of another individual or organization. Contracting organizations and those involved in joint business ventures often require valuable or sensitive information that belongs to another party, especially government contractors. A business in the role of a contractor may create or use records, which then become the property of the contracting organization.

A business is responsible for the proper use and control of others' information and for compliance with any provisions set forth in a licensing agreement, contract, law, or government regulation. Failure to maintain adequate security for these records and information, including proper disposal of the documents, may result in a law violation, litigation, and other consequences.

Dozens of seismic data industry firms filed suits against big oil conglomerates over theft of the small firms' seismic survey data. These firms make money by setting off blasts and recording the sound waves under the earth's surface, and the data help pinpoint the location of deposits of oil and gas under the earth's surface. Because data collection is so expensive, leasing the information reduces costs to the oil companies. But even leasing fees can be as high as tens of thousands of dollars per mile of data. The alleged thefts occurred when oil companies shared with other oil companies the data they individually leased from the seismic companies. One company even used the data as an asset to lure buyers of its separate subsidiary companies. Judges have ruled that the data are trade secrets warranting protection from being shared, sold, or made public without the consent of the information's owner and without compensation to the seismic companies.

Unless it is in the company's best interests to possess others' records and information, not doing so allows companies to obviate the necessary obligations to protect such information and avoid potential risks.

Litigation and Investigation Records

Records and information relevant to potential, current, or past litigation or government investigation are considered sensitive and, in some cases, valuable. These records must be protected from alteration or loss, and—depending on whether the records are sensitive or valuable—a number of restrictions may be necessary regarding their disclosure to others. (See Chapter 5, "A Day in Court," for more information on litigation and investigation records.)

Vital Records

In the event of a natural or manmade disaster, certain business records are critical to the organization's ability to continue operations or to resume business after the disruption. These records, as well as any records required to handle the crisis situation, are considered vital in that they preserve the company's rights and help fulfill company obligations. (Chapter 2, "Preservation of Legal Rights and Business Assets," discusses records and information required to ensure business continuity. Appendix I, "A Vital Records Program," describes methods to protect those records from disaster.)

Historical Records

Business records, as the corporate memory, provide an accurate portrayal of business development and activities over time. Examples of records that may be considered historical include

- advertising materials
- architectural drawings
- board minute books
- financial records
- materials unique to the business or industry

- newsletters and other publications
- officers' and executives' correspondence
- oral histories
- photos
- scrapbooks and clipping files

Each business determines the relative value of corporate history and the extent to which historical records are collected, indexed for future reference, and preserved. Historical records are frequently original source materials for biographies or histories, or they may be used for public relations and marketing functions such as

- trade and other public exhibits
- museum exhibits
- corporate identity programs
- commemorative histories
- centennial celebrations

Legal departments sometimes need historical records to document legal positions. Historical records can establish rights to a trademark registration, justify a tax position, or place legal matters in a historical context of policies and events.

A corporate archive may be a tangible asset in the negotiation of the sale of a business, or it may be a tax write-off when donated to a non-profit museum or university.

INFORMATION SECURITY THREATS

Threats to the security of business records and information may originate from sources both internal and external to a company. Environmental threats to information security range from earthquake and tornado to power failure and fire. Even the very medium on which information is recorded (the information carrier) and the means to process the information (the information processor) may threaten continued existence of the information.

The most common source of information security threats is people. Through intentional or unintentional behavior, human threats to information security may include

- computer operator error
- unauthorized computer access
- filing error

- dumpster divers
- criminal activity
- vandalism

Employees

People inside a business are a greater information security risk than outsiders. Current and former employees have the skills, knowledge, access, and opportunity to cause information damage and loss through negligent or through intentional behavior.

Inadvertent disclosure of valuable or sensitive information occurs when an employee is careless or is unaware of what needs protection or how it is to be protected. For instance, valuable information might be left out on desks, on meeting room walls, and in wastebaskets. When janitorial staff moonlight for the competition, they may take home more money selling trash than emptying it.

Businesses may go to great lengths to prevent unauthorized access to their computers, but they sometimes neglect the unshredded printout tossed into trash dumpsters or the confidential report left on a photocopier—all data that could wind up in the wrong hands.

One brokerage firm found itself in an embarrassing—and legally vulnerable—situation after its trash blew onto the property of a neighboring business. When the brokerage company refused to pick up its trash after receiving complaints, the neighbor simply mailed the discarded customer balances to the brokerage firm's clients. Many customers, outraged at the irresponsible handling of their personal financial information, transferred their investments to another firm.

Yet another embarrassing moment was documented in the February 5, 1996, issue of *Fortune*. A photograph showed bank employees rummaging through trash at a landfill to recover important documents that had inadvertently been tossed out. Adding insult to injury, a bank spokesperson admitted that the bank had had to do so before.

People love to talk about their jobs to professional colleagues, potential employers, job candidates, suppliers, and the media. Sometimes in their excitement they slip, revealing more than they should. Occasionally, sensitive conversations are within earshot of strangers in restaurants, airports, and trade shows. Or "need to know" becomes "everybody knows" when a conversation leads off with, "I shouldn't be telling you this, but . . ." Such acts of negligence are akin to locking a safe and leaving the valuables on the floor next to it. Although it is possible that the valuables might not be disturbed, the likelihood of loss or damage is greatly increased.

Employees are more mobile than ever before. More often than not, this mobility is not of their own choosing as mergers and layoffs continue in today's business environment.

With the erosion of the kind of company loyalty that existed twenty years ago, employees who leave a company to work for the competition or to set up their own competing business may be an information security risk. A disgruntled worker may, for instance, exact revenge on the employer.

When one computer programmer saw he was going to be fired, he tampered with the company's computer system. Two days after he was terminated, a computer virus destroyed 200,000 data files.

Occasionally an employee unwittingly takes intellectual properties and knowledge to the competitor, unaware of their proprietary nature. Or a worker might go to the competition to spite an employer, with or without the intent to disclose proprietary information or engage in illegal or unethical activities.

Competitors have been known to lure away key personnel expressly for the purpose of obtaining marketing plans or customer lists.

Dow Chemical sued General Electric for allegedly stealing trade secrets by hiring fourteen employees from its plastics division. General Electric was ordered to return any documents it might have wrongfully obtained, to transfer one mechanical engineer to a new job, and to take other specific actions.

With so much information stored electronically and capable of being instantly transmitted outside the company, employees do not have to work very hard to steal some of the most vital information a company owns.

Gates Rubber Company claimed a competitor stole copyrighted engineering and marketing data. An injunction was granted barring Bando American Inc. from using a computerized marketing program that appears to be a copy of a Gates program. The court noted that a Bando software designer, who had formerly worked for Gates, was said to have "brought with him to Bando all the computer files he could get his hands on before leaving Gates."

Criminal Actions

Both insiders and outsiders may pose information security threats through criminal, malicious, or mischievous actions. White collar crime is more widespread and uncontrolled today than it was twenty years ago. New technologies are making it easier for disgruntled employees, greedy competitors, and adventurous computer hackers to violate information security measures.

There are crimes by computer, in which the computer is the criminal's tool, and there are computer crimes, in which the computer is the target of the crime. Thieves use computers to steal intellectual properties or private data. Hackers are the most notorious criminals who victimize computers and networks. Today's easy transfer of electronic information leads to effortless theft of intellectual properties, compromise of privacy policies, fraud, and the like.

Digitized information can be deleted, modified, and transmitted—often without detection. Security risks associated with theft of laptops and handheld organizers grow with the volume of data they hold. Computer hackers lock up a system to prove a point. Industrial spies sell trade secrets to the competition. Computer bulletin boards provide individuals a safe, anonymous venue to post sensitive and valuable information, infringe on others' copyrights, or even attempt to manipulate stock prices. Terrorism, once deemed a threat only to a company's operations in foreign countries, has in recent years hit U.S. business at home.

The magnitude of information crimes and security breaches is difficult to document because most crimes go unreported. Such attacks—be they mischief, sabotage, espionage, or a crime—are often not reported so as to avoid embarrassment, inconvenience, the potential of additional damage from a public trial, or loss of customer confidence. Concerns about a damaged reputation when a reported crime hits the news may go by the wayside when stockholders or others clamor to hold someone accountable for criminal actions that cause severe harm to a business, its employees or customers, or the general public.

One company chose to pursue prosecution of a former executive for theft of intellectual property:

A General Motors Corporation (GM) executive in Europe took cartons of confidential data worth millions of dollars and several other GM executives with him to his new job with Volkswagen. The 10,000 GM documents, worth millions of dollars, included supplier information, a study for a proposed auto plant, and photos and descriptions of future car models. German prosecutors launched a criminal investigation and charged the executive and several of his colleagues with industrial espionage. Criminal charges in Germany were dropped when the executives made charitable donations to fulfill a requirement to resolve the case. GM and U.S. federal prosecutors continue to examine their options.

Competitor Intelligence and Industrial Espionage

Every year billions of dollars are lost, reputations are smudged, and market shares are reduced as a result of stolen trade secrets and technology.

Industrial spies can be state-sponsored or commercial. Corporate spies today have the help of governments that have converted cold war intelligence networks to help support their own industries, and their jobs are facilitated even more by today's sophisticated and affordable technologies.

Executives traveling abroad are cautioned about the possibility of undercover flight attendants and to keep a tight grip on sensitive documents to prevent hotel staff from copying information or stealing laptop computers left in a room.

After examining patterns of competitive bids coming in too close on its overseas bids, many international manufacturers and other companies now encode their overseas communications and data transmissions.

Various methods of gathering information about other businesses are legal, but some are not. Yet other tactics may be questioned on ethical grounds. Competitor intelligence gathering may be based on overt and covert tactics. Measuring the amount of rust on a train track to determine the volume of shipments into and out of a plant is one of the more covert tactics used in the past. Additional covert tactics are

• electronic surveillance
• unauthorized computer access
• extortion or blackmail
• theft
• dumpster diving

Active documents in wastebaskets, especially wastebaskets by copy machines, are a gold mine for competitors and criminals. The U.S. Supreme Court ruled that dumpster diving for documents is legal when trash is in a public location and the trash is open to scavengers.

One company did not understand why a competitor seemed to anticipate its every marketing move. One day when the owner saw its dumpster overflowing, he called the trash hauler. The hauler said that the previous year the competitor paid him not to pick up the company's trash and that the man currently paid to poke through the mail, printouts, and other documents in the trash was probably ill that week.

Mountains of valuable competitive information can be gathered without resorting to cloak-and-dagger tactics. Corporate detectives, market research firms, and competitive analysts—of the ethical variety—rely on public information to do their jobs. Their sources include

- direct contact with knowledgeable individuals
- published and unpublished public records and government information
- corporate public relations packets
- trade shows
- information service providers
- disassembly or chemical analysis of a rival's product

Environmental Threats

Threats to the security of records and information can arise from environmental conditions.

The worst—and probably the most ignored—environmental threat is a natural disaster such as a rain or wind storm, hurricane, flood, tornado, or earthquake. The "it won't happen here" sentiment tends to make a business discount the potential consequences of such an event. Even if a tornado does not make a direct hit on a business, the company may suffer serious damage if the tornado hits its power source or communications network.

In addition, facility problems could affect information security. A flood caused by a broken pipe or sump pump failure can damage computer hardware and records in all media. An air-conditioner breakdown might cause an unexpected computer shutdown, or ravenous rats might cause a short in wiring and cabling.

The electrical power that lets us do things faster and more efficiently is the same power that can damage or destroy expensive equipment, cause data loss, and even cause fire. From static discharges to power spikes and lightning strikes, hardware and data can suffer immediate damage or delayed damage when the cumulative effect of line noise, brownouts, and minor power surges takes its toll.

Florida is notorious for its severe thunderstorms. During one of those storms, a business reported that its uninterruptible power system (UPS) came to its rescue thirty-four times in one hour.

Increasing demands for power to operate and cool the equipment caused energy crises that forced power companies into brownouts and blackouts on both coasts in recent years.

Media Permanence, Durability, and Portability

Another credible threat to information security may be the very medium on which the information is recorded. Increasingly more records and information are in electronic form, which is significantly easier to copy, transport, and transmit than other information media. Millions of dollars' worth of research and development can be carried out the door on a disk or in minutes can be sent over phone lines or wireless networks to an external computer.

Microfilm, paper, and computer systems are vulnerable to aging, adverse environmental conditions, and abuse. From paper, photographs, and microfilm to optical disk and audio tape, the quality of processing and the quality of materials affects the future life of the information. The physical characteristics of an information carrier determine its susceptibility to information damage or loss as a result of environmental conditions, use, and aging.

Permanence and durability are significant issues for records that need to be retained for an extended period of time, or even for a few weeks. Of particular concern are those records that must be retained for ten years or longer. Deterioration of many information carriers can begin as early as three years after storage under normal conditions. Abnormal storage conditions and use will speed the deterioration process.

(More detailed information on records storage media is in Chapter 8, "Integrating Media Choices.")

Computer and Network Catastrophes

Computer and network catastrophes result from fire, operator error, system malfunctions, power supply problems, criminal actions, and more.

A computer disaster, intentional or otherwise, will cost time and money in terms of downtime, restoration of lost data, and repair or replacement of equipment and software. Even if a company is able to salvage its data from a disaster of some kind, it may not be ready to resume operations in a timely manner if the disaster destroyed the hardware, software, or networking capabilities required to use the data.

In addition, obsolescence of hardware and software may threaten the existence of electronic information. As systems are updated and replaced, consideration is not always given to the ability to access the older data files, which may need to be retained for potential future use.

Today's business environment thinks first and foremost: access and connectivity to the rest of the world. The ability of individual computers and networks to communicate with one another enables fast exchange of information. But the very ease of this interconnectivity also offers greater opportunity for information security breaches.

Among the many physical points of entry to computer systems are desktops, laptops, intranets, wireless networks, and the Internet. Wireless networks connect computers through radio signals similar to those used by cellular telephones. As prices of wireless networks fall, their use increases. But all it takes is a laptop, fitted with a wireless networking card and a small antenna, to access the network's e-mails and files from a nearby location.

The source of computer virus threats only a few years ago was the sharing of files on diskettes. Today's primary source is e-mail through the Internet. The Sixth Annual FBI Computer Crime and Security Survey found that 70 percent of those surveyed experienced security breaches through the Internet, and 65 percent suffered financial losses.

Until the Internet's coming of age, most computer break-ins were by insiders. Now unauthorized access from around the world to networks and computers is through Internet connections. The Internet is used as a tool for immediate transmission of trade secrets or unlimited illegal copies of copyrighted information. It is also used to destroy electronic information or to tamper with web pages.

High-speed Internet connections present an easy target because they are always on, giving computer hackers more time to find and attack a computer. Once upon a time hackers were generally youthful pranksters wanting to demonstrate their technical prowess. The fun and sport of computer hacking began to take on a criminal tone when systems were accessed at financial institutions, telecommunications companies, and government installations. Today hackers from around the world are intent on theft of proprietary information, invasion of privacy, alteration or destruction of data, and disruption or shutting down of operations.

A worm is a virus-like program that does not always cause damage, but it can travel from computer to computer through a network. Criminals use worms to gather secret data and not leave behind evidence of the worm.

Code Red and its subsequent variations is a worm unleashed in 2001 that entered computers through a vulnerability in Microsoft software. It caused more than $2 billion in damage.

Hackers can also hijack a machine to launch an attack against a web site, such as a denial-of-service attack. The Computer Crime and Security Survey reports that nearly 80 percent of e-commerce firms reported hacker attacks that flooded their servers, thus preventing legitimate users from gaining access.

In one attack on high-traffic web sites by a 15-year-old Canadian, later sentenced to a youth detention center, the estimated damages were $1.7 billion.

Viruses are a form of terrorism that may strike at any time; they are indiscriminate about their victims, and it is difficult to identify the perpetrator. The ICSA Labs Sixth Annual Computer Virus Prevalence Survey in 2000 reports that companies are experiencing an increasing number of virus incidents and growing costs per incident. It is estimated that there are more than 160 virus encounters per 1,000 machines each year.

More than half of those surveyed experienced a virus disaster. Recovery from a disaster requires as much as twenty days, and the costs to recover from a virus are accelerating—direct labor expense to clean up infected hard disks and networks, loss of productivity during downtime and cleanup, and corrupted or lost data.

Business, government, and other organizations and individuals spend more time and energy to prevent viruses, yet the virus experience is worsening. The propagation of Internet-enabled viruses allows infection of more systems in shorter periods of time.

(See Appendix II, "Records and Information Security Program," for more on protection of sensitive and valuable records and information.)

4

Employer Rights and Responsibilities

Personnel costs are the single greatest expense for most businesses. These costs include salaries, benefits, taxes, training, management, and turnover. There also are costs in the forms of:

- compliance with laws and government regulations
- litigation and government investigation
- employee threats to intellectual properties and information security
- risk of liability for employee bad behavior

Employee recordkeeping is necessary for business management planning and decision making. Records preserve the many details to be remembered year after year for a changing number of workers. Maintaining accurate employee records is also a good business practice that meets various government requirements and protects a business.

Employers have a number of rights and responsibilities regarding their workers relating to personnel actions, employee safety and privacy, protection of business assets, and more. Records are created, reported, maintained, and protected in order to comply with government recordkeeping requirements or to show that the business is in compliance with employment laws and regulations. Records are also created, maintained, and protected to preserve certain rights of the employer:

- the right to a proper defense
- the right to minimize business liabilities

- the right to file a claim against another party
- the right to protect business assets

EMPLOYERS ON THE DEFENSE

Not every business is affected by all federal employment laws, but an employer may be subject to the requirements of every state in which it has employees. State laws tend to pattern themselves after federal laws, and they usually extend their impact to companies smaller than those affected by federal laws.

The intent of employment law is to protect the innocent worker. Regulatory agencies, legislation, and the courts stepped in to the historical role of organized labor to protect the worker as the economy evolved from an industrial to a services and information economy. Government advocacy of employee rights is the strongest ever, so employment law has become a measurable threat to even the fairest and most generous employer.

Claims and charges by employees and government agencies have become an inevitable part of doing business in today's regulated and litigating business environment. Economic downturns, sympathetic juries, and media hype contribute to increasing employment litigation risks for employers. The risk of being sued rises each time a court defines what constitutes unfair, unethical, or discriminatory behavior.

Most businesses are eager to settle employee claims out of court because of the

- expenses involved in defending themselves,
- potential of a damaged reputation,
- risks of additional similar suits, and
- tendency of juries to be sympathetic to the worker.

Employment laws and regulations directly or indirectly influence personnel recordkeeping practices. A number of them stipulate that a business must create, collect, and maintain or report certain records. Government reporting or information disclosure requirements apply to payroll, benefits, taxes, equal employment opportunity, safety, health, and other business functions or activities.

Other laws compel the creation of records in order to show compliance with the law. It is in the best interest of a business to collect and maintain accurate and complete records that demonstrate compliance with an employment law, even if the law has no recordkeeping requirements.

Documentation of compliance with the law and other good recordkeeping practices help prepare for litigation and government investigation or audits. Complete, accurate, and indisputable records minimize risks and losses when they deter an employee or government agency from filing charges in the first place, or when they encourage a claimant to settle out of court or to drop unfounded charges.

When a target of an investigation has not created and maintained records according to a government requirement, it could have serious difficulties defending itself and may be subject to fines and penalties.

Under the Immigration Act, every employer must verify that all persons hired are eligible to work in the United States. The employer must document that verification on the Employment Eligibility Verification form, or the I-9 form. Each I-9 form must be retained for three years from the date the employee is hired or for one year past the employee's termination, whichever is longer. Not properly completing, retaining, or presenting an I-9 form for inspection by government officials carries a fine of $100 to $1,000 for each violation.

The Department of Labor, the Equal Employment Opportunity Commission (EEOC), and the IRS are among a number of different agencies that rely on records documenting wages, taxes, and other employee payments. When a question arises regarding payment of minimum wage or taxes, overtime practices, discrimination in pay or benefits, and similar claims, the following records may be among those reviewed:

• wages, overtime, sales commission and other employee payments
• income tax withholdings
• benefit plans and payments

Business often uses independent contractors for staffing flexibility and reduced costs. The waters remain murky about what constitutes an independent contractor, in spite of the IRS's twenty questions to help determine the distinction between contractor and employee. To defend itself in an IRS review, a business should consider documentation of practices that respond to the IRS criteria for independent contractors, including records of scheduling, hours worked, training, and location of work. If the IRS determines that contractors are employees, a business may need to cough up back taxes, interest, and penalties for all workers in the position reviewed. The business may also be vulnerable to liabilities in any claims for employee benefits.

Liability for Employee Bad Behavior

Because employees are agents of a company, employers may face liability for the actions of their workers. Inappropriate employee behavior may lead to information security breaches and civil or criminal liability. Numerous employee actions increase employer risks, including

- installation of unlicensed software on a company computer
- transmission of trade secret information through the Internet to a competitor
- unauthorized copying of copyrighted publications, music, software available in the work environment or through the Internet
- posting of sensitive company or employee information to Internet bulletin boards or chat rooms
- downloading of pornographic materials from web sites
- sending of harassing e-mail messages to other employees
- destruction of property or physical assault on other workers in retaliation for a disciplinary action or termination

Employers thus need to ensure that their workers comply with international, federal, state, and local laws and regulations to avoid civil or criminal charges against the employee and/or the company.

Federal Sentencing Guidelines codify fines and penalties for corporate wrongdoing at the federal level. Fines can be especially hefty if a company does not have internal programs to detect and prevent illegal acts.

In 1995 Lockheed Martin Corporation agreed to pay a $24.8 million fine and to plead guilty to conspiring to violate U.S. antibribery laws. The company was placed on a three-year probationary period in which it is required to turn over periodic ethics reports. It now has mandatory training on security, software license compliance, and other federal compliance concerns.

Fines, penalties, and other business risks can be reduced if a company takes reasonable steps to detect and prevent any criminal activities. Among the company policies and practices to document in a company's defense are

- property and facility security systems
- mandatory employee, contractor, and supplier training on company policies, ethical behavior, and compliance with laws and regulations
- employee hiring practices
- employee monitoring policies and practices
- information security program
- program and policy audits

Documentation of these and similar risk reduction systems may help convince a prosecutor or regulator not to pursue charges against the company.

Worker's Right to Privacy

Worker privacy concerns exist in two primary areas: employee monitoring and employee private data. This section addresses only employee private data. Later in this chapter is a more in-depth discussion of the use of employee monitoring to protect corporate assets and to minimize risks of liability.

Issues about employee privacy keep showing up in courts. From reference checks and drug testing to employee surveillance and searches, there are many areas in which an employee may charge a company with invasion of privacy.

Summary personnel records that do not identify individuals are created most frequently for management purposes and to show overall compliance with laws and regulations, as discussed earlier in this chapter. Individual employee records contain personal information that is protected by privacy and other laws or regulations. A number of federal, state, and international privacy laws exist to protect the individual by controlling the collection, maintenance, access, use, and dissemination of personal information.

Employers are required by law to inform job applicants when a credit history is being used to evaluate them.

One corporation agreed to settle charges that it failed to tell job applicants that information in their credit reports influenced the decision not to hire them. The FTC said the employment reports marketed by credit-reporting agencies often contain more information than do the standard credit reports used by banks and retailers.

Under the consent agreement, the corporation is required to mail letters to applicants who were denied jobs because of a credit report, stating the reasons they were not hired and the name and address of the agency that supplied the company with the damaging report. The company must comply with the Federal Fair Credit Reporting Act and maintain documents to prove its compliance for the next five years.

Employers routinely create and maintain records specific to individual workers. Among such records are

- personal data such as date of birth and Social Security number
- employment history
- performance appraisals
- payroll information (wage and salary data, payments, deductions)
- benefits program enrollments and claims
- illness and accident reports

- skills inventories and training histories
- employment actions such as promotion, demotion, and termination

In general, the right to access employee records belongs to the employee, the government, law enforcement authorities, and company employees with a legitimate need to know. State laws often specify when access is allowed to certain records. Collective bargaining agreements may provide additional guidelines for access to employee information. A business is subject to penalties for any damages that may occur as a result of a willful or intentional action that violates privacy rights.

ForwardThink Corporation has a corporate policy on employee records. This policy states that the individual employee and others with a business need to access employee information may access that employee's records. (Those with a legitimate need to know include payroll and human resources staff, an employee's supervisor, and management personnel.) The policy goes on to state that individuals have the right to know what records are maintained about them and who has access to these records. Employees may submit written requests to review their records and may request amendment to those records to correct any errors found. Procedures are established for adequate safeguards to prevent unauthorized disclosure or misuse of the information. An accounting of nonroutine information disclosure, such as to law enforcement authorities, is maintained.

(More information on safeguarding employee records is provided in Appendix II, "Records and Information Security Program.")

Health and Safety

Inadequate and inaccurate records are especially harmful on matters regarding worker health and safety issues. Prosecutors are bringing more criminal charges, and executives are receiving jail sentences, for reckless endangerment of lives. Efforts to comply with health and safety regulations must be demonstrated in court or in government inspections, audits, or investigations.

At one manufacturing plant OSHA found 221 violations. Of the 130 willful violations, 129 involved faulty recordkeeping. The penalties assessed against the plant totaled $1.4 million, of which the charges for poor recordkeeping were $1.29 million. The case was then turned over for criminal prosecution.

Safety program records that may provide evidence of compliance include

- risk management and safety program documentation
- company policies, procedures, and standards to eliminate or reduce hazardous practices and conditions
- employee education and training activities
- vehicle and equipment maintenance and accident reports
- employee accident and illness reports
- medical files and benefits payments

Worker exposure to toxic substances is a high-risk area for employers. In its defense, a business must have records relating to

- hazardous conditions and substances (air quality tests, spills and clean-up operations, etc.)
- efforts to adequately warn employees of the risks and to train them to handle materials properly
- actions taken to improve safety conditions
- effects of exposure on workers

Ergonomics is a relatively new workplace safety issue. Its impact extends beyond manufacturing environments to even the smallest of office sites.

One manufacturer was hit with a $1.6 million fine for alleged flagrant violations of workplace safety regulations at its plant. After on-site inspections, OSHA cited the corporation for 264 violations, all but 2 of which were considered serious. OSHA reported that work conditions resulted in repetitive motion disorders requiring 300 employees to seek medical help; of those, 25 underwent surgical procedures. Among the charges were 100 recordkeeping violations, each of which was assessed a fine of $2,000. The manufacturer had improperly recorded, or failed to record, the cumulative trauma disorders as required on an OSHA log of injuries and illnesses.

Employment Actions

An employer cannot generally foresee when and if a hearing or lawsuit will occur regarding an employment action, but events and practices must be documented just in case. Employment actions to be documented include

- selection for hire, promotion, layoff, recall, education and training opportunities, early retirement, and so on
- determination of pay and other compensation
- performance appraisals

- employee grievances or complaints
- disciplinary action or demotion
- termination

A paper trail of evidence to back up a company's reasoning and actions may be necessary one day to reconstruct the decision-making process in a credible manner. The key to avoiding problems and reducing risks is to begin recordkeeping efforts at the inception of employment. From the hiring process, throughout the term of employment, to termination, documentation of employment actions may show that employee policies and procedures were applied consistently and equitably.

Records should be created consistently and in the normal course of business for all employees. Documentation of events should be direct observations (not hearsay) and should be completed in a timely manner—that is, as close as possible to the time of their occurrence. Both positive and negative job-related performance should be recorded. All documentation should be accurate and factual.

A company's personnel records are used not only by the company in its own defense but also by a plaintiff to support the case against an employer. Judges traditionally grant plaintiffs broad access to defendant records in bias cases because the employer, not the worker, has all the facts and records. Government agencies also have access to employer records and information for audits and investigations.

The Department of Labor and individual state labor departments sometimes broaden a discrimination complaint review to include additional employees. Evidence necessary to refute allegations of discrimination may include

- job group profiles
- job placement files (job requisition, advertising copy, applicant files, the review and selection process, any testing results, etc.)
- guidelines, reports, and analyses on compensation and salary plans
- a history of employee transfers, layoffs, promotions, educational and training opportunities, and so on, and their related decision processes

Among the top claims filed today are claims of sexual harassment and age discrimination. Jury trials and compensatory and punitive damages for harassment and discrimination complaints hit companies hard. Complaints must be promptly investigated, thoroughly documented, and treated with confidentiality.

Documentation becomes even more critical when a termination follows shortly upon any sensitive occurrence, such as an employee claim for worker compensation or a complaint made to a government agency about discrimination, work conditions, or company misconduct. Such a termination may be construed as retaliation, which is forbidden by law. A termination found to be in breach of public policy is considered a wrongful discharge.

Termination in breach of a contract—express or implied—is one basis for wrongful discharge claims. Express contracts are those written agreements signed by both the employer and employee. Implied contracts may be verbal agreements, employee handbooks, or other promises made by the employer or employee. Breaches of contract violations typically result in payment of back pay and lost benefits. Frequently, damages regarding emotional distress and punitive damages are also awarded.

In one major oil company, a homosexual employee had left a personal document on a copy machine that other employees found to be repulsive. The document was a party invitation with the "house rules" for a gay party. The company fired the employee shortly after that incident despite the employee's record of exemplary job performance. A California Superior Court judge found the company had violated assurances it would not fire any employee except for unsatisfactory job performance and consequently the court awarded the terminated employee $5.3 million in damages.

EMPLOYER RIGHTS

Efforts to preserve an employer's right to a defense often overlap with the efforts to preserve the right to protect its business assets and the right to protection under the law. Among the efforts by employers to exercise and preserve its rights are policies and employment agreements, prevention and enforcement activities, and standards that address personal records.

Policies and Agreements

Just as government promulgates regulations to protect workers, so do companies establish policies and contractual agreements to protect their assets, workers, customers, and the general public.

Policies and employment agreements may address any of the following issues:

- protection of a company's sensitive and valuable information
- protection of others' sensitive and valuable information, such as copyrighted materials or another's trade secret
- protection of employee private information
- standards and practices for records and information in all media

- proper use of company resources, including laptop computers, e-mail, and Internet access
- proper business conduct
- sanctions for noncompliance with corporate policy

Both organized labor contracts and individual employment agreements spell out the rights and obligations of the employer and the employee.

The rules of business contracts have been applied in certain court cases involving employment contracts.

The House of Good Intentions asked one of its top managers to relocate to another site, which was having serious financial difficulties. After only six months the company closed the site and terminated the employee. The employee took the House of Good Intentions to court because prior to negotiation of the relocation he had not been informed of the serious financial difficulties. Based on business contract law, the court decided this information should have been disclosed to the employee as information the plaintiff needed to decide whether to enter into the contract.

Most employment agreements stipulate the compensation and benefits for performance of designated job duties. Many go beyond that to include clauses such as the right of the employer to terminate the employee at any time for cause or in the event of the sale, merger, or discontinuance of the business. Some employment agreements make compliance with corporate policies about recordkeeping, information security, and proper use of company resources a condition of employment.

A separate agreement may be executed to protect the organization's sensitive or valuable information. In a nondisclosure or confidentiality agreement, the employee is obligated not to disclose certain information to unauthorized parties during and after employment. The contract may also stipulate injunctive relief or legal damages for breach of any of the contract's provisions. Some employment agreements also include a "loyalty and due care" clause that prohibits any personal actions that would be unlawful or that would be in conflict with the company's interest.

Headlines in recent years are about high-profile trade secret disputes arising from executive defections to competitors. Competitors are luring away key employees and all the trade secrets the workers can carry or transmit.

General Electric Company (GE) made headlines in recent years as it defended itself against charges of stealing employees from competitors. In one case, Dow Chemical alleged GE hired fourteen Dow employees for the purpose of obtaining trade secrets. One piece of evidence presented was a marketing study written for GE that was nearly identical to a confidential marketing study written by that same person while he was employed at Dow.

In another claim against GE, Bayer AG of Germany charged that one former Bayer employee stole trade secrets before he left Bayer for a job at GE. Bayer charges that the employee made special efforts to become knowledgeable of more company secrets from the time after his job interview with GE's chief executive officer until he resigned from Bayer to work for GE.

Employees are also stealing trade secrets for their own personal gain.

One Kodak engineer retired and became a consultant to Kodak's competition. The FBI discovered a recipe book of Kodak secret formulas for making film in his home.

Generally, an employee's violation of a nondisclosure agreement will not destroy the right to protect the trade secret. However, the trade secret owner must act to stop the leak and to enforce its rights to trade secret protection as soon as it is aware of the problem; otherwise, the rights will be lost.

Another risk of proprietary information loss is departing workers who believe they own any intellectual properties they developed on the job. To avoid confusion about ownership of information, employment agreements must formally assign to the employer the rights to inventions, writings, and other products developed in the course of employment.

The language of employee handbooks, policies, and agreements must be clear and precise to minimize the risk of having a judge or jury interpret their wording. All policies and agreements should be reviewed periodically to ensure they accurately reflect the business and technology environments in which they exist.

The documentation of policies, procedures, and contracts, as well as the documentation of compliance with them, may be critical to a proper defense against any claims or to the ability to file a claim against another party. An employer may need to show how employee policies are applied equally to all employees.

Prevention and Enforcement

Without appropriate employee education on recordkeeping and information security policies and practices, the employer will not be able to hold the employee accountable for compliance with those policies and procedures. Without enforcement of its policies, a company may lose its right to protect its assets.

To prepare for information security violations, an organization determines procedures to be followed in the event of security breaches and any sanctions for violation of security procedures. When a violation occurs, an incident response team may determine what steps are necessary to minimize the damages and to prevent further violations of a similar nature. This team—including an investigator, legal advisor, computer specialist, and auditor—should be trained in company information policy and basic investigative techniques to collect and properly handle the evidence necessary to file charges or claims against an offending party.

An organizational change that affects the job status of individual employees—such as a merger, downsizing, or relocation—may create conditions ripe for employee sabotage and other threats to records and information. Information security should be a higher priority during such times to guard against threats from disgruntled employees.

For white collar crime by employees, prevention has been more effective than attempts to obtain restitution. Useful preventive measures include

- employee background checks
- employee standards of conduct
- security programs
- methods to remove temptation and opportunity
- employee monitoring

(See Chapter 3, "Threats to Sensitive and Valuable Records and Information," and Appendix II, "Records and Information Security Program," for more on employee threats to information security and on information security practices.)

One controversial prevention and detection measure used increasingly more by business is employee monitoring. The 2001 American Management Association (AMA) Survey on Workplace Monitoring and Surveillance reports that three quarters of U.S. firms now monitor employee telephone calls, e-mails, Internet activities, and computer files.

Generally, employee monitoring serves legitimate business purposes such as the following:

- to evaluate job performance
- to measure quality of customer interactions
- to prevent or detect criminal action such as theft of trade secrets or use of company resources to commit a crime
- to protect the company from legal liability for employee actions such as copyright infringement or espionage
- to prevent or detect policy violations such as sexual harassment

The Electronic Communications Privacy Act (ECPA) generally prevents monitoring of electronic communications, but with some exceptions. Employers have the right to monitor stored electronic communications if there is reason to believe a crime has occurred or when they need to protect their business, rights, or property. The right to monitor electronic communications also rests with employers because they provide the systems and other resources for their employees' business use.

The monitoring of computer data and electronic communications more than doubled over four years while video security surveillance and monitoring of phone conversations and voice mail messages increased only nominally.

Electronic communications monitoring is not without its controversies. Only a few years ago most employees believed they had a reasonable expectation of privacy in their e-mail communications. Today they tend to hold the same belief about their Internet surfing activities. The reality is that for business reasons, a business has a legitimate right to monitor employee use of its communications systems. How that monitoring is accomplished and to what extent it is implemented vary from one organization to another. As electronic information and communications technologies continue to evolve, so must their monitoring policies and methods to achieve a balance between employee privacy and business interests.

In August 2001 the *New York Times* reported on "rebels in black robes" who fought back at computer surveillance in their place of work. The intent of the monitoring software was to enhance security and to reduce computer use that was not related to judicial work and that was clogging the system. A group of circuit judges based in San Francisco argued with the Administrative Office of the Courts in Washington, D.C., that such monitoring violated their privacy. The conflict deteriorated to the point that a council of judges ordered their technology staff to disconnect the monitoring program for a week, pending a temporary compromise.

The approved compromise allows limited tracking of Internet use, such as downloading of pornography and music. Web sites, such as Napster—the center of controversy over music copyright violations—will be blocked. When suspicious activity occurs, such as lengthy downloading times, supervisors will be notified.

Of the AMA-surveyed businesses that conduct electronic monitoring and surveillance, more than 80 percent inform employees that e-mail, Internet connections, and computer files are subject to monitoring. The more information about monitoring provided to employees, the better the employer-employee relationship. Employees need to know if, when, how, and why they may be monitored, as well as what happens with information gathered during the monitoring.

More and more employers obtain employee consent in writing, such as through an employment agreement. Electronic consent may be obtained every time an employee must click "OK" at a policy statement banner before logging on to a computer system.

Under the Communications Privacy Act, there is one area of risk where the company may be prohibited from auditing its corporate data. Corporate information stored on a computer that is the personal property of an employee may not be auditable by the employer. To deal with this issue, a policy is needed to prohibit employees from maintaining business records on their own computers. A policy is also needed to address hardware, software and data issues for telecommuters who work out of their homes.

Personal Records

Any record created by an employee that documents activities performed within the scope of employment or that uses company resources should be considered a company record. Corporate policy, with the involvement of legal counsel, should clearly state what a business record is. In addition, employees should be educated about business records and what policies apply to them.

Without proper education, employees mistakenly believe that the following are their own personal records and, as such, are not subject to the review and control of the organization:

- calendars and itineraries
- meeting schedules, agendas, and notes
- managers' employee files
- electronic and voice messages
- electronic documents on desktops and laptops
- files in desks and credenzas

In addition to misinterpreting what a business record is, employees tend to set up records systems that are not in compliance with corporate recordkeeping standards. Employees do so primarily because they lack confidence in the company's records systems. Some employees want the convenience of having records close at hand; others simply find it difficult to throw out anything.

A growing concern is the lack of company standards for managing electronic files on desktop and laptop computers, as well as on mainframes and servers. (See Chapter 9, "Electronic Records and Information," for a more detailed discussion of the business risks related to the lack of management and control of electronic records.)

Serious problems may develop when employees are allowed to maintain their own records and information systems separate from those established for official company records. Costly recordkeeping inefficiencies are only one consideration. Individuals destroy their records only when they see fit, and not according to the company's records retention schedule. This action may jeopardize the integrity of the company's records retention program and be interpreted by a court as selective destruction. (See Chapter 7, "Retention and Disposition" for more on the risks of selective records destruction.)

Occasionally, for a self-serving purpose, an employee creates and maintains records separately from official business record systems. Employees have created or maintained records to document mistakes by other employees or in anticipation of filing a wrongful discharge claim. Headlines in recent years are about records found in an employee's basement or garage that find their way into a government investigation or court proceeding. Most often these records should have been destroyed according to the company's records retention schedule, or they are trade secrets. Since these records have not been in the control of the organization, they may easily be misinterpreted or taken out of context in a courtroom.

In short, personal records do not usually help a company. They may, in fact, prove to be harmful. A records management program must have control over the creation and management of all business records, including those in employees' offices and desks.

5

A Day in Court

Records are a principal form of evidence used in judicial and administrative proceedings and in government agency or other audits. They provide a trail of evidence that may be more trustworthy than the memory
of witnesses regarding increasingly complicated business transactions.
Lawsuits concerning events of one, five, or twenty years ago must rely
more on records than witnesses. When a legal proceeding involves the
word of one against the word of another, a favorable decision is more
likely for the party that can make the better showing in court through
witnesses and documents.

Companies with high turnover and those experiencing fast-paced and
extensive change will need to rely more on documents than witnesses.
The originator of a record may no longer be employed or may not otherwise be available as a witness.

A New York Court of Appeals found a written document of a verbal agreement
to be more trustworthy than the memory of a telephone conversation. When one
party disputed the terms of a deal made over the phone, the court said written
confirmation of the conversation is the only reliable evidence of transactions
where the likelihood of remembering the details of any one agreement, among
scores of similar deals each day, would be small.

A witness normally sets the foundation for admission of a document
into evidence. This could be the person who created or received the

document, the individual responsible for a department, or even the records or information systems manager.

CONSEQUENCES OF IMPROPER RECORDKEEPING

Timely and efficient response to document discovery requests is achieved through a comprehensive records and information management program, as well as through litigation management strategies. Documents must be collected, organized, and reviewed by attorneys without delay and with minimal disruption of business.

A well-functioning records and information management program ensures the existence of valuable and legally required records that will support company claims as well as defend against others' claims. It also reduces costs and exposure to liabilities by destruction of records that are no longer necessary or valuable. Without appropriate recordkeeping practices, a business may discover it has too many records, not enough records, or records that are not admissible as evidence.

Too Many Records

Warehouses or entire rooms have been filled by records and information related to cases involving complex financial transactions, product development, engineer designs, construction projects, long-term pollution, and multiple plaintiffs and defendants. The following are examples of the paperwork burden experienced by different companies:

The direct cost to one employer to retrieve, copy, and deliver documents required by an EEOC subpoena was an estimated $90,000.

The securities firm, Drexel Burnham Lambert, Inc., spent well over $40 million to copy, collate, and cross-reference 1.5 million pages of documents for its insider trading defense.

One attorney rented a U-Haul truck to carry his client's files across the country to the trial site.

Perhaps overdoing it a bit, 150 attorneys shipped 680 cartons of documents to the FTC overnight on a rented DC-9, in response to antitrust regulator requests for information on a $25 billion acquisition of RJR Nabisco, Inc.

Business executives and corporate attorneys tend to want to keep every record "in case we're sued." However, this defense strategy could backfire on a company. In addition to the unnecessary records storage and handling expense, the document production process for any litigation will be all the more costly and burdensome.

The Quick 'n' Dirty Company was faced with thousands of liability claims and class-action lawsuits. The corporation had a records retention schedule, but it had failed to implement it prior to initiation of the legal actions. Warehouses full of paper and microfilm records had to be searched in an effort to locate records relevant to the actions. Hundreds of backup computer and e-mail system tapes had to be restored for searching. Forensic computer technicians screened desktop and laptop computers for any deleted files that were not erased.

Too many corporations today have rooms or warehouses full of unidentified boxes of records. The boxes may be from an acquisition or facility closure. Often the boxes contain records and other items packed up from a former employee's office—marked, for example, "Joe Smith's Office." Because the contents are unknown, no one can apply a retention schedule to them, and so the boxes often are retained "just in case." But "just in case" can never happen without knowledge of what is in the boxes. The litigation risk related to these records is the inability to comply with a discovery order to search *all* records for pertinent information.

Computer tapes also create litigation risks related to discovery because all tapes are subject to review for discovery. Years of e-mail system backup tapes are abandoned in a storage room. Other tapes contain data from obsolete systems, so the organization may be forced to pay hundreds of thousands of dollars to restore the hardware and software needed to read the data.

Retaining records for periods beyond business and legal requirements may senselessly expose a business to additional liabilities when those documents are taken out of context in a legal proceeding. Or perhaps they contain unfavorable or damaging information. Because records of a creating party are considered an admission of truth by that party, they carry weight in a courtroom and are used more and more to the advantage of opposing parties.

The author is not advocating destruction of potentially damaging or unfavorable records. Destruction of records must be performed according to a formal records retention and destruction program based on an established records retention schedule and destruction procedures performed in the normal course of business.

Too Few Records

Attorneys cannot adequately represent an organization when records are not properly created and protected.

A business may be forced to settle or to pay a damages claim when documents critical to its defense cannot be found.

A jury slapped Chrysler with damages of $265.2 million, of which $250 million was to punish to company. The jury had difficulty understanding why the auto manufacturer could not produce documentation of a decision to make a mid-year vehicle design change. In addition, some films of safety tests had been destroyed according to the manufacturer's retention policy, but others created at the same time were still available. (Chrysler claimed that although two lawsuits were pending at the time of destruction, the records were destroyed because they were unrelated to those cases.) Finally, two lines of data from an electronic log of anomalies had been deleted.

When an organization is unable to produce certain records, it loses its right to file a claim against another party.

The Quick 'n' Dirty Company delivered more than $5,000 worth of equipment to another firm, but it was having difficulty obtaining payment. Unable to find the sales agreement or even proof of delivery of the equipment, Quick 'n' Dirty decided to write off the equipment as a loss because it would be fruitless to file an unsubstantiated claim in court against the customer.

Failure to comply with a court or government agency order to produce records may result in one or more of the following consequences:

- obstruction-of-justice charges
- contempt of court charges
- a court's inference that documents were destroyed in bad faith because they contained damaging information
- a finding in favor of the party obtaining the order

When documents are destroyed before their time, or when some and not others are retained beyond stated requirements, a business may suffer negative consequences in both civil and government actions.

In a 1984 court case, except for the destruction of potentially damaging records, there was no evidence presented by the defendant that employees complied with any document retention procedures. Useless and unacceptable documents had been retained, but important documents could not be produced because they had been disposed of earlier. Finding no evidence of document destruction pursuant to a consistent and reasonable policy, the judge concluded that the company intentionally destroyed documents to prevent their production, thus preventing a fair hearing of this product liability case. The defendant was prohibited from introducing evidence in support of its defense, and the judge issued a default judgment in favor of the plaintiffs for $10 million.

Courts do not look favorably upon document destruction, even when it is by accident or negligence.

Prudential Insurance Company was fined $1 million for allowing destruction of documents covered by a court order. The company also had to pay plaintiffs' attorney fees and costs associated with the motion for sanctions against the insurer. Thousands of agents in a number of different locations had destroyed some records relevant to the proceedings, and the company delayed notifying the court about the document destruction problems. Some time after that, more than 4,600 boxes of records were destroyed in a fire at a commercial records center. Because the company claimed it had phoned the judge's chambers shortly after the fire to notify him of the loss, the judge did not impose additional penalties.

Regulations for certain industries, such as public utilities, require that the circumstances of any inadvertent document destruction or loss be documented. Other businesses may be wise to adopt this practice.

Trustworthiness Challenges

Management should become familiar with the federal and state rules of civil and criminal procedure that apply to their business. As long as business records meet requirements of the various rules of evidence, records in any medium—paper, film, and electronic—are admissible in a court of law. They must be accurate and reliable.

Business has a responsibility to create and maintain records that satisfy the conditions of admissibility as defined in federal and state laws and rules of evidence. Records that best meet admissibility and trustworthiness standards are records of fact—not opinion. They are records

- prepared by a knowledgeable person at or near the time of an event
- created in the normal course of business
- created and maintained to serve an independent business purpose or to meet a legal requirement
- created by an independent third party
- created before litigation is foreseeable

Testimony by the creator of the record, the records manager, or other qualified witnesses may be necessary to show that these requirements are met. In addition, a company may be called upon to establish in court the existence of a records management program.

The trustworthiness of records may also be determined by the processes and systems used to create, maintain, and produce them. The methods necessary to authenticate records as accurate and reliable will vary slightly from one information system to another. In general, documentation of the following strategies will help support the claim that the organization's information systems are trustworthy and reliable:

- written records and information policy and procedures
- records retention program development and administration
- audit trails of procedures to create, process, and produce information
- certifications of authenticity for document reproduction processes such as filming and electronic document imaging
- records and information management program training activities
- records program audits confirming that what was supposed to happen did in fact happen and noting any remedial action that was taken
- sanctions for employee noncompliance with records policy

(See Chapter 9, "Electronic Records and Information," for more on electronic records and digital signatures.)

LITIGATION MANAGEMENT STRATEGIES

More and more attorneys are advising their clients to implement a records and information management program for all records, including electronic records. These same attorneys are challenging and scrutinizing their adversaries' records and information systems.

Records called upon during pretrial discovery and as evidence during a trial may be either a blessing or a curse. If the records contain sufficient data substantiating the company's claims, charges against the business may be dropped or a reasonable settlement may be reached. The records may, however, contain information used successfully by the opposing party. How well records are created, maintained, and destroyed will determine how well the program reduces certain risks and losses from any court proceeding.

Based on an assessment of costs, risks, and benefits of various record-keeping practices, legal counsel can determine the best approach to litigation management, an approach that provides flexibility within legal, ethical, and practical constraints.

Generally, litigation risks that may exist as a result of poor records and information management practices include the following scenarios:

- failure to preserve records necessary to file a claim or to support a defense
- maintenance of too many useless records, resulting in excessive litigation costs and exposure to risks
- inability to locate paper, film, electronic, and other records
- inability to produce electronic documents because of hardware or software obsolescence, or degradation of information storage medium
- opposing party's ability to recover deleted electronic data

To minimize such risks, litigation strategies typically involve records retention and destruction, information security, information retrieval, and other records and information management program practices.

Regulatory requirements and rules of evidence may affect records management practices that support litigation strategies. Information media selection and management may be governed by government requirements regarding record forms and rules of evidence. Information security, preservation, and indexing requirements may be found in laws, regulations, or contracts. In addition, retention requirements ensure that records remain in existence for as long as required by law or as long as necessary to demonstrate compliance with the law.

Retention Decisions

As discussed in Chapter 7, "Retention and Disposition," various laws and regulations specify a retention period for certain records. In the absence of a clearly stated records retention requirement, a business should analyze other legal considerations in order to make retention and destruction decisions that support litigation strategies.

Essentially, risk analysis and a best effort to interpret the law will lead to appropriate decisions about what records to create and how long to maintain the records in order to protect the business and to show compliance with the law. Legal counsel must weigh the costs, litigation risks, and benefits of retention time periods to determine the most reasonable retention for individual record categories.

Lawyers do not always agree on legal strategies regarding records retention. Retaining records as long as possible is a strategy based on the assumption that the records will be more helpful than harmful to the company. Some lawyers argue that if records do not exist—and their nonexistence does not violate a law or create an adverse inference—no charge may be brought against the organization. Still others believe that any corporate document, no matter how innocent it is, may become a weapon in the hands of opposing counsel. Somewhere between these extremes is the more reasonable approach.

Legal research of requirements relevant to the organization includes review of retention requirements in laws, statutes, and regulations. It also encompasses considerations such as limitations of action and case law. Additional areas of risk may include the likelihood of litigation, investigation, or audit, as well as the organization's past experiences with such actions.

A statute of limitations establishes a time period during which a claim may be filed, so a litigation strategy to retain records for all or part of that time period will be based on how important it is to preserve the company's right to a proper defense against any claim and the right to file a claim against another party.

There are circumstances in which retention of specific records for the entire statute of limitations is advised. If a company is likely to be a plaintiff, or if an adverse party would have sufficient information to file a claim without the need for discovery, it may be advisable to retain relevant records for the full statute of limitations.

If the risk of a claim and loss against the company is small or non-existent, or if there is little prospect of being a plaintiff, counsel may advise retention of records only long enough to meet business needs because the extraordinary administrative burden to retain them out-weighs the risks of any losses. The risks of a shorter retention period may also be acceptable when an excessively long statute of limitations is in a state in which the company does little business.

Litigation risks related to retention of electronic records and e-mail are significantly greater than risks related to paper documents. Unfortu-nately, the records retention principles applied to paper, film, and other readable records are not always applied to electronic data, even though they should apply from the time a computer system is turned on.

Most electronic records and information systems are designed to proc-ess, store, and transmit large amounts of information. To date, few are designed to accommodate records retention policies. Litigation risks spe-cific to electronic records retention include:

Vast amounts of data retained in a number of different systems and on different information storage media must be searched.

Electronic information systems are not as well inventoried and organized as pa-per documents, so they are difficult to search for a timely response to a dis-covery request.

Security backup copies contain information that is different from current ver-sions.

Multiple copies and different versions are not managed well.

Pressing the delete key does not erase a computer file.

Of particular concern in litigation are e-mail messages. Many organi-zations do not have clear guidelines about the appropriate use, manage-ment, and retention of e-mail messages and their attachments. When there are guidelines, little is done to audit for compliance.

A number of steps may be taken to minimize litigation risks related to retention of e-mail and electronic records:

Preserve only what continues to have a legitimate business value as per the records retention schedule.

Use software applications and other processes to completely erase deleted files.

Keep system and data backups to the minimum required to restore them in the event of a computer disaster.

(See Chapter 9, "Electronic Records and Information," and Chapter 11, "E-Mail," for more on electronic information systems.)

Discovery and Electronic Evidence

The discovery phase in a lawsuit allows each party to provide relevant information to the other party to prepare for trial. Frequently, pretrial discovery leads to settlement before trial.

The discovery process involves depositions, interrogatories, and document production. Until Rule 26 of the Federal Rules of Civil Procedure was revised in 1993, each party had to ask for specific information from the other party. Now, very early on in a federal suit each party has a duty to identify relevant records and to make information about those records available to the other party.

In a typical lawsuit or government investigation, a formidable volume of documents and electronic data may be in the possession of the business, adversarial parties, and third parties. A party may object to a discovery request when the burden and costs outweigh the benefits, but proving the burden meets the court's standard is difficult. To prevent one party from uncontrolled rummaging around in its records, an organization may also request the narrowing of a subpoena whose scope is too broad, or it may object to a request for its proprietary information.

Information technologies are changing the scope and complexity of the discovery process burden. Although business has embraced the technology revolution for many years, not until recent years did electronic records play a significant role in lawsuits. Historically, both parties in litigation make their paper recordkeeping systems available in the search for relevant information. Now computer disks and tapes are being requested by opposing parties.

The word is spreading quickly to litigants that discovery of electronic information and e-mail is a potent weapon in litigation. It is such an effective litigation tool for plaintiffs primarily because most defendants do not have control over the voluminous electronic data they generate and store.

The processes to search e-mail messages and other electronic files are expensive and complex, but a growing number of companies are making it their business to dig up potentially useful and damaging electronic tidbits.

E-mail messages often harbor the smoking gun for which every litigating attorney searches. E-mail tends to be a spontaneous communication that its creator mistakenly believes will remain private or will disappear when it is deleted. Jokes that were humorous distractions from work for some individuals are now evidence in harassment or discrimination cases. E-mail is also used effectively in today's courtrooms to support wrongful discharge and antitrust claims.

Prosecutors relied in part on internal company documents and e-mail to build the government's case against Microsoft in its antitrust suit filed in 1997. A former Justice Department trial attorney reported that about 70 percent of the 1,500 exhibits accumulated by the government were found in e-mail messages. Boxes of printed e-mails came from Microsoft backup tapes. Among the smoking gun memos and e-mails were a list of enemies and threats to "crush" a competitor. E-mail messages were also used to reconstruct meetings between Microsoft and executives of other companies.

Litigants prefer the original electronic record to a printed copy as evidence. Today computers create the vast majority of paper documents, so the electronic file is the source data and the best evidence. Adding to production expense may be the need to provide the means to the other party for access to its mainframe tapes—the hardware and software necessary to retrieve the information.

Another reason the original electronic records are preferred is that the electronic form has additional bits of often useful data, commonly referred to as metadata. An e-mail's metadata includes information about the sender, recipient(s), dates and times of transmission and receipt, and more. A word-processing document's metadata may include who made what edits and when, previous versions, and more, depending on the software settings.

The original electronic files are also used to discover what information may have been deleted and to recover it (deleted electronic documents have many lives). Electronic evidence discovery is most costly and risky when the opposing party searches through hard drives to retrieve deleted files not completely erased.

The ForwardThink Corporation hired an electronic evidence discovery firm to examine the Quick 'n' Dirty Company's electronic records. The consulting firm discovered that many files had been deleted. The firm could have taken it a step farther to resurrect the deleted information, but instead it took a picture of the hard drive to show where large portions of data had been erased. Shortly after opposing counsel saw the photograph of the hard drive, the case settled.

Electronic records may have been deleted and erased, but they continue to survive on backup tapes or on paper on another employee's desktop computer. As well, e-mail messages are forwarded, printed, backed up, and deleted—but not erased—every day.

Litigation Preparedness

Case law indicates that an inadequate records program is not an excuse for failure to comply with discovery obligations. An organization must be prepared to demonstrate its good faith efforts to create, retain, and dispose of records in a responsible manner and in accordance with established business practices. Systems must be in place to identify, locate, and preserve all relevant records in all locations and in all media in a timely manner for litigation and investigation.

In one case, both parties in a lawsuit destroyed records. There were no sanctions against one party because the destruction was pursuant to a records retention policy, and records were destroyed only after a review to make sure documents were not relevant to this litigation. The other party did not fare as well. Records destruction occurred when a lawsuit should have been anticipated, and the destruction continued even after the suit was filed. A default judgment was entered against that party because it appeared the destruction was in bad faith.

An organization can do much to prepare for litigation. Records and information policies and practices need to be reviewed for changes necessary to reduce litigation risks and costs.

When an organization has an effective litigation response mechanism in place before discovery happens, costs and time necessary to search for relevant records will be minimized. The following records and information practices help support a litigation preparedness strategy:

Know what is in the organization's records and information systems.

Index and organize records and information for timely retrieval of relevant and important information.

Adopt a retention policy for all records and information systems, including e-mail communications and electronic files on mainframes and desktops.

Systematically destroy records and information that have met their retention requirement and are not needed for litigation or investigation. Document destruction activities. Shred or otherwise destroy sensitive paper and microfilm, and erase electronic data.

Minimize copies, superseded drafts, and security backups through standard practices and training.

Implement procedures to halt destruction of all records and backups related to investigation, audit, or litigation.

Be prepared to provide to the other party information on systems and procedures to create, copy, index, store, backup, and destroy records and information.

Develop policies on the proper use of print and electronic information, as well as communications systems.

Educate employees on company policies and standard practices regarding records and information.

Monitor and audit for compliance with company policies and practices.

Special attention must be paid to electronic information and e-mail systems. Discovery of electronic evidence can be more expensive and complex than discovery of paper documents, so employers must be prepared for litigation involving scrutiny of electronic records. Employers can prepare against such litigation by

- conducting an electronic data risk assessment,
- developing a business relationship with litigation support firms, including electronic evidence discovery firms, and
- preparing records and information systems managers for depositions by other parties who want blueprints of records and information systems.

Special attention must also be given to the records centers full of boxes from an acquired or divested company. The discovery process mandates a review of all records and information to identify what may be relevant to a lawsuit. When boxed records and computer tapes are tucked out of sight without an adequate inventory and index, an organization cannot state in good faith that it has searched all available records and information systems.

Protective Orders

From traffic court to the Supreme Court, court records are normally open to the public. So are most congressional hearings. Transcripts, testimony, evidence, and judgments of criminal and civil cases are public record. Records routinely unavailable to the public are those of cases involving juveniles, some unresolved criminal cases, trade secrets, and records protected under the right to privacy. Certain state courts allow disclosure of records only when the requestor demonstrates a legal interest in the case, when the requestor is a taxpayer in the state, or when there exists a potential business relationship with one or both parties.

A business will need to show good cause before court records are sealed. Requests to seal court documents are routinely approved when both parties agree. Court proceedings on trade secret theft may present a dilemma to the violated trade secret owner. In some situations, the defendant insists on disclosure of the secret information in question in order to prepare its defense. In other situations, litigation costs rise when the litigation is shrouded in secrecy.

Trade secret information not the subject of the proceedings is generally

protected from public access. In determining whether to seal court proceedings and documents, however, a judge reserves the right to consider
the public interest. Records not generally sealed are those considered to
be of public interest, including those dealing with possible health, environmental, and other public hazards. Settlement agreements often include confidentiality clauses to prevent future disclosure of sensitive or
valuable information.

LITIGATION SUPPORT

As discussed earlier, implementation of various records and information management policies and practices prior to litigation or investigation gives an organization a strategic advantage. Among those
preparedness practices that limit expense and litigation risks are the routine records destruction according to a retention schedule and the organization of the remaining records for their timely retrieval and
production at the lowest costs. The collection, organization, and reproduction of records for discovery are thus accomplished at the lowest
possible cost, with minimal disruption of normal business activities or
delay.

The sophisticated records management program also has a step-by-
step guide to litigation support, from the discovery process through the
proceedings.

Destruction Hold

An organization has a duty to preserve records related to foreseeable
or pending litigation, government investigation, or audit. A destruction
hold on records is a procedure to suspend destruction of those records.
Even if no legal requirement exists to create or maintain a record, that
record cannot be destroyed within established, routine records destruction procedures if it relates to litigation or investigation.

Irresponsible destruction of records related to a legal action greatly
increases the risk of being forced to settle a claim or the risk of other
losses in the proceedings. Any indication at all of an existing action or
of one looming in the future is a signal to cease document destruction;
otherwise, the violating party may be charged with obstruction of justice.
An adverse inference may arise if a party proceeds with records destruction when it knows, or should have known, the documents are relevant
to an action. Obstruction of justice or other charges may also be brought
when someone advises others to destroy records or when that person
knowingly permits record destruction.

Among headlines-making stories that continue to unfold at the time of this writing, records destruction at the accounting firm Arthur Andersen resulted in a felony conviction of the firm. Indictments of individuals may follow.

Journalists report the records destruction began after Arthur Andersen hired a law firm to prepare to defend itself in cases that could arise related to its client Enron Corporation. Destruction may have continued after the firm learned the SEC was about to request Enron documents. Upon receipt of the SEC subpoena, Andersen management reminded employees of the firm's policy to preserve records when a subpoena is issued.

The Arthur Andersen firm's future is bleak. This particular crisis could have been avoided if employees had not destroyed Enron records when they should have known those records must be preserved for future litigation and government investigations.

Yet to play out is the role of document destruction at Andersen's client Enron Corporation. When Enron filed the largest bankruptcy case in U.S. history late in 2001, company officials knew—or should have known—there will be related lawsuits and government investigations. An Enron spokesperson said that four e-mail messages were sent to employees about company policy not to destroy documents when government inquiries or litigation were imminent. Evidence shows, however, that records destruction began and continued long after knowledge of congressional, SEC, and Justice Department probes into the company's collapse.

The box of shredded documents taken home by a laid-off Enron employee to use as packing material became an exhibit in testimony before the House Energy and Commerce Committee. After piecing together strips of documents, it appeared they contain financial information about controversial partnerships allegedly established by Enron to hide debt and inflate profits. Paper and electronic documents—shredded and deleted alike—are now being retrieved and restored. They eventually may be used as evidence against the company and its executives, and the evidence of records destruction may lead to obstruction of justice charges.

Whether or not destroyed documents may have contained damaging information, evidence of document destruction may be a more serious litigation and business risk than the documents themselves. The following scenarios illustrate this point.

As part of its defense against a sexual harassment lawsuit, one soft drink maker claimed that sexually explicit materials were not present in the workplace. Yet a computer forensic technician discovered that a strip poker program had been intentionally deleted from a computer, but not erased. Consequently, the judge increased the jury's award from $450,000 to $1.7 million.

In a discrimination case, the judge found that destruction of documents was so prejudicial that he inferred they would have demonstrated discrimination.

In a case about trade secrets, a special master was appointed by the court to investigate possible document destruction. He found evidence that the destruction was done by officers and employees of a company charged with trade secret theft. The court said that because documents that should have been turned over to the plaintiff were altered or destroyed, the company did not deserve a trial on the merits of the case. The court ordered a $65 million judgment against the defendant.

A judge presiding over a product liability case allowed jurors to be told about missing internal documents regarding the Bronco II that Ford said it inadvertently destroyed. Jurors were left to draw their own conclusions about whether the documents might have been incriminating. In early anticipation of lawsuits, attorneys should have included the missing documents in a roundup of engineering and safety documents before the vehicle was marketed.

In another discrimination lawsuit, Texaco was forced to settle for $176 million. Subsequent to conclusion of that proceeding, an investigation was initiated into possible conspiracy and obstruction of justice charges against one or more executives. Audio tapes in the proceedings captured discussions of ways to keep information from the plaintiff, including document alteration and destruction.

Columbia/HCA Healthcare Corporation would have had trouble convincing a jury that it discarded documents according to a retention schedule. In the midst of a federal investigation of Medicare fraud that was later settled, a citizen notified authorities that Columbia documents were found in a garbage dumpster at a gas station several miles from the nearest Columbia facility. Even if the documents were not related to the investigation, the circumstances certainly appeared suspicious.

To reduce the risks of loss or alteration, unintentional or otherwise, many businesses remove relevant original records to a secured location. Duplicate copies are left in their place for normal business use. Additional security procedures, such as higher levels of security for communications and information transmission procedures, may be necessary as well.

A 1991 lawsuit involving 9,000 plaintiffs and ten different defendants suffered a serious setback before jury selection was even completed. Three weeks of painstaking juror selecting involved the screening of more than fifty prospective jurors. A defense team psychologist had prepared a document that analyzed the prospective jurors. When a defense attorney's employee inadvertently faxed this revealing document to a plaintiff's law firm by mistakenly pressing a speed dial number, that law firm in turn faxed the papers to other plaintiffs' lawyers.

The defense argued that the document was a privileged work product, but the judge found that the defense had not taken reasonable precautions to prevent the mistake, thus constituting a waiver of confidentiality based on attorney-client privilege. Because this particular disclosure threatened to taint the entire trial, the judge dismissed the prospective jurors and ordered the jury selection process to begin again.

Document Production

A subpoena duces tecum, the order to appear and produce documents, may be for a proceeding to which the recipient may or may not be a party.

Third parties are sometimes required to produce information in cases involving other parties. Consider these examples:

One mining company had to produce invoices for an antitrust investigation of one of its vendors.

Five motion picture studios spent more than $2 million to produce 600,000 documents in response to a subpoena for litigation involving other parties.

Competitors and business partners of Microsoft were compelled to produce e-mail messages and other documents for the antitrust investigation of Microsoft.

When document production is for a lawsuit in which the organization is a party, corporate attorneys and outside counsel may turn to a litigation support services firm for case management services. To avoid expensive and disruptive changes as the case proceeds, it is best to plan first which activities will be handled by in-house legal staff, outside counsel, or the litigation support firm.

Normally a copy of a paper or filmed document is provided to the other party or is introduced as evidence at trial. When the opposing party requests original paper or electronic documents, the information owner will want to make duplicates for its own business use and to prepare its case.

Unless a subpoena specifically states that records are for use outside the office, it is preferable to furnish the records for on-site examination. Documentation regarding the summons and what information was furnished should be maintained in the event this information is needed later.

Each party in possession of relevant documents has an obligation to organize and format those materials in a way that is useful to the party seeking discovery.

The tobacco industry turned over 9 million pages of internal documents for plaintiffs in one state to sift through for evidence that tobacco companies manipulated nicotine levels in cigarettes to hook smokers. The tobacco companies spent tens of millions of dollars to create computer databases to sort, index, and identify documents, but they did not turn over the databases with the documents. When plaintiffs complained that they were forced to look for a needle in a haystack, the court ordered that the computer databases be turned over to the plaintiffs.

Failure to produce records required by a subpoena may result in court sanctions.

GM has been sanctioned more than once for refusal to obey court orders to turn over documents to plaintiff attorneys. In one case, the company was barred from presenting any defense exhibits. GM had no choice but to settle the case only days before trial. In another case, the court threw out GM's entire defense because GM continued to ignore the court's orders to turn over records.

The court sometimes rules in favor of the opposing party when it believes a company intentionally withheld evidence.

One of the largest ever judgments of bad faith against a major insurance company occurred in 1991. The judge found the discovery abuses were knowingly and willfully carried out to prevent the plaintiffs from obtaining relevant evidence. He held the insurance company liable for the entire face amount of the policy. Jurors, who tend to favor the little guy over the large corporation, were left to determine the punitive damages against the company.

Case Management

All relevant records must be identified, collected, organized, and maintained so they are readily accessible throughout the course of a proceeding. Among these litigation records are

- pleadings (the plaintiff's complaint and the defendant's answer or counterclaim)
- identification and tracking of company records for review in case preparation
- identification and tracking of records the organization has a duty to preserve
- written objections to the court for a protective order or to limit discovery
- identification and tracking of documents and electronic data produced by both parties in discovery
- sworn depositions of witnesses
- interrogatories and answers
- physical examinations
- trial briefs, transcripts, and other records

A litigation case management firm describes the typical document review and production process in the following scenario:

More than one million documents in both paper and electronic form are available for review in the search for information relevant to the proceedings. There may also be thousands or millions of e-mail messages and attachments. These records are located in a number of facilities and locations across the country.

Computer programs are used to assemble and sort through electronic documents such as e-mail messages and financial reports. Documents are indexed and coded by date, author, recipient, subjects, and key words for sorts and searches, and duplicates are filtered out. Attorneys can then focus more of their efforts on analysis of the 200,000 items that may be relevant evidence.

Legal counsel selects records needed to make a case, those needed to respond to requests by the opposing party, and those to be included in a case management database. Critical records are retrieved, copied, and delivered to the appropriate parties. An estimated 50,000 deposition documents and 4,000 listed trial documents are added to this database. Of all these documents, only about 30 are considered key trial documents.

The capability to retrieve documents is critical to a company's own case management. If a document is not found because of poor filing, the company may wind up unprepared when the opposing party produces the record, or it may lose its case. Experts in litigation case management note that accurate, detailed indexing and efficient organization of records may provide savings of thousands of dollars, along with the ability to prepare detailed complaints and responses earlier than would otherwise have been possible.

The coding, indexing, and cross-referencing system used to track documents may be manual or automated and may vary according to the nature of the case. Objective document coding and indexing extracts only information that requires no judgment, such as names and dates. Subjective document coding and indexing requires ranking the document for its relative merit, coding the issue(s) addressed in the document, and creating an abstract.

Plaintiffs began using computers to manage litigation during the era of breast implants lawsuits. Then came the tobacco litigation, facing more than 30 million documents that span decades. Automated systems that may be used are database or text management, optical character recognition, or imaging systems.

ForwardThink Corporation used a document imaging system to help control more than 115,000 documents, or one-half million pages of text, for one of its cases. In a matter of minutes, the system helped attorneys locate a single page of a document that forced the opposing party to offer a $35 million settlement.

A database of as many as 20,000 case-related documents may be stored on a single CD-ROM (compact disk-read only memory), capable of key word searches and cross-references. An alternative to creating new CD-

ROMs with database updates, documents and other court records are made available through the Internet. Digital document storage and retrieval services use the Internet as a delivery vehicle to registered parties. Each repository is client specific, and only those registered and verified by the system can access the files. The files are encrypted for additional security protection.

New and changing roles of technologies in litigation are becoming more visible. The litigation that began in 1997 over once-popular diet pills has been characterized as the nation's first significant cybersuit:

- Attorneys advertised for clients over the Internet.
- Computer-driven presentations and depositions were used in the courtroom.
- Warehouses of documents were indexed and stored on computer disks for access on laptop computers.
- Lawyers vacationing elsewhere monitored court proceedings and sent advice via e-mail.
- Some of the most embarrassing evidence against the defendant was in employee e-mail exchanges.
- The judge created his own web site to post his orders and to allow lawyers and the public to track the case.
- A plaintiff's computer consultant developed a program to search the defendant's consumer complaint database and found dozens of patients with side effects that may not have been reported to the FDA.
- A collection of articles on diet pills was assembled in a laptop computer for reference during depositions of doctors and scientific experts.
- A collection of electronic depositions and evidence was used to challenge the credibility of witnesses.
- Enterprising attorneys boiled down the best evidence against the defendant to a database on a double-CD-ROM package for sale to interested plaintiff attorneys.

Technology today helps attorneys do their jobs, but the organization must still manage all the relevant records and information throughout a proceeding and beyond, when the records revert back to the rules of the organization's retention schedule. So much material ends up on paper, and that means a warehouse of paper will not go away soon.

In complicated cases and those involving a number of plaintiffs or defendants, it is common to have a separate facility dedicated to document production and litigation support. Such a facility can be designed to accommodate a number of litigation support functions:

- record and data storage and processing
- record duplication and document imaging

- communications and computer equipment
- meeting rooms and offices

A separate facility limits disruption of normal business activities and can be designed with appropriate security measures to protect the sensitive and valuable information inside.

6

The Roles of Records in Corporate Change

Managing change in today's business climate is complex and challenging. Good business information systems help identify changing business conditions and support the necessary response.

Business must be able to respond quickly to changing conditions and expectations among a wide range of constituents: customers, employees, government, shareholders, suppliers, and the general public. A records and information program supports the organization throughout the change process from conceptualization and decision making through the transition to operations under the new business conditions.

Records and information systems also help ensure compliance with relevant laws and regulations, as well as the fulfillment of obligations to individuals and other entities. This becomes especially important during times of change, which tend to breed more litigation and government investigation. A business may need timely access to records created prior to the change, records that document the change process, and records after the change in order to defend itself against charges or to file any necessary claims.

The demand for information retrieval, processing, and production increases during each phase of any business change:

- analysis
- negotiations
- decision making

- implementation
- post-change conditions

Records and information management activities should be closely co-ordinated with the activities of legal, finance, and other departments, along with the activities of any outside advisory resources.

INFORMATION SECURITY

One of the first considerations during times of corporate change must be information security. Security risks tend to increase during such times, so security measures need to be strengthened or modified. Compliance with the new practices should be monitored, and confidentiality agreements must be executed.

New Business Ventures

No strategic alliance, merger, or acquisition can be considered without the sharing of sensitive and valuable information. This information is disclosed to the potential partners or buyers, and to employees, suppliers, and investors. Outside professional advisory services also may need access to extensive financial and proprietary information to assist buyers in their analysis of the proposal. These parties may be accounting firms, investment bankers, business brokers, acquisition specialists, business appraisers, and even corporate detectives.

An enterprise will want to protect itself and its secrets to prevent unauthorized disclosure of the information to others. This opportunity to learn about technologies, management, and financial status may become a serious business risk, especially if a deal goes sour.

If a business opportunity proposal fails, sensitive and valuable information has already been exchanged. This is particularly risky when the potential partner or buyer is a competitor. Pre-deal confidentiality agreements should include a clause that prevents the parties from exploiting what they learn about each other in the event the deal fails.

Every individual and organization that will have access to sensitive or valuable records should sign a confidentiality agreement that provides for the protection of the company's intellectual properties, trade secrets, and sensitive information.

Publicly held companies will want to take special care in guarding information about the proposed venture. Confidentiality agreements and other information security practices should extend to outside suppliers who are exposed to insider information as part of their work.

A graphics and production company, for instance, must take unique security measures when preparing a public announcement of a merger or acquisition: It must

- maintain in house as much production equipment and as many employee amenities as possible to limit employee contacts with the outside world
- restrict access to the part of the building where the most sensitive work is done
- ban or encrypt e-mail communications
- restrict cell phone use to conversations that use only code names.
- download at the printer any documents on a password- and firewall-protected web site
- switch clients' and projects' code names to the real company name only at the last possible moment

(See Appendix II, "Records and Information Security Program," for more on security measures that may be implemented during sensitive business negotiations.)

Organizational Change, Layoffs, and Liquidations

Records and information security becomes more urgent than normal business conditions when an enterprise is expanding, contracting, relocating, or closing.

In the fast pace of business expansions, sometimes information security measures are forgotten in the dust of change. It is at this time that extra precautions may be needed to prevent trade secrets from falling into the hands of a competitor.

Security measures will need to be stepped up in preparation for relocation of a facility, during the move, and throughout the settling-in period. Security threats from outsiders tend to increase during the chaos and confusion of a move. Computers containing sensitive and valuable information should not be left unattended on a loading dock, for instance.

If employees resign or are terminated as a result of a facility relocation, the probability of employee sabotage grows. (Chapter 3, "Threats to Sensitive and Valuable Records and Information," and Chapter 4, "Employer Rights and Responsibilities," discuss employee information security threats related to terminations and other circumstances.)

Information security concerns do not end when a business is about to be liquidated. Intellectual properties are available for sale, including patents, customer lists, registered trademarks, copyrights, and Internet domain names. Those intangible assets need to be protected until their sale.

There may also be litigation risks related to how to dispose of certain proprietary information. If the dissolved organization's web page privacy policy promised not to sell customer information, there may be claims of breach of contract or unauthorized disclosure of private information.

The risk of employee theft of computers is at an all-time high during dissolution of an organization.

Not too long ago, dot-com companies—those businesses dependent on the Internet as their home base—were the darlings of investors. The widespread failure of so many of them so soon after their creation is a bitter pill for their employees to swallow. At one failed company, an employee stole a server. At another, employees walked off with $35,000 worth of laptops, handheld computers, monitors, and laser printers before the failed company could organize an asset auction. An investigator said the employees believe they were entitled to the equipment, since they had been promised millions in stock options.

Theft prevention is not solely for the purpose of preserving the tangible asset for sale at auction. Computer assets must be stripped of all intangible assets and legal obligations as soon as is possible. Licensed and proprietary software programs should be removed or erased. All company proprietary, customer, and employee information must be erased or otherwise be made irretrievable by any means.

NEW BUSINESS VENTURES: ANALYSIS TO CLOSURE

Mergers, acquisitions, and strategic alliances continue to be a significant part of the business landscape. The need for quality information to support these new business ventures is critical. Whether one is buying or selling, accurate and complete records of assets and liabilities must be assembled for review and analysis by the teams of attorneys, accountants, and others.

Business Valuation

Activities preparatory to a business sale begin with an accurate valuation and assessment of the condition of the business to be acquired. This process is usually referred to as due diligence.

To determine a fair asking price for the business or the portion(s) of the business to be sold, records will be required to identify assets, liabilities, and other obligations such as warranties or other agreements. Even the archives of a business may be treated as an asset in the negotiation of a sale, or they may be treated as a tax write-off if a decision is made to donate the archives to a nonprofit organization.

A potential buyer will want to evaluate the past track record, present outlook, and future potential of the target business. Other records that may be needed include

- marketing plans
- management practices
- policies and procedures
- organization charts
- personnel files
- financial and legal information about current owners

Records will be assembled, processed, and created for the critical financial and legal audits necessary in this evaluation process. Also appropriate may be an analysis of external information regarding current and future market conditions that may affect the business.

In a financial audit a wide range of financial records from the preceding several years may be compiled for review, and new records may be created for the review in the following areas:

- profit-and-loss statements
- debts
- mortgages and leases
- utilities and other expenses
- status of various tax filings and payments
- bank accounts and safety deposit boxes
- securities and cash equivalents
- age, cost, depreciation, and insured value of assets
- age of accounts receivables
- monthly sales for thirty-six months
- sales fluctuations over twelve months
- accounts that may be lost with a change of ownership
- intangibles that may generate profit (intellectual properties, franchises, etc.)
- age and turnover of inventories
- production and labor costs
- price lists, discounts, previous increases
- employee benefit plans, insurance and wages payments
- insurance coverage types and premiums

A legal audit will require the review of a number of company records. Title documents and public records may need to be scrutinized to confirm that the assets for sale are free of encumbrances and use restrictions.

Are there any pending or foreseeable claims, lawsuits, or government investigations? Are there any contingent liabilities, such as warranted products? What is the extent of compliance with various government requirements for safety, labor, environment, wages, taxes, retirement plans, and more? What are the rights and obligations stipulated in contracts, agreements, leases, permits, and licenses?

Among the documents and information required for other legal considerations are

- a list of all states where the target company is qualified or authorized to do business
- deeds and titles
- intellectual properties, including trademarks, patents, and copyrights
- product or service agreements and warranties
- powers of attorney
- contracts for the purchase of materials, supplies, and equipment
- lists of creditors

The following example illustrates how inaccurate and incomplete records may be a litigation risk involving its customers, subcontractors, or the acquiring company.

A national telecommunications firm decided to sell its business operations and customer base in a number of states so it could concentrate on a targeted region of the country. When the time came to assemble an information package for potential buyers, corporate headquarters found it had to resort to estimates of business value. The inventory records of fixed assets, vehicles, equipment, and materials were current and accurate, but the records of the rights and obligations of the company, its subcontractors, and its customers were not. A corporate database reflected a picture of business commitments to customers and subcontractors, but the original agreements and warranties to back up that information were incomplete and inconsistent.

If information disclosed for analysis is inadequate, the organization may be sued for breach of contract or fiduciary duty, or for negligence.

As the analysis and negotiation process continues, additional records are processed and created on top of the existing records made available for review. Financial models may be developed to evaluate a number of different scenarios. The effects of alternative structures or the timing of a transaction on taxation may be documented for study. There may be other records created in support of certain legal considerations, and records may be produced for disclosure to certain parties or filed with a government agency in order to comply with a government requirement.

Government Requirements and Legal Considerations

Throughout the analysis of a proposed acquisition or merger, government requirements or other legal considerations will compel the review, creation, or disclosure of certain records. The burden of compliance with antitrust, securities, taxation, environment, consumer protection, and other legislation must be assessed. If the proposed deal crosses the border, international treaties and regulations must be reviewed. Issues of timing, financing, and other strategies must also be considered.

There may be a requirement of prior notification to the Department of Justice or the FTC regarding a merger or acquisition. The shareholdings of a target business may need to be traced to ensure compliance with SEC regulations or appropriate blue-sky securities laws of the state(s) involved. A merger may require approval by the seller's shareholders and the shareholders of the buyer, unless the buying corporation already owns a majority of the stock. Federal and state laws require a franchiser to disclose designated information to a potential buyer within certain time frames associated with the payment of deposits and the signing of an agreement.

Mergers of companies that are competitors or that produce similar goods or services will need to pay more careful attention to antitrust regulations than will mergers of companies that will form a conglomerate. Document filings with the Department of Justice's antitrust division or the FTC will be required when a merger or acquisition meets certain legal criteria, including transaction size and the degree of control being acquired.

Other legal or government actions may be necessary before final closure of a deal. Businesses may need to be prepared to justify their actions in response to government investigations or complaints from competitors, suppliers, customers, or shareholders. Third-party actions against one or more parties to the merger may result in a temporary restraining order or preliminary injunction, litigation, or further government investigation. Existing records and new documents required for any litigation or investigation will have to be organized, indexed, duplicated, and forwarded to the appropriate government agencies or court.

Sale Agreements

When one business completely takes over another business, it generally assumes its assets and liabilities. A business sale agreement typically specifies

- assets to be transferred, including intellectual properties
- assignment of responsibility for preexisting, current, and future liabilities such

as tax obligations, product and environmental liabilities, and employee retirement benefits

• assignment of rights and obligations related to contracts
• purchase price and financing arrangements
• any noncompete or consulting arrangements
• provisions for arbitration

A sale agreement may or may not stipulate that the buyer will assume certain or all debts and liabilities or that they will be retained by the seller. Clarification of which assets and liabilities form part of the agreement is critical to the avoidance of lawsuits farther down the road. Separate employment contracts often supplement a sale agreement to ensure retention of key personnel.

It is highly recommended that the sales agreement include a clause specifically addressing each party's responsibilities for the business records in all forms—paper, microfilm, and electronic. Absent a clause that speaks to records responsibilities, logic dictates that the party assuming assets, liabilities, or obligations, also assumes responsibilities for the relevant records. Any large volume of inactive records should be mentioned in the agreement, as it may represent a significant expense to the party responsible for maintaining those records for as long as needed for legal or government purposes.

Under the agreement, the target company may be responsible for preparing records for the new owner by organizing, consolidating, segregating, duplicating, imaging, and even packing the affected records. Time frames should be established for any duplication and transmittal of the records to support the acquired portions of the company. Procedures should be determined for records and information searches that are required because certain records were not provided at the time of cut-over.

AFTER A MERGER OR ACQUISITION

Information demands continue at a high level under post-acquisition conditions. To support its assumed customer and employee bases, assets, liabilities, and other terms and conditions of the agreement, the newly formed organization will require immediate access to important company data from all acquired segments of the business.

Information from each company is required to identify and resolve transition issues, including

identification and notification of all customers and suppliers

elimination or consolidation of redundant or obsolete business functions and activities determination of personnel requirements for the new organization and qualifications of existing personnel

management and resolution of different employee pay scales, benefits programs, and retirement plans

disposition of duplicate assets, including equipment, vehicles, and properties

collection and indexing of documents relevant to pending and potential litigation and government investigation regarding the merger, as well as activities of the individual acquired companies

development of budgets and realistic timetables for transition activities

Unfortunately, problems with information retrieval normally arise because of incompatible or inadequate records and information systems. Incompatible methods of collecting and organizing data may present difficulties for timely access to useful information. A merged organization may need to seek outside assistance from a computer and software business that specializes in helping merged companies consolidate or separate their electronic information.

Ideally, the preacquisition planning process addresses records and information management issues. Planning becomes more important when the time frame to complete the integration process is compressed from years to months. Managers will find it especially helpful to

- assess and compare the records and information management programs of both organizations
- determine ownership status for business records and information
- develop a records and information systems transition plan
- identify staff members from both organizations who will be available for the transition
- conceptualize the scope of the new records and information management organization

Timely integration of the various information systems into a seamless network of efficient information systems is critical to the transition process and to the new organization's ongoing operations. All employees need training on changes in information systems. More frequent compliance audits may be useful to identify problem areas and to give positive feedback when systems work well.

Disposition of Records

When the ownership and disposition of an acquired company's records is not clarified by an agreement, the issue is normally resolved by default. Generally, records and information that support legal rights and obligations remain with those rights and obligations—whether they stay with the original organization or are transferred to the new owner. Certain records may be required by both organizations if the assets and obligations are divided among the organizations.

The new owner should identify records associated with the assets, liabilities, and other business functions it has now assumed, based on the sale agreement, to determine the proper disposition of records.

When The House of Good Intentions acquired the subsidiary of another business, property and equipment leases were renegotiated or officially transferred through the individual vendors and lessors. The acquired organization forwarded lists of the acquired products, parts, and equipment to the House of Good Intentions, along with ownership documents, tax records, and user manuals related to those assets.

Although The House of Good Intentions did not assume either the customer liabilities or the revenues related to transactions prior to the sale, the firm requested duplicate copies of selected customer files to support its future efforts to provide products and services to the acquired customers. Some customer files contained records that were the property of the customer, so customer agreements regarding records were updated to reflect the records transfer to a new business.

The House of Good Intentions did not agree to assume responsibility for any past employee actions related to the employees it agreed to hire from the former company. Forwarded to The House of Good Intentions were copies of only basic employee information—name, address, length of service, job title, and salary.

If an audit of the target company's records during the acquisition analysis was not practical or feasible at that time, the new owner should initiate a records and information management program assessment immediately after the close of the sale. If the former organization had a records management program, the records documenting the program will need to be retained in the event of litigation or investigation regarding records from that company.

It is preferable to do a records inventory before any records are shipped to the new organization. Vital, sensitive, and valuable records must be identified and appropriately protected. Certain records may be destroyed. The remaining records should be accurately indexed and clearly labeled for proper disposition by the new organization.

Removal and appropriate destruction of duplicate and valueless documents will avoid unnecessary transportation expense and reduce storage and handling costs. A record destruction review may be conducted if the acquired organization has an adequate records retention schedule. If no retention schedule is available, the acquiring organization's schedule may be used only if a review determines that regulations in all jurisdictions relevant to the organization are included in the legal research that underlies the retention decisions. Documentation of any retention schedule modifications and record destruction must be retained to support future audit and compliance needs.

If the acquired records are well indexed, it is possible to compare those records with an inventory of the new owner's records to identify any duplicate records that may be purged. Clearly identified and indexed active records may be merged with similar files belonging to the new owner, such as customer or supplier files.

The Quick 'n' Dirty Company came into being as the result of a merger of three separate businesses. Three trucks dumped business records into a warehouse several weeks after the merger was finalized. There were no packing lists with the boxes, and many boxes containing folders, binders, and computer disks and tapes had no labels. The firm's cash flow was reaching critical condition because it could not find records to bill customers. A team of temporary employees had to be hired, trained, and sent to the warehouse to find the records necessary to collect on past sales transactions and the records necessary to generate new sales from the existing customer base.

Poorly organized or unindexed records in storage rooms or commercial records centers are an unwarranted expense because the records are not easily retrieved. Labels on boxes that read, "John Doe's Office" or "Project Files" are not useful. Poorly indexed records are also an ongoing litigation risk, as discussed in the previous chapter, "A Day in Court."

Generally, important active records and information are merged into the new organization's records and information systems. Inactive records of the acquired business tend to be maintained separately from all other records. A system to retrieve inactive records must be established so they may easily be recalled for the inevitable audits, government investigation, or litigation.

LIQUIDATION OF AN ORGANIZATION

Legal obligations related to finances, contracts, employees, environment, shareholders, and more, live on after an organization is liquidated. Records continue to be needed to support the former entity in litigation, government investigation, and audit.

Accounting records are needed to support tax returns and their audits. Employee files may be needed for future litigation. Asset documents may be needed to file insurance claims for incidences of property theft before the assets are sold. Other records must continue to exist to satisfy a regulatory requirement to retain them.

The parent company, board of directors, general partners, or owners are responsible for the maintenance of a company's records when an organization is dissolved. These individuals may be sued or fined for any improper recordkeeping practices.

Appropriate measures are necessary to safeguard information that must be retained by law, to show compliance with the law, to defend the organization, and to file a claim. Following is a summary of one of the earliest court cases that demonstrates how an IRS audit is a foreseeable action and that an organization has a duty to preserve the related records.

The records of a liquidated firm were left in the care of one of its partners, who stored them in the basement of an office building. Two years after the firm's liquidation, a flood caused substantial damage to the basement's contents. The firm's books and records were discarded, along with damaged merchandise and other items stored in the basement. The judge determined that this seemingly careless treatment of records at a time when the IRS would need them supported the inference that the information would have been harmful to the defendants.

When an organization that will be dissolved has a records retention schedule, a records destruction review should take place at the time of dissolution. Prior to any destruction, records should be reviewed to determine if they are needed for litigation, investigation, or audit.

More records can be destroyed when a business shuts down than can be destroyed during a routine annual destruction review. Duplicate copies, drafts, and reference materials are no longer needed for business use. Records with a retention requirement of active may no longer be active and may be destroyed.

Certain records about assets are transferred to the organization that purchases the asset. Other records, such as employee hazardous exposure monitoring records, may be transferred to a regulatory agency for their ongoing maintenance. Record destruction and records transfers to other organizations should be documented for future reference.

The Resolution Trust Corporation (RTC) was created to resolve failed savings and loan institutions and dispose of their assets. Although much of the work accomplished by the RTC is completed, responsibilities for the RTC records continue. The successor agency to the RTC is the Federal Deposit Insurance Corporation (FDIC). Managers for both organizations examined their different records management programs and made adjustments to achieve a more efficient organization of the new records program.

If there is no retention schedule, the liquidation process will need to finance storage of all records until all legal and financial obligations are satisfied.

ORGANIZATIONAL CHANGE

The more dynamic a company, the more difficulties it will have keeping its information systems current and responsive to its end users, government requirements, and legal obligations. Government investigations and litigation tend to increase during organizational change, and records must be readily available for these proceedings. When a business changes, grows, or shrinks, easy-to-use records and information systems become even more critical as energies of a changing workforce are diverted to new endeavors.

Growth and Change

A start-up business often experiences a fast pace of change and growth in its first few years. Ideally, a records and information management program should be established along with other internal systems and processes at the time of start-up.

The House of Good Intentions began business operations with five employees. In two years it grew to 1,200 employees in twenty-five office sites. As early as one month after incorporation, the firm hired a consultant to design a corporate-wide records and information management program. The consultant worked with top executives and managers to establish a subject list of anticipated or probable records groups for indexing purposes. An outside law firm used this list to research recordkeeping requirements and develop a records retention schedule. A records manager was hired later to continue program development and to coordinate records activities in each facility through the office managers, designated as the records coordinators.

Responsibility for certain records management tasks was assigned to corporate headquarters, relieving the field offices of these responsibilities. Information security, e-mail, retention, and other policies were established for implementation in every facility. A standardized records filing and storage system was designed, which later proved to simplify the opening, consolidation, and eventual closing of facilities as the business matured. Record transfers between locations required no additional processing other than changing the location data field in the records management database.

As a business changes, the records and information management program must be updated so it may continue to support changing business functions. A well-designed records and information program will be flexible enough to adapt easily to organizational change so it may continue to be compatible with and supportive of new organizational directions.

One retailer experienced spectacular growth, from 2,000 square feet to 40,000 square feet within only a few years. Along with the physical expansion of its inventory and facilities was an explosion of its paper-based information systems. Paper document systems struggled to track an inventory of 200,000 merchandise items, thousands of customers, and 9,000 vendors. A customized computer information system was installed to achieve timely receipt of merchandise and to enhance customer service.

Facility Moves

Relocation of a facility presents many challenges and opportunities for records and information management. The challenge is to minimize disruption of daily activities. The opportunity is to settle into a new location with a new or updated records and information management program in place.

Good planning for an office move begins far in advance of the move. Records and information managers should be involved in planning to determine the appropriate space, equipment, and environmental conditions to accommodate all the organization's records and information needs.

Only necessary records should be moved to the new facility. Unnecessary and valueless records should be purged to avoid the expense of moving them to the new facility. All other records and electronic information systems should be reviewed for possible disposal within the existing records retention program. If a move is across state lines, the records retention schedule may need to be revised to reflect the new state's recordkeeping requirements. Prior to any destruction, confirmation should be made that the records are unrelated to litigation, investigation, or audit.

To further reduce space requirements for records in the new facility, it may be appropriate to transfer inactive records to a records center. Designated records may also be converted to microfilm or optical disk prior to or during the move.

The remaining records and information should be organized and indexed for easy retrieval and to facilitate future applications of the retention schedule in the new facility.

Workforce Reductions and Facility Closures

When a business decides to reduce expense, it often turns to workforce reductions and facility closures or consolidations. Information is required to analyze what tasks, jobs, functions, or business sites may be eliminated in the new business strategy. Because of the higher risks of litigation or government investigation in these circumstances, more careful attention must be given to accurate and complete recordkeeping throughout the change process. In addition, government information disclosure requirements may be applicable, as in the federal law that requires sixty days' notice to employees and local governments of any plant closing or major layoff. Employees must also be notified of their right to continue health insurance coverage.

The principle that elimination of tasks and the streamlining of internal processes should go hand in hand with elimination of workers also applies to a records and information management program. The organization's records and information systems should remain strong and may need to be made stronger to offer the support needed by the surviving employees of a workforce reduction.

When a facility is closed for reasons other than a sale or liquidation of the business, the company remains responsible for the assets and liabilities of that facility's operations. Many enterprises have a tendency to dispose of records from a facility as part of its closure procedures. However, without the records necessary to clarify its position, it would be difficult for the business to defend itself or to file claims against another party should the need arise.

The House of Good Intentions decided to close one of its poorly performing facilities. Prior to the closure, final paperwork was processed on invoices and customer bills. Suppliers were notified of final invoicing procedures. Records of employee terminations or transfers to another site were created. Technical manuals, handbooks, and other company information and property were collected from those employees to be terminated. Additional records were created during the closure process to document the disposition of records, vehicles, furniture, equipment, hardware, software, and other assets.

The data on personal computers targeted for sale as surplus equipment were transferred to tape, and the hard drives were reformatted to completely erase the data. Duplicate and other unnecessary records were destroyed.

Certificates of records destruction, records transmittal notices, and all other records created during the closing process were collected for retention along with other records from the facility. Records most likely to be recalled within eighteen months for financial, legal, or customer support purposes were transferred to a corporate headquarters temporary staging area. All other records were transferred to a records center for storage until the company's records retention program guidelines authorize their destruction.

7

Retention and Disposition

A typical executive, tax manager, or corporate attorney would sleep better at night knowing that the company is documenting every business transaction or process and is maintaining those records forever. But storage of the billions of new documents created every year is simply not practical in terms of costs, efficiencies, and litigation risks. Few businesses can afford to store and properly preserve all paper, microfilm, and electronic records they receive and generate for extended periods of time. Costs mount up in terms of space, environmental controls, hardware, software, equipment, supplies, personnel, and information security and preservation.

The tendency to want to keep records permanently stems from a reluctance to make decisions. Keeping records is easier than having to determine what to destroy and when to destroy it. But the evidence is piling up against keeping everything "just in case." It is costly to maintain records that are no longer useful, valuable, or required. Records retained longer than necessary are being subpoenaed, adding unnecessary records to the already burdensome document review and production process. Worse yet, a risk exists that the content of records may be taken out of context, misinterpreted, and used against their owners by an opposing party in litigation or investigation.

MANAGING VOLUMES OF RECORDS AND INFORMATION

Studies show that more than 80 percent of filed records are never referred to again and that 40 percent are completely without value. But which records have real value, and which have no value at all? Which records lose their value after a period of time, and how long is that interval?

It is irresponsible for a company to be overzealous by clearing out boxes of records or dumping magnetic tapes without appropriate guidelines. A systematic approach to record destruction is especially important in companies likely to be involved in litigation or government investigation. Any haphazard or ad hoc approach can be construed as selective destruction and thus have negative consequences, such as obstruction-of-justice charges.

A records retention and disposition program helps a business regain control over the proliferation of its records and information. The program maintains that delicate balance of having enough of the right records and not having too many records.

A records retention program, the very heart of records and information management, identifies

- valuable and necessary records to be retained to meet business and legal requirements
- the appropriate information carrier for specific records and information
- official record and unofficial, or duplicate, copies
- when it is best to convert certain records from one information carrier to another
- when it is more economical to transfer records to a less costly storage facility
- when it is appropriate to permanently dispose of records and information

Although a retention program may be costly to develop and administer in terms of human and capital resources, the costs of not having a systematic program in place are greater. Aside from the costs to manage unnecessary records, the legal justifications for a records retention and disposition program are quite persuasive.

Certain records must be maintained in order to comply with the law or to show compliance with the law. If business does not follow the rules—including maintenance of records to show its compliance with the rules—it may lose its legal rights or be subject to civil or criminal charges and penalties. Other records no longer necessary are destroyed to prevent unnecessary legal costs and liabilities. As awareness of the benefits of a records retention program grows, more and more attorneys are advising their clients to establish such a program.

The Records Retention Schedule

At the heart of a records retention program is a records retention schedule that is based on legal requirements, litigation risk management, and business needs. The schedule and its supporting policies apply to all records and information, regardless of their storage media.

A retention schedule is a vehicle for conducting the activity of records retention and disposition in a systematic, rational manner. The development of a retention schedule forces management to make hard decisions based on long-term business needs and legal requirements. The ultimate objective of a retention schedule is to meet business needs and legal requirements, as well as to destroy records at the earliest possible time in the best interests of the business.

In its purest form, a schedule identifies which records are to be maintained, in what form(s), and for how long. A more advanced retention schedule includes instructions for disposition other than destruction, such as conversion to another information carrier or transfer to another location. As a management tool, the schedule not only controls the volume of records but also organizes the remaining records for better access.

ForwardThink Corporation's retention schedule covers records in all media. The schedule is based on a subject listing of the company's records and the appropriate retention requirements for each group of records. Some record groups have instructions for when inactive records are to be transferred to the records storage facility. Instructions for certain records to be converted to microfilm at a specified time include what to do with the original paper or electronic record. E-mail messages are automatically erased from the server and desktop computers at the proper time. A retention and destruction guide exists for each electronic information system. The schedule also prescribes frequencies and methods of backing up electronic records and transferring the backups to the computer data security center. Upon expiration of the final retention period for a group of records, those records are retrieved in all of their various forms and destroyed by trashing, shredding, and electronic data erasure.

A retention schedule must apply to all records that have a real or potential impact on the business, its employees and customers, government relations, court proceedings, and the general public. This includes paper and electronic records, microforms, audio and video tapes, and photographs.

If a retention and disposition program is not applied to all records, a court of law may challenge the systematic destruction of records according to an established schedule when records that should have been destroyed continue to be available through a computer, microform, paper, or other record form.

At The House of Good Intentions, the retention schedule for paper and microfilm records is not coordinated with the Information Systems department's procedures for computer records. As a result, COM and paper printouts of computer data are not routinely destroyed when the original computer data are erased.

Electronic data continue to exist when the related paper and microfilm records are destroyed according to their retention schedule. In some cases, a file on a computer diskette is deleted under the assumption that a paper or microfilm copy is being retained, when in fact it is not.

If the integrity of the records retention program of The House of Good Intentions were ever to come under scrutiny in court, the company's inability to apply the same retention and destruction procedures to all records in all media could jeopardize any claim of a systematic records destruction program.

Just as it is important to apply a retention schedule to all records in all media, it is important to apply such a schedule consistently throughout an organization. One retention requirement applies to each record category, even when those records are in different departments or facilities in different states. For example, an accounting department budget is retained for the same time period as a law or marketing department budget.

The subject of one company's security investigation sued the company and subpoenaed the investigator's report from four years ago. The Colorado plant retained its security investigations for three years, so the report had been destroyed. The plaintiff discovered that company plants in another state had security investigation reports dating back five years. The plaintiff claimed an appearance of wrongdoing, because evidence was purposefully destroyed at the Colorado plant.

RETENTION AND DISPOSITION DECISIONS

The creation and maintenance of records is compelled by business needs and legal requirements. When taken one step farther, these needs, requirements, and other considerations determine when those records have served their useful purpose(s).

A retention schedule is a blend of user needs, stated and implied legal requirements, and various legal considerations. Legal considerations are based on the amount of risk the business is willing to assume, interpretation of the intent of the law, contractual obligations, statutes of limitations, and litigation strategies. The overall value of records and information is assessed according to their actual and anticipated uses by the business, the government, or a court of law.

Business Needs

Every business has its own needs for records and information. Records are necessary for planning, resource management, and management of daily activities and business transactions. If a vital records schedule exists, some of the work has already been done regarding record transfers and disposition of superseded vital records. Interviews of record creators and users help determine business needs in the basic functional areas, including

- administration
- corporate history
- finance
- human resources
- manufacturing and production
- marketing, sales, and customer relations
- research and development
- securities and shareholder relations
- strategic planning
- tax and legal matters

Record creators and users may also be consulted on suggested record storage media, but the final decision should include factors such as legal and retention requirements. Record users throughout departments will have a good idea of how long individual record categories should be maintained. They also know when a record becomes inactive and ready for transfer to a lower-cost records center. The decision to transfer inactive records to another location is strictly a business decision and is not based on any legal requirement.

Legal Requirements

Compliance with the law regarding records retention is not as difficult as it might seem. Most laws tend to reflect good business practices. As an example, in order to meet its own information requirements, every business normally creates and maintains many of the financial records needed for tax returns. A retention program simply makes sure these records are protected and maintained at least as long as necessary to satisfy legal requirements.

Recognizing that telephone companies maintain records in the normal course of business, the FCC eliminated hundreds of its recordkeeping requirements, including records retention requirements. The commission now requires telecommunications companies to develop their own retention schedules.

Government regulations do exist that deviate from generally accepted business practices. These differences between government and business needs primarily occur in situations where the public interest is not yet fully defined or where government purposes for the records differ from those of business. For example, the government requires a much longer retention period than most businesses prefer for employee hazardous exposure medical records because the government's interest is in monitoring problems that may not develop for many years.

Government requirements may contain clearly stated recordkeeping instructions, implied requirements, instructions that are confusing or that contradict other recordkeeping requirements, or no instructions at all. State requirements may exist where federal requirements do not, or they may be different from federal requirements.

More than half of the stated requirements to create or maintain records do not specify how long to retain those records. There are requirements that specify the acceptable media form(s) of a record and the conditions under which each form is acceptable. A few government recordkeeping requirements go so far as to specify storage conditions and information security methods. Many statutes and regulations do not specify any recordkeeping requirements at all, but it would be in the best interest of a business to anticipate the implications of its recordkeeping practices regarding rules of evidence and the ability to demonstrate compliance with a regulation.

There are certain records that may be affected by more than one law or regulation. For example, the same payroll records necessary to support tax claims may also be needed to show compliance with equal pay regulations. Or one regulatory agency may require that certain records be maintained for six months, whereas those same records may be needed for eighteen months to satisfy Department of Justice requirements.

Not all of the thousands of federal, state, local, and foreign records retention requirements affect every business. Companies must comply with those federal requirements applicable to all businesses and those related to their industries and specific business activities. Every location where the company is doing business, where it has a facility, property, or employees, or where it is incorporated, is subject to a number of state, local, and international requirements.

The TechTrack firm, for example, is doing business in fourteen states. Research of federal and state requirements turned up 900 applicable federal and state recordkeeping requirements.

A company must make an effort to be reasonably informed of laws that affect its recordkeeping practices. It must also stay current on the changes in statutes, regulations, and case law. Most businesses already have some of that knowledge scattered throughout their organization: A safety manager is familiar with OSHA regulations, a human resources manager is aware of employment requirements, and a contracts administrator knows contract requirements related to records and information.

Centralizing this knowledge, confirming and updating it, and filling in the blanks can be a relatively simple task.

There is no single source to identify all international, federal, administrative agency, and state recordkeeping requirements that govern an individual organization. Hampering a thorough search is poor indexing of requirements or the absence of published requirements. On the international level, English translations may not be available.

Publications that include suggested retention schedules should be used with caution. They may not be current, and they may not include industry-specific requirements or all jurisdictions in which an organization operates.

Corporate or outside counsel, a records retention consultant, or the organization's records management professional may complete research of recordkeeping requirements. Most corporate legal departments are reluctant to devote the time necessary for research and interpretation of the laws as they apply to business situations. Outside counsel is sometimes used for this service—at great expense.

A records management professional who undertakes this task can use one of the few commercially available publications and databases of recordkeeping requirements. Legal counsel should review and approve the results of research completed by anyone not formally trained in conducting legal research.

Regardless of who does the research, it is important to make a reasonable attempt to find, interpret, and apply the law. The research should be updated every year or so.

Contracts and Agreements

Legal requirements regarding recordkeeping may be found in contracts and agreements.

Records belonging to one party that are in the possession of another party frequently are covered by a contract of some sort. Hospitals, clinics, and law, accounting, and engineering firms may not modify, destroy, or turn over to a third party the records belonging to others without permission of the owner or a court-ordered subpoena.

Responsibility for the records of one company acquired by another will normally be covered by the acquisition agreement. If this is not made clear in the agreement, the organization responsible for the assets and liabilities of the acquired company should be responsible for the records.

Federal contractors have recordkeeping requirements, as stated in various federal laws and regulations applicable to all contractors. They may also have additional requirements specifically stated in the contract.

The House of Good Intentions has a contract with the federal government. Regulations regarding federal contracts require retention of records for three years after completion of the contract. Exceptions to this retention period are cost accounting and procurement records, to be retained for four years, and time cards, to be retained for two years. A review of the contract reveals that in addition, specific employee records must be retained for five years to be in compliance with federal contractor requirements.

Statutes of Limitations

Statutes of limitation, or limitations of actions, are found in federal and state statutes and regulations. A statute of limitations specifies the time period during which an organization or individual may sue or be sued after an event. It is important to identify (1) the relevant limitations of actions in every state in which a company does business and (2) when each statute of limitations time period begins.

Statutes of limitations do not impose a legal requirement to retain records, but they are a legal consideration that must be part of the retention decision-making process. They define the scope and time frame of risk for the organization. For example, because a discrimination complaint may be filed within 180 days of an action, records of employment actions should be maintained at least for this time period to defend against any discrimination charges.

If no record retention requirement exists, the statute of limitations becomes an especially important legal consideration.

Most tax regulations do not state a record retention requirement. Retention decisions for tax-related records must factor in the limitation of assessment time period and the retention requirements applicable to those records that support a tax return, such as property, sales, and insurance records.

The federal limitation of assessment time period is three years after a return is filed or the tax becomes due. During this time the IRS may assess or collect taxes or initiate legal proceedings. In addition, the taxpayer may demand a refund or a credit during this time. An exception to this limitation of assessment time period may be the extension of the time period to six years if the taxpayer mistakenly—or otherwise—understates the gross income by 25 percent or more.

Because most states use the federal tax return as the basis for their own income tax, a business will need to retain the federal return's records for as long as they are necessary to support the state income tax return.

When no legal requirement and no legal consideration are found for a record category, the best strategy may be to retain the records for three years. However, a retention period longer than three years might be necessary for historical, research and development, and other records that are critical to long-term business needs. This suggested three-year retention is based on the Uniform Preservation of Private Business Records Act and, with some exceptions, affects federal recordkeeping requirements and the requirements of the states that have adopted the law as of this writing.

Litigation strategies may be developed that result in a decision to retain a records group longer than business needs dictate, or longer than the government requires, in order to protect the company's interests within a statute of limitations. If a statute of limitations allows legal action within six years and the business wants to retain the right and the opportunity to take action or to defend itself within this time period, it will consider maintaining related records for all or part of the statute of limitations, even when that time period is longer than other recordkeeping requirements. (See Chapter 5, "A Day in Court," for litigation strategies that relate to records retention decisions.)

Finalizing Retention Decisions

Retention decisions reflect how long a time is reasonable to maintain records to conduct business, to protect the organization and its assets, and to demonstrate compliance with the law.

Every decision to retain or not to retain a record category involves analysis of the costs, benefits, and risks involved. To provide a full and equitable analysis, attorneys may need to become educated on records management principles and the benefits of controlling large volumes of records for manageability and efficiencies.

Retention decisions should be based on sound business practices and should allow for as much flexibility as possible within the existing legal, practical, and ethical constraints.

The final records retention schedule must be approved in writing by the departments responsible for individual records groups, by legal counsel, by the tax administrator, by the records and information management professional, and by others as appropriate. Written approvals of the final retention schedule will demonstrate both systematic development of the retention schedule and company-wide support of the program.

The selected retention periods are not cast in concrete because record categories, legal considerations, and business activities change over time. Any changes in the retention schedule must not be treated casually. Changes must be justified and approved by the appropriate management personnel and by legal counsel. The process must be fully documented.

Once it is determined how long records are to be maintained, efforts must be made to preserve those records for their full retention period. Knowing how long a record will be retained becomes a major factor to consider when selecting the record's storage medium. All records designated for retention must be protected from damage or loss. This includes making sure that computer data, hardware, software, and indexing are preserved so as to be able to access and produce electronic records for as long as necessary.

The retention schedule should be distributed throughout the organization to those employees with responsibilities for record creation, maintenance, transfer, media conversion, and destruction. Procedures must be in place for routine and systematic implementation of the records retention schedule, as well as for documentation of the process.

RETENTION PROGRAM MANAGEMENT

The chief executive officer and general counsel should authorize a records retention program. A policy statement defines the scope and purpose of the retention program, authorizes implementation of the program, identifies the individual(s) responsible for its development and implementation, and prescribes sanctions for noncompliance with the policy.

But a program that exists only on paper is not good enough. Every employee must clearly understand the importance of recordkeeping and the guidelines for records retention and destruction. Any destruction outside of the policy appears more corrupt than random destruction in the absence of a program because ill-timed records destruction is subject to misinterpretation. Annual audits or compliance reviews help ensure enforcement if sanctions for noncompliance are provided for in the company policy.

At ForwardThink Corporation, the clout to obtain compliance with the records retention and disposition schedule comes from top management. When a department audit reveals problems, the offending department is prohibited from purchasing any new equipment, and no facility improvements are authorized for that department. In addition, department employees are not eligible for annual bonuses.

One individual is responsible for keeping the retention program current and for ensuring that microfilming, record transfers, and destruction are done in an orderly manner. In large organizations, this person typically is the records and information management professional, who oversees department coordinators with these responsibilities.

The retention program director develops procedures for smooth operations, for uniform treatment of records, and for periodic reviews of the program. Regular reviews of the retention schedule and disposition practices determine if retention periods are still appropriate, if new regulations or statutes are now in force, or if clarification is needed. Changing business activities or legal requirements may affect the way records are maintained, and new record categories may be needed in the retention schedule. The retention program director should also be familiar enough with the program to be capable of testifying about it in court if necessary.

Program Documentation

A business may need to demonstrate to a legal or regulatory authority its good-faith efforts to retain and dispose of records in a responsible manner and in accordance with established business practices. Documentation of the records retention and disposition program should be maintained to show systematic development and administration of the program in the normal course of business.

The process of program development and the practices and guidelines to implement the program should be documented, along with the approval signatures, legal research, and lists of destroyed records. Retention research documentation shows a best effort to find, interpret, and comply with relevant requirements. Changes to the retention schedule and program should be documented. Records of audits and any follow-up actions or program modifications also should be maintained.

Program documentation should be retained for a reasonable period of time, or as long as is deemed necessary to substantiate the claim that best efforts were made to determine appropriate requirements and that the program was well conceived. Documentation will establish that a program has been implemented in the regular course of business over a period of time.

A ForwardThink Corporation client filed a claim against the company and requested documents in pretrial discovery that were only four years old. As it turns out, the desired documents had been destroyed only eight months earlier under the firm's records retention and disposition program. Crying foul, the client asked the court to bring sanctions against ForwardThink because of deliberate destruction of damaging documents.

ForwardThink Corporation was able to show the court that its records destruction program had been implemented consistently for the last nine years, and that its legal research had found no requirement to retain the documents in question for longer than three years. The judge found in favor of the defendant on this point because of the firm's established program and because there was no evidence that ForwardThink was aware the client intended to file a claim at the time the records were destroyed. Because the plaintiff was unable to support his claim without those documents, the charges against the firm were dropped.

Premature Destruction

Occasionally a record is lost or destroyed before the expiration of its retention period. Such a mishap occurs primarily through accident or negligence, but occasionally the loss is purposeful. Special procedures may be needed to handle this situation for records in all media.

If a duplicate of the lost record exists, the duplicate becomes the record copy. It should be marked as such and stored so that it is subject to the original record's retention requirement.

Perhaps the record is available for duplication from an outside source, such as a government agency, customer, or supplier, or the record may be re-created from other existing records.

Legal counsel may deem it necessary to document any premature destruction or loss of a record. In fact, this procedure is required by federal regulation for certain industries, such as a public utility. A statement of accidental loss includes a description of the record, under what circumstances the record was lost, and when the record was lost or when the loss was discovered. One copy of the statement may be stored in the place of the original record, and records management and the organization's litigation support group may maintain additional copies. If the original record is needed at a later date for any legal reason, this document is submitted in place of the original.

Records Organization to Facilitate Program Administration

How well records are identified, indexed, and organized determines how efficiently records disposition is accomplished. (The functional retention schedule described in Appendix III, "High-Performance, Low-Maintenance Records Retention," can be used as a framework to identify and physically organize records.)

Legal requirements and business needs for records and information are based on their function(s), so when their organization is consistent with their functions, retrieval is simplified for routine business use and for disposition or destruction. Retrieval is further expedited when records are clearly identified by title, date, subject, and so on.

The ability to physically isolate records having different retention requirements is especially important for electronic information, microfilm, and large paper files. The impracticality of applying different destruction dates for record categories contained on a unitized CD-ROM disk or on a single microfilm reel will result in improper administration of the retention schedule.

The ForwardThink Corporation uses a functional and subject listing to organize its records. Very large series of records are further organized by year, such as accounts receivables, OSHA reports, policy manuals, job placement files, fixed asset reports, and payroll tax reports.

Corporate standards for computers require that computer disks and tapes contain only similar records groups that have the same destruction dates. They must be clearly labeled to facilitate retrieval and destruction at the appropriate time. Microfilming standards are similar in that a microfilm reel will not contain records that have different destruction dates.

Closing active files is a standard procedure that also facilitates implementation of a retention program. When a contract expires or a project is completed, steps are taken to pull all related material together and to assign a close date to the records so that the retention requirement can begin.

Duplicates and Non-Records

Because duplicate records may be called into evidence, they must be controlled in much the same way as official records. Any method that clearly distinguishes a designated official record copy from a duplicate will ensure its timely and proper destruction.

However, the proliferation of photocopiers, computers, and other office technologies makes it more difficult to adequately administer a retention program. Numerous copies and different versions of e-mail and other electronic records are found in various paper and electronic record systems. A retention policy may need to state clearly what is not a record and therefore is not governed by the retention schedule.

Duplicate records and information especially must be controlled to reduce storage and handling costs and to preserve the integrity of a systematic retention program. A duplicate record normally has the same legal significance as an original under the rules of evidence, so it is deserving of the same attention as that given to designated record copies. A guideline instructing a specific retention period for duplicate records that clearly spells out acceptable exceptions will help control them. Taking a hard line on duplicate records, ForwardThink Corporation has established this policy:

Duplicate records must be destroyed within one year from their creation. Exceptions are authorized by the office of record and by Information Management. Exceptions to this policy permit longer retention of duplicate copies in these record categories: Budgets (2 years); Accounts Receivable (3 years); paper copies of General Ledger reports that are on microfilm (4 years); Employee Training Records maintained in field offices (3 years).

All other records and information not described in the retention schedule or related policies are considered nonessential and should be disposed of immediately or as soon as they are no longer in use.

One word of caution about duplicate records: A duplicate record is considered an official record copy when it has significant marginal notes; it should be retained for the full applicable retention period.

(See Appendix IV, "Records and Information Management Best Practices," for a discussion of official records and duplicate records.)

Suspension of Destruction

The routine destruction of records relevant to any foreseeable or pending legal action or government investigation must be suspended as soon as the business is aware of the action. This suspension of routine destruction—a destruction hold—is commonly referred to as a legal, audit, or tax hold.

As soon as anyone in the company becomes aware of possible investigation or litigation, legal counsel must be notified immediately. Because initially it can be unclear which records will be involved, it is best to stop destruction of all records until legal counsel can determine which records are relevant to the case. Legal counsel should notify all employees of what records are related to a case and that routine destruction procedures should cease. Counsel may, in addition, grant permission to continue destruction of all other nonrelated records according to the retention schedule. Every effort must be made to protect the records from alteration or loss.

Chapter 5, "A Day in Court," presented certain facts about the class-action suit in which Prudential Insurance was fined $1 million for destruction of records related to that action. This scenario presents background for the court's decision.

The judge said the blame for record destruction "rests squarely on the shoulders of senior corporate officers." According to top management testimony, no executives had an active role in formulating, implementing, communicating, or conducting a document retention policy. Officers should have advised employees of the importance of preserving relevant documents and should have advised them of potential civil and criminal sanctions for noncompliance with the court order to produce documents. He concluded that document destruction was inevitable because there was no comprehensive document retention policy, and e-mail communications about preservation of documents were inadequate.

There was no proof that Prudential, through its employees, engaged in intentional destruction to thwart discovery, but the company's "haphazard and uncoordinated approach to document retention indisputably denies its party opponents potential evidence to establish facts in dispute."

The company was ordered to mail a copy of the court order to all employees and to submit to the court within thirty days a written manual of the company's document preservation policy. This policy on what to preserve and when to destroy records must be distributed to each employee, and a hotline must be set

up for reporting document destruction. The company must also establish a certification process for compliance with the document retention policy.

(More information on the suspension of routine record destruction because of a legal, tax, or audit hold is in Chapter 5, "A Day in Court.")

Record Disposition

Standardized procedures for records disposition will simplify training
and ensure uniform handling of similar records in all media and in all
locations. These instructions may be found in a retention schedule.

The retention schedule may call for a particular record group to be
transferred to inactive storage, be microfilmed, or be disposed of at a
certain time. Internal procedures for record transfers should be designed
for efficiency and to ensure that any system used to identify the locations
of records be updated.

The standard procedures used to convert records from one information
storage medium to another should be followed and documented when
the schedule calls for media conversion, such as microfilming or document imaging. These record conversion procedures are based on government, legal, and business recordkeeping requirements. The retention
schedule should indicate whether or not the original record may be disposed of at the time of conversion or at a later date, depending on business needs and any related government requirements.

When the retention schedule calls for destruction of a record group, it
should also indicate the appropriate disposal method for that record category. Private and proprietary records are normally shredded. Special
software applications may be used to permanently erase electronic records.

If the retention schedule indicates destruction of fifty categories of records at a given time, all fifty groups must be destroyed—not just thirty
or forty record groups—in order to prevent any negative inferences as
a result of selective destruction.

All documents and records groups slated for destruction must be destroyed unless there is a compelling reason not to destroy them, such as
foreseeable litigation or government investigation.

Lists of records destroyed according to the retention schedule are
maintained to document compliance with the retention program and policies. All program documentation may be used to show that records are
routinely destroyed in the ordinary course of business according to consistent, standardized procedures.

In one case in which the plaintiff questioned the destruction of a record, the
defense persuaded the judge that the record was destroyed for a legitimate rea-

son and without improper motive. According to the judge, "The records, having been retained for a reasonable and legally sufficient period and no longer needed for any purpose, were destroyed in the normal course of business."

When a records retention schedule is well developed and regularly updated, there is normally no need to obtain further approvals for destruction after all the appropriate departments have signed off on the schedule. However, a business might consider a final review by legal counsel and/or the tax manager prior to destruction in order to discover any recent changes in the law or to determine if litigation or government actions have been initiated but records management has not yet been notified to suspend destruction. If in this final review a decision is made to retain the records longer than the retention schedule indicates, the reason must be justified and documented.

It is irresponsible—and risky—to clean house on a whim or when there is a crisis for space, especially when litigation or an investigation is imminent. A retention schedule is a necessary guide to all records disposition, including a one-time record destruction or microfilming project. There should be no haphazard or selective destruction of business records.

The House of Good Intentions has a warehouse full of records from a company it acquired years earlier. The records have not been used and appear to be of no value. Because the records have not been organized and indexed for a comparison with the company's own records retention schedule, random samples are selected to assess their value. A record is made of the categories of files found, including identifying which ones are now slated for destruction and why. The few records found to be of some legal or historical value are microfilmed according to the firm's standard microfilming procedures, and the originals are destroyed. The retention and destruction decision-making process and the filming processes are documented.

ELECTRONIC RECORDS CHALLENGES AND RISKS

Companies that implement retention policies for retaining and destroying records have been fairly successful at their application to visible records like paper and microfilm. Few organizations have applied those policies to electronic records and information for the following reasons:

Electronic information systems were not designed to accommodate retention and destruction because organizations mistakenly believe that records and information management principles do not apply to electronic information.

It is easy to store vast amounts of electronic data on relatively inexpensive information storage media.

Every organization must acknowledge that its information technologies create business records and courtroom evidence. With that in mind, the organization must do what is necessary to accommodate the records and information retention and destruction function.

A number of records and information management principles that traditionally support retention and disposition of visible records are equally appropriate for electronic records. Electronic information systems must have the following capabilities to incorporate those basic principles:

- Identify what is to be retained, for how long, and in what information storage media.
- Retrieve data for conversion or migration to another information system or information storage media.
- Retrieve data for erasure at the proper time.
- Preserve electronic data and the ability to retrieve the data for the full retention requirement.
- Preserve, manage, and disclose to others electronic records related to litigation, investigation, and audit.
- Differentiate between pre-record, non-record, duplicate, and official record.
- Identify and minimize redundant data and multiple versions that exist in numerous information systems—paper, film, server, desktop, computer tapes and disks, backup tapes and disks, and so on.

Knowledge of how to apply retention, preservation, and destruction functions to electronic records continues to evolve. Retention program implementation challenges continue, as do the risks of not managing electronic data according to records and information management principles.

Retention Program Implementation Challenges

Information systems departments do not generally consider electronic records retention until e-mail messages fill the servers to capacity. That is neither the appropriate time nor the right reason to contemplate records retention and destruction. Retention and destruction should have been considered when e-mail and every other electronic information system were designed.

Not all electronic information systems are designed to accommodate electronic records retention and destruction. Generally, it is very difficult to retrofit a system to accommodate the need to identify and extract an electronic record for migration to another information carrier, for conversion to another information system, or for destruction. Most information systems departments are overloaded with design modifications and system maintenance projects, so only top management support will move electronic records retention and destruction to a higher priority.

Information systems administrators are the most knowledgeable individuals who have the technical expertise to apply a retention schedule to centralized electronic records and information systems and their backups. This is not an easy task because too many information systems were designed without the capability to destroy designated records at a specified time while retaining others.

Electronic records under the control of an individual employee are those on the employee's desktop and laptop and those saved to a server by the employee. Guidelines for retention and destruction reviews are important tools to assist the individual in complying with the retention schedule and corporate policies. These guidelines should cover

- e-mail and e-mail attachments: possible locations, how to delete and erase, and procedures for transfer from the e-mail system to a separate recordkeeping system
- tips on searching the possible storage locations to be reviewed: hard drive directories and files, and removable media such as diskettes, CD-ROMs, and backup tapes
- suggested methods to organize electronic files to simplify normal retrieval and retention reviews
- definitions of pre-record, non-record, duplicate, and official record

Application of a retention schedule to shared records on a system must be a team effort by those who create and access them. For example, those individuals working as a team on a project must determine the appropriate guidelines for centralization of information, elimination of duplicates, and application of the retention schedule.

At the time of this writing, the most useful approach to electronic records retention is a combination of the following:

- system design and redesign to accommodate retention and destruction functions
- records management software applications
- electronic document management and electronic document imaging systems with retention and destruction capabilities

Risks of an Inadequate Program

A records retention schedule is more than a set of rules to follow. A schedule is the result of a thoughtful decision process about what business information must be retained and for how long.

An organization has a business need and a legal duty not only to retain but also to preserve information for the specified time period. Preservation is a more challenging prospect for electronic records than for most paper records because the nature of electronic information systems is problematic for preservation. Electronic records are highly susceptible to a number of information security threats to their continued existence. In addition, electronic information does not have as long a life expectancy as that of paper and film records.

Preservation issues can become business and litigation risks. Records needed in the future must be retrievable for business purposes and for litigation, audit, or investigation. Yet, keeping electronic records longer than necessary exposes the organization to unnecessary discovery expense and risk of information being used against the organization by another party.

When an organization does not consistently apply its retention policies throughout the organization, the litigation risk is an appearance of selective record destruction. Another litigation risk is keeping electronic records longer than necessary.

Whether business records are paper, film, or electronic, courts have no sympathy for an organization that does not have control of its records and information.

(See Chapter 9, "Electronic Records and Information," and Chapter 11, "E-Mail," for more on electronic records and e-mail.)

8

Integrating Media Choices for the Ultimate Information System

Organizations experience information overload as their information systems expand from paper and microfilm to electronic information. In today's and tomorrow's information systems, the most common media used are paper, microform, and electronic. Records and information within each information system often migrate to and from other information systems. Paper moves to microform and electronic. Microform moves to paper and electronic. Electronic moves to paper and microform.

To further complicate matters, there are a number of information subsystems in each of the media-based information systems. They are rarely connected to each other to minimize redundant data. Electronic information systems have a number of information subsystems, such as e-mail, desktop computers, web sites, and individual business applications, such as payroll.

Information users today need to know what information is on what system, and they need to know how to use each of those systems. This information retrieval burden is minimized when information users can go to a single interface on a single platform to retrieve needed information.

The need for more and better information, and the wide range of available information systems, makes it imperative that organizations manage the information in all its forms as a single information resource.

AN INTEGRATED INFORMATION SYSTEM

Management of a multitude of information systems is both simple and complex.

The first premise to accept is that an organization's information systems are corporate assets to be managed as such. They must be managed and controlled to protect the organization and to add value to the enterprise. This means that information ownership issues must disappear. Records and information in a department, on a desktop or mainframe computer, in a record center, and in an electronic vault, are all corporate resources to be managed.

The second premise to accept is that the medium is not the message. Instead of focusing on a specific medium, the driving force behind all recordkeeping practices must be the content and purpose of records and information. Information users care only about getting the right information at the right time. They do not want to have to first determine which information media system to query when searching for information.

The third premise to accept is that connection of now independent information systems adds value to the corporate information resources. For example, when an employee terminates, a procedure in place to automatically notify all information systems containing employee information adds value to those systems. Individuals accessing those records know that the employee is no longer with the organization, and records that must be retained for a specified time period after employment termination can begin their countdown to destruction.

Transforming Media Systems into Information Systems

Historically, management focus has been more on the record form than on the record content. The physical and technical attributes of paper, microform, and electronic information systems continue to drive their organization and management.

When an organization focuses management of records and information on their *content*, achievement of the following business objectives naturally follows:

- retain useful, valuable, and required information as long as necessary
- eliminate unnecessary information to minimize expense and business risk
- organize records and information for timely and efficient retrieval
- protect sensitive and valuable information

It is more important than ever that all information systems are managed within a framework of records and information management principles. The following questions should be asked—and answered—before any new information system is created:

What information must be recorded, and for what purpose(s)?

Who will have access to use the information, and how will they find it?

What information storage media is best for retrieval in a timely manner at a reasonable cost?

Will user requirements change over time?

Are there legal requirements or legal considerations related to media choice for this information?

How long must the information be retained to satisfy business and legal requirements stated in the records retention schedule?

What equipment or technologies will be required to access, process, and produce the records?

Is the system capable of maintaining, processing, and retrieving records for their full retention requirement?

What storage media are best for short-term, mid-term, and long-term preservation of the information?

What controls will be necessary to ensure that information is systematically and accurately collected, created, maintained, retrieved, produced, distributed, and destroyed?

Will parts, service, and system support be available for as long as they will be necessary?

What information must be protected, for what reasons, and for how long?

What security procedures are necessary to protect information from damage, loss, or unauthorized access?

Is an interface needed with other technologies or information systems for related information and transactions?

Is the information system compatible with other information systems (including computer, paper, and microform)?

These questions should also be asked periodically throughout the life of an information system as business needs and legal requirements change. The sooner these questions are answered, the better. It may be too cost-prohibitive to respond to them at a later date.

System Design

Every organization needs an enterprise-wide information system that is easy to use, easy to manage, and easy to change. End users want their information as quickly and as easily as possible. The various media systems in numerous locations must be integrated into, and managed as, a single information system that adds value to and supports the enterprise.

The individual organization must determine the best mix of information-recording methods to meet its needs. Each information system needs to coexist and be integrated with other systems. No individual system should compete with or contradict other systems.

Clearly defined records and information management policies and practices support management of information resources in a decentralized environment. An integrated information system has added value when there is management and control of recordkeeping practices from the point of record creation or receipt through final disposition.

Value is also added to individual information systems when they are integrated into a single information resource. Problems related to information systems that are organized and administered independently of each other may be avoided. The task to satisfy recordkeeping requirements is simplified, and the ever-so-important element of consistency will be there.

Information management standards are needed to connect each information system with other manual and automated systems. As with the application of computer standards, all records and information systems must be able to interface with each other for the sharing and distribution of information when information needs demand that sharing and access.

Each information system must have a useful indexing system compatible with established, uniform indexing standards. Without an adequate indexing system, even a stand-alone information system is not a cost-effective information resource.

Indexing Standards

The volume of information available increases exponentially every year. Tools are needed to find what is relevant.

Search capabilities are only as good as the indexing. A current example of this is searches on the Internet using search engines. Often the search yields hundreds or thousands of results. The search results may not even include what is really needed, and the information user does not know if the desired information even exists.

Standard identification, classification, and indexing are the architectural framework to construct an integrated information system. It supports information access and retrieval, and it improves access to information as it migrates to and from individual systems. It is used to identify and minimize unwanted redundancies.

Indexing systems facilitate proper storage, retrieval, and processing of records in all media. Records are identified with distinctive and meaningful titles. Cross-indexing and key word search features enhance the ability to retrieve specific or similar records in all media efficiently.

When information creators and records users talk the same language, common search strategies will improve productivity. Otherwise, differences in data definitions may lead to layering of inconsistent or outdated information and a failure to make relevant associations among records groups and media systems.

When systems are fragmented in such a way that data sources cannot be simultaneously updated or searched, unsuspecting users may reference an outdated or incomplete version of information.

A bank installed an electronic document imaging and document management system. Among its many applications are accounts payable, mortgage loan insurance files, consumer loans, and credit card management. A uniform indexing system allows a single search path for all documents, regardless of whether they are stored on optical disk, microfilm, or paper. The work of seven file clerks is now done by one employee, turnaround time for system users decreased, and customer service improved.

Records Management Software Applications

Tools often used to manage an integrated information system are records management software (RMS) applications. Similar to a fixed assets inventory program, the automated technology provides management and controls with fewer resources. It can also provide access to records and information in multiple information media systems.

At the heart of RMS applications are indexing standards and capabilities. Through standard indexing, the software application improves access to all inventoried and indexed information resources. RMS applications can support multiple classification schemes transparently when department classifications are translated for wider use.

Such systems offer controls and capabilities to apply records and information management functions to other information systems. They are a good start at improving access to and better management of records in all media, from the time of their origination through their eventual disposition.

MEDIA DECISIONS

The design and management of information systems requires continual analysis of how well various information carriers satisfy records and information management requirements specific to the content of records and information. No single information carrier is the answer to a company's records and information needs. Selection of an information carrier is based on a number of factors.

From legal and security requirements to media durability and cost considerations, the records and information management issues described below must be considered when deciding what information carrier is best for specific records at various points in their useful and their required lives.

Legal Requirements

A number of legal requirements may affect media selection, as well as related procedural and technical requirements.

A contract between two parties may have requirements related to record media forms. For example, a contract may allow one party in the possession of another party's records to convert those records to another information carrier, but the contract may prohibit the destruction of the original records. Federal contractors typically may not destroy the original unless certain conditions are met.

Most regulatory requirements today that directly affect media choice relate to microfilm records. Agency requirements for electronic record forms began being issued in recent years.

The IRS has rules for both microfilm and data processing records. Microfilming must meet industry standards, procedures must be documented, and the film must be preserved. The capability to produce a visible, legible record must exist for as long as the record remains material in the administration of any IRS law. All support records must be identified and made readily available.

Electronic records must be preserved in a retrievable, machine-readable form for IRS review and audit to determine reliability of the system and data. System documentation and an audit trail of the steps from data entry through printout are necessary. Media must be clearly labeled and maintained in a secure environment with backups maintained off site. Periodic inspections of storage conditions and the condition of electronic data tapes will ensure information integrity. The IRS must be notified immediately of damaged or lost computer information.

(The IRS Revenue Procedures specify the conditions under which these and other requirements exist.)

Government regulations may prohibit destruction of original records converted to another information carrier. There are occasions when the original must continue to be maintained and made available for inspection by an agency or court. In other situations, a regulation may state that the original may be filmed and then destroyed only after a designated number of years.

If there is no requirement to retain an original record after it is filmed or digitized, the original may be destroyed after completion of a quality control inspection. Depending on the value of the records, an organization may choose to send the original records to a remote site as a security backup.

Evidentiary Requirements

Rules of evidence specify the conditions under which a duplicate, microform, or electronic record is the best evidence. Generally any record form is admissible as evidence when it is accurate, reliable and authentic. Some media may be more susceptible to a trustworthiness challenge than others. When the trustworthiness of a record is challenged, the party producing that record as evidence will have the burden of proof of authenticity and reliability.

When a record produced for evidence is a duplicate, its owner may need to show that it is an accurate reproduction of the original record. When charges of fraud are highly probable, as in financial transactions, an original record has a higher degree of reliability. Litigants prefer original electronic records because of the related metadata stored with the original record. Technical experts prefer the original paper records when an accurate determination of age or a handwriting analysis is ordered.

As the traditional information carrier, paper is challenged the least often regarding its authenticity. An original paper record is most valuable when the record's authenticity is questioned. Sometimes paper is the only means to provide a legible duplicate record. Occasionally it is preferable to maintain an original paper record, such as a stock certificate, in order to preserve its physical characteristics, such as paper texture, age, color, or size.

Microforms generally are admissible as original or as duplicate records. However, the reproduction process may be questioned. Microform process documentation to support a trustworthiness claim may include the following information:

- statement of subject matter on the film
- indexing and arrangement of the information
- name of the department or person authorizing the filming process
- camera operator name and date
- certificate of authenticity
- reproduction procedures, timetable, and film odometer readings
- quality inspections of records
- film-splicing procedures

When a microform was created electronically, that information processing system's documentation would be useful.

The trustworthiness of electronic records is more likely to come under scrutiny because so many electronic records are easily altered without a trace. Nonerasable electronic media are often relied on to avoid a minitrial on trustworthiness of evidence.

System documentation that may be needed to dismiss any electronic record's trustworthiness challenge includes

- record creation or conversion procedures
- verification of data validity
- software and operating systems documentation
- data-processing procedures
- computer operations log
- audit trail from data entry to production of a visible record
- database modifications
- production of visible records in the ordinary course of business
- file and document listings
- source and object codes
- make and model numbers of tape and disk devices
- interface capabilities and requirements
- system operators and users training

System documentation is necessary, also, for routine business purposes such as current and future information systems management.

Record Permanence and Durability

A record's retention requirement and the record's anticipated use determine what permanence and durability characteristics will be necessary in the information carrier.

If a record has a very short retention period and multiple users do not need it, it is more cost-effective to create and retain that record on the least costly information carrier. The longer the retention requirement for a record, the more important the permanence and durability characteristics of its selected information carrier and any information processing equipment or technology.

A business may need to take steps to prevent technical obsolescence and degradation of its information carriers and processors. All information carriers and information processors are vulnerable to aging, obsolescence, harmful environmental conditions, and misuse.

Some information carriers are self-destructive. Acidic paper, poor duplication techniques, inadequate information-processing methods, and computer tapes and diskettes are examples of self-destructive information carriers. The physical properties of audio recordings are such that they last only a few years, so the information must be transcribed to some other more dependable medium. Video recordings are subject to degradation and are also dependent on a compatible mechanism to view the recording.

Optical disks are not yet proven to be archival storage quality, but their general expected life is ten years. Diskettes begin to deteriorate within eighteen months. Computer tapes generally last less than ten years. Government data from twenty years ago has decomposed to the point where the carrier will fall apart if run through any surviving equipment from that era.

For long-term retention, the organization must plan to transfer electronic data to new data storage devices and/or to schedule migration from a soon-to-be-obsolete format to a newer, more viable format or technology.

Data on disks and tapes may be copied and recopied to other media as needed to preserve the information. Note, however, that migration of digital signatures may not be appropriate. Digital signatures in electronic documents, such as contracts, are now recognized as legally binding. A problem may arise if in the future it becomes necessary to migrate the electronic document to another technology for its ongoing preservation. Migration may affect the digital stamp or other cryptographic techniques, leading to invalidation of the electronic contract document.

Assuming the electronic data on a storage device survive as long as needed, the greatest risks regarding preservation of electronic data lie in the hardware and software necessary to access and process the data. Hardware and software become obsolete or dysfunctional in relatively short periods of time as organizations struggle to remain current with new information technologies. Without careful planning, information is left stranded on tapes and disks from primitive or discarded computer systems.

- The 5.25 inch drives, for example, have now almost entirely disappeared from the office scene. Any data remaining today on 5.25 inch diskettes should be copied to another information carrier that works in a more accessible drive.
- Not all software application upgrades offer backward capability, in which the new software version can read and process data created and stored in the earlier version. Ideally, records of the earlier version should be converted to the upgraded version for preservation until the end of their retention requirements.
- Records from a system replaced by a new application can sometimes be con-

verted to the new system. Conversion programs are designed to move data from the old system to the new one.

- An organization may need new software to decipher old programs and to reorganize the data before a new system is able to analyze and process the information. If the information storage media are not properly labeled, however, and old system documentation is unavailable, the information may be rendered useless.

If the older data cannot or is not converted to the new system, the old system and its documentation must continue to be maintained so the information is accessible and retrievable for as long as it may be needed by government or by the business.

Security

Individual record categories may have different security requirements. An organization will want to safeguard certain information to preserve its legal rights and to meet its own business needs. Federal contractors must comply with federal guidelines for the equipment and facilities that house government classified information. Certain government agencies may have other information security requirements.

Records and information in all media need to be protected from loss, damage, alteration, or unauthorized access. Some media are more secure than others for protection of records from specific threats.

Security measures will vary from one information carrier to another. Sight-readable records will require equipment and facility modifications to prevent unauthorized access, damage, or loss. Electronic records require security measures unique to the information system to prevent unauthorized access or accidental loss.

(See Appendix II, "Records and Information Security Program," for more on information security practices.)

Organization and Use

Understanding the function(s) of a record and how it will be used helps determine what information carrier is most appropriate and how best to organize it.

Access to large volumes of paper records is often inefficient. An overriding need for simultaneous and instantaneous access by multiple users is typically the justification for an electronic records system. Microforms may not be as costly as electronic records, given their low duplication and distribution costs, but access is not as fast as with electronic records.

Electronic information systems are commonly used for access to current information. When online access is no longer necessary but the information must be retained for a significant period of time, the information may be converted to microfilm. Computer output microfilm (COM) is safer and more cost-effective than electronic records when the retention requirement is significantly longer than the active life of the information.

Indexing and organization of the various information media will vary somewhat, but they should be consistent with standard guidelines. With a sophisticated indexing system, electronic records can be retrieved more quickly and more accurately than microform or paper records. Microforms provide for more convenient and accurate filing than do paper records because of their uniform sizes and fixed-file continuity characteristics.

Record groups that have different retention requirements should be physically organized on separate tapes, diskettes, film reels, microfiche, or file folders to avoid compromising the integrity of a records destruction program.

Cost Considerations

Cost is a significant factor to consider in the selection of a record's medium. Among the costs to consider are access, storage, security, and any process necessary to convert records from one information carrier to another.

Paper records are costly to store and retrieve in terms of space, equipment, and human resources. Duplication and distribution of microforms are less costly than distribution of large volumes of paper. Records in both microform and electronic form require hardware or equipment to create, read, process and produce the records.

Although microform and electronic records cost less than paper to store, other cost considerations could rule them out as a media choice. Computer system development and installation costs may be prohibitive.

It may be difficult to justify conversion of paper records to another media when the costs to store the original paper record are less than the costs to convert and store the records in the new information storage form. Paper conversion costs include preparation of the paper documents, filming or scanning, film processing, quality control, indexing, and the subsequent storage, handling, use, and equipment necessary to read and produce the records. These costs increase when documents are stapled or folded, images are on both sides of a document, images are faded, or there are variations in the size, color, or weight of the papers.

INFORMATION CARRIERS

This section describes the three primary information carriers used in business today. It summarizes their positive and negative attributes as record and information storage media.

Paper

Paper is an information carrier that business will be managing well into the twenty-first century and beyond. Even companies that use optical disk technologies today will not convert all their paper records that are stacked in storage areas.

Paper is not always the archival-quality medium one expects. It may suffer damage or loss from physical deterioration attributable to biological, chemical, or mechanical causes. Natural disasters and planned or inadvertent actions by people may also affect the continued existence of paper records.

The acid content in paper, for example, weakens and breaks the paper's fibers, causing the paper to yellow and become brittle before its time. Today's newspaper is yellow next week and brittle enough to break into pieces in a few years. Acids in paper originate from the chemicals used in the manufacturing process, printing inks and dyes, human hands, air pollutants, and other materials with which paper comes in contact.

The method used to record information on paper may contribute to permanence and durability problems. Certain inks can contaminate an otherwise permanent paper. Dark blue and black inks are preferred for signatures because they resist fading. Durability of carbonless paper copies can be an issue. Letters printed by certain typewriter ribbons are susceptible to lifting off of the paper, thus obliterating the information.

Until organizations replace their thermal paper fax, cash registers, and other machines with plain paper machines, thermal paper is not a satisfactory information carrier either. The paper turns brown, and the print fades with age or exposure to sunlight and heat in a very short period of time.

Microform

Microform is a generic name used to describe any of the various forms in which the use of microphotography reproduces a record. A microform may be a microfilm, a microfiche, or an aperture card.

Microforms are most suitable when

- filing and space problems exist
- information integrity must be preserved
- records are to be retained for six or more years
- the same records are needed in separate locations
- security copies of vital, electronic, or other records are necessary

The type of microform to select depends on the anticipated uses of the records and how frequently the records may need to be updated. If information security and file integrity are more important than the ability to update the information, unitized film formats such as microfilm rolls and microfiche are recommended. Roll film is serialized on open reels, cartridges, or cassettes and may be updated by splicing; some microfiche is now erasable.

Microfilm jackets containing filmstrips are easily updated and, like microfiche, permit direct access to the desired image without having to advance through a roll of film. Computer-assisted retrieval (CAR) systems can film documents in random order, index and code them as the batch of records is filmed, and then enter the indexing information into a computer system. Functioning as a computer database manager, a CAR system allows efficient updating and cross-referencing of records to direct a user to the specific frame that contains the desired information.

Information is filmed directly from paper records through source document micrographics, or microforms are created directly from electronic records; COM is created by the transfer of data directly from a computer to microfilm without the necessity to create paper. Production costs are greatly reduced when paper record creation is eliminated.

Microforms are a safe information carrier that may last for hundreds of years. The quality of the film and the processing, storage conditions, and use of microforms affect the life of microforms. Conformance with microfilm industry standards eliminates the concerns about obsolescence and compatibility of associated equipment.

Silver halide film supports permanent or archival standards of quality. Diazo film has an inherent dye fade, but it is less expensive and more suitable for temporary use. Any existing nitrate-based film records must be copied to another film and disposed of properly. Nitrate-based film can spontaneously combust at temperatures of 106 degrees Fahrenheit or higher and release toxic gases.

Electronic

The use of computers in business first started with data-processing applications on mainframe computers. Information technology is now applied to management of databases, text, images, video, and audio as well as transmission of information between systems.

Hybrid systems combine electronic, photographic, and microform information systems. Advanced systems can scan, film, digitize, read, print, transfer to disk, and transmit records and information through communications lines and radio signals.

As storage and retrieval systems, electronic information systems reduce storage requirements, protect records from loss, deliver immediate access to multiple users of the same record, and distribute information faster to end users.

Electronic information systems store computer-generated, paper, or microform images on high-capacity optical disks. With an adequate indexing system, filing and retrieval costs are low and there are few "lost" files. Specific system functions are employed to protect data from alteration or loss caused by users.

Electronic document imaging systems are cost-effective for large-volume, high-use records that do not need to be updated. When permanence and durability issues are resolved, electronic document imaging will be hard to beat for records storage and retrieval economies.

Computer drives and erasable data storage disks allow data changes. System documentation and documentation of the procedures followed for information updates and conversions help demonstrate accuracy, reliability, and trustworthiness of the records.

It is unfortunate that application of records and information management principles has largely been ignored in the rush to install information technologies. (More in-depth discussion of related issues is covered in a number of chapters in this book.)

STORAGE CONDITIONS AND HANDLING REQUIREMENTS

Storage conditions and how records are handled will affect access capabilities and the permanence and durability of a record media. The appropriate storage and handling conditions and practices must exist to help preserve records and make them accessible for as long as they are needed. Periodic inspections to check the condition of each information carrier for deterioration or damage from storage conditions or handling may be necessary.

Environment

Storage conditions that are the enemy of information carriers are high temperatures, humidity extremes, ultraviolet light radiation, atmospheric pollutants, and various biological entities. Damage to media from a hostile storage environment generally is not reversible.

Temperature and humidity levels that are consistent with energy conservation and worker comfort guidelines are generally acceptable for records. The lower the temperature, the better. High humidity promotes mold and bacteria growth and accelerates deterioration caused by acids in materials. Mold degrades paper cellulose fibers and will stain and discolor records. If humidity is too low, materials tend to become brittle. High temperatures and humidity also favor the propagation of pests that eat paper, glue, photos, and other materials.

Wide fluctuations in heat and moisture will stress materials as they expand and contract. A stabilized temperature of between 55 and 65 degrees Fahrenheit and a relative humidity of 40 to 50 percent are close to ideal for a multimedia storage facility. Fluctuations of more than 10 degrees or 15 percent relative humidity from hour to hour, day to day, or season to season should be avoided.

The heat given off by light sources is relatively insignificant when compared to the damage caused by the ultraviolet radiation from natural sunlight and fluorescent light. Records should be stored away from direct sunlight, or the windows should be covered. Incandescent lighting should be used whenever possible because it emits no harmful radiation. Fluorescent lighting tubes may be fitted with ultraviolet radiation filter sleeves.

A number of air pollutants and destructive gases emitted from building materials, equipment, and a growing number of records themselves need to be controlled. Any dust or grime in the presence of moisture can act as a corrosive poultice. Gaseous and other particulate pollutants in the air may soil paper, contribute to acidic deterioration of paper or microfilm, or obliterate data contained on microform or electronic media. Air pollutants may cause damage to equipment, which could then damage the information carrier.

Fire, heat, and water, like pollutants, take their toll on paper, microform, and electronic records. A business may want to take any steps necessary to prevent or minimize threats from a number of disasters and to produce backup records for storage elsewhere in the event of record loss. A business continuity plan should address salvage procedures specific to the record media to be preserved.

Preservation and Handling

Record preservation encompasses the efforts to retard or control deterioration or to prevent the loss of records. The extent of preservation efforts for different records will depend on the value(s) of the records and how long they must be maintained. How they are preserved varies from one information carrier to another.

The equipment, hardware, and software required to read, process, produce, and store information in various media must be well maintained and functioning properly to prevent damage or loss of information. Harmful acids, oils, and dirt easily migrate from media containers or hands to records, so consideration of plastic or acid-free folders or boxes may be appropriate to house certain records. Electronic and magnetic media should be kept away from magnetic or static sources. Excessive records handling should be avoided.

9

Electronic Records and Information

Electronic records and information are everywhere. They are on desktop and laptop computers, mainframe computers, file servers, intranets, and the Internet. They are stored in jukeboxes, electronic vaults, and record storage warehouses.

Computers create, store, process, and retrieve information. There are word-processing and spreadsheet software applications, transaction processing systems, database management systems, knowledge management systems, and more. Systems can be single user, multiple users, and connected systems.

Information technologies allow organizations to better manage, process, use, and store information. These technologies have positive attributes that make valuable contributions to the bottom line. Information technologies in business today also present challenges that do not always have positive consequences.

This chapter discusses the positive and the negative aspects of electronic records and information. An overview of records and information management solutions to the challenges is found at the end of this chapter.

THE GOOD

Technological applications help business work faster, more efficiently, with fewer resources. They help us manage a rapidly increasing volume of records and information, and they help us communicate faster.

Legal Status

Until recent years the legal system lagged far behind the swiftly moving technological innovations. Slowly the legal system is filling the voids related to intellectual properties protection, agency acceptance of electronic documents, privacy, and more.

Government agencies began publishing regulations about records in electronic form several years ago. Some regulations state what records may be created and preserved electronically, standards to be met, any information security requirements, and other recordkeeping necessities. Federal agencies are required to begin accepting regulatory filings and other information submitted to them in electronic form. Amendments to the Freedom of Information Act now require agencies to provide information electronically when so requested.

The IRS has revenue procedures and regulations that have electronic recordkeeping requirements. Among those regulations are requirements related to electronic data interchange (EDI) technology. EDI is often used for electronic transactions in which one party purchases a product from another party.

The taxpayer that uses EDI technology must retain machine-sensible records that, in combination with other records (e.g., the underlying contracts and price lists), contain all the detailed information required. The extent of the detail in the electronic records must be equivalent to the level of detail contained in an acceptable paper record. The taxpayer may capture this information at any level within the accounting system provided the audit trail, authenticity, and integrity of the retained records can be established.

Electronic records generally are admissible as evidence. An electronic record's reliability and accuracy, like that of a paper document, may be challenged in court.

Federal and state laws now recognize digital signatures as being the same as written signatures. Conditions under which a digital signature is acceptable may vary from one jurisdiction to another. Legal acceptance of electronic signatures now opens the door for even more business transactions to take place entirely in electronic form.

As of this writing, there are no tested standards for the technical method and format for digital signatures. Careful thought and planning are needed to use this relatively new technology and to ensure that all electronic files and data necessary to recreate the digital signature and the document to which it is linked are preserved for as long as is necessary within the corporate records retention program.

Productivity and Customer Relationships

Most electronic information systems are tools that enhance productivity. Business processes are reengineered to improve workflow and to support decision-makers.

Some information systems support the offering of higher-quality customer service. Workers have instant access to customer data so they can respond to customer inquiries without delay. Technical product information is readily available to solve customer problems in real time.

Other systems support compliance with government requirements. Information that must be filed with government agencies is created and sent electronically. Electronic records are a more reliable method to maintain control over large, complex volumes of records.

One airline's electronic document imaging system saves dollars for record storage. It also avoids FAA fines for not producing maintenance records when requested by the FAA. When maintenance records are not produced upon request, the FAA can impose a fine of $10,000 every time the airplane takes off and lands. The airline can be fined for every part on the plane for which maintenance records are not produced.

Multi-user information systems allow collaboration of teams of employees on specific projects, such as an engineering design project. Each team member has access to a central depository of information that is shared, referenced, and processed.

Data warehousing tools and technologies support access to and analysis of data. A data warehouse is built by importing targeted data from various information systems. For example, a customer and sales data warehouse is available for use in marketing and product development activities.

Knowledge management is a discipline that promotes an integrated approach to identification, management, and sharing of an organization's information assets. Eventually knowledge management software applications will be part of the records and information management solution that integrates the organization's various information systems for end users.

Intranets

Corporate intranets are growing in popularity throughout the business world. They are a private network inside an organization that uses the same software employed for Internet content and connectivity. Typically, various electronic documents and information are stored on an intranet server for access by users through Internet web browser applications.

Electronic files from corporate applications are converted into a standard format, such as hypertext markup language (HTML), which can be read by every desktop computer with the browser installed. The HTML format allows for hypertext links—those pointer links in a document that take the user to the referenced document.

An intranet can be used as a collaborative tool by which individuals can work together by sharing and accessing the same information. It can also be an excellent tool for communicating to employees. Employee policies, procedures, and training materials are often posted in corporate intranets.

Records and information management functions must be incorporated into the development, maintenance, and retention of intranet technologies and content. Records and information management professionals help determine what information posted on an intranet should be retained as an official record within the guidelines of the records retention program.

If a corporate policy is posted on an intranet, should an electronic copy of that policy be retained, or should another form of the policy be retained as the official record? Is it necessary to document when the policy was posted and for which employees? Who will ensure that revised policies are retained along with previous policies for as long as each policy statement must be retained?

Security of sensitive and valuable information must also be addressed. What information is and is not appropriate to post on an intranet? Who has authorized access, and what security is required to prevent unwanted intruders?

One judge waived the trade secret status of information posted on a company's intranet because 3,000 people had access to it—including employees, suppliers, and customers.

Because intranets often hold business records and information, record-keeping practices must be applied to their content.

THE GOOD AND THE BAD

Much of what is good about information technologies also has negative aspects. The good and the bad may be attributed to certain characteristics inherent in the technologies. For example, the feature of easy document manipulation and modification improves productivity, but it can pose authentication problems in litigation.

Technological changes result in progress and innovation. They also result in challenges to play catch-up with change. It is difficult to develop and achieve any standards because of the rapid changes and constant innovations. System users rarely have the time to master current tools before they are replaced with newer and better tools. Productivity declines when employees are constantly learning how to use functions and features of hardware and software applications.

Electronic information systems have many good attributes intentionally built into them, but the systems can be bad when records and information management functions are not designed into them. How records and information management functions can offer solutions is discussed in a section at the end of this chapter. This section briefly describes the good and the bad of individual characteristics and functions of electronic information systems.

Wide and Instant Access

Digital technologies and the connections between them offer a solution to the need for instant information access and distribution. The ability to transmit information instantaneously means the pace of business is quickened. Simultaneous access by multiple users improves productivity.

Remote access complicates information security. Valuable and sensitive information can be transmitted without being noticed. The risk of unauthorized access, damage, or loss increases with the number of access points available.

Business computers used to be mainframe computers locked away in rooms with limited access. Now every employee has access to numerous information systems, increasing the risks of insider misdeeds such as trade secret theft or sabotage. Connections to the outside world extend those security risks as well. (Security risks related to the Internet are discussed in Chapter 10, "The Internet.")

Storage Capacity

The good news is organizations can economically store vast amounts of electronic information. The bad news is organizations can economically store vast amounts of electronic information.

If growth of stored electronic information can be measured by the volume of media storage capacity shipped, the following numbers tell the story of exponential growth of electronic records.

One petabyte of data storage is approximately the equivalent of 400 million books 500 pages in length. In 1996, 400 petabytes of data storage were shipped to consumers. An estimated 2,000 petabytes of data storage were shipped in the year 2000.

The ability to store more in less space has tremendous benefits of improved productivity and storage cost savings. It is good to store hundreds of thousands of document pages on a single CD-ROM because it is easily portable and consumes little storage space. It is bad if that CD-ROM is the only copy of the documents and it is stolen, lost, or damaged.

It is easy to ignore the growth of electronic files because the accumulation of electronic files is not as obvious as boxes of paper files. Inexpensive digital storage fosters an attitude that application of the corporate records retention program is not necessary. So systems fill up with outdated, useless information.

Even electronic information storage costs can escalate beyond budgets. Servers fill up with e-mail messages, abandoned software applications and their data, and individual employee inactive files. System performance and employee productivity can deteriorate with too much unnecessary information to sort through. Over time, the methods to preserve electronic information storage media and the systems needed to read the information become costly.

Litigation costs rise unnecessarily when large volumes of data must be searched. When electronic records are not destroyed according to the corporate records retention program, that noncompliance is selective destruction and a litigation risk not to be taken lightly.

Decentralized Environment

Electronic information systems in most organizations are in a decentralized environment. The information systems department oversees mainframes, servers, and specific information system applications. Often they also oversee internal and external communications systems. Specific software applications are sometimes under the control of other departments, such as accounting or human resources. And individual employees control their desktop and laptop computers to accomplish more in less time as they create e-mail, correspondence, spreadsheets, and other potential business records.

This decentralized environment has incompatible information systems and systems that are not linked to other related systems. Typically, there are no organization-wide standards or disciplines for the creation, storage, and deletion of electronic records. Few organizations have detailed guidelines for what kinds of information storage media to use in specific situations, for backup procedures, or for methods of obliterating electronic records in accordance with the records retention policy.

Consequently, end users perform electronic recordkeeping activities in a discretionary manner. Electronic records are saved to hard disk, server, backup tapes, CDs, and other locations. Unlimited copies and multiple versions of the same documents saved in numerous locations are rarely managed or deleted. Or a record exists in only one place, and only its creator knows where it is.

Individual users who did not organize their desk and credenza files do not organize their desktop computer files. Problems of retrieval and application of the retention program exist when electronic files are not organized and when there is no motivation to purge electronic files. Litigation risk is high when an organization must review desktop computers in addition to all the mainframes, servers, and data stored off site.

"Delete" Is a Misnomer

Software developers make it easy for users to fix mistakes through "undo" or "recover" functions. Deleted e-mail messages are saved to a "deleted" folder in the e-mail browser. But those user-friendly functions make it difficult to eliminate electronic files when it is appropriate and necessary.

Deletion of electronic files is not assured unless the files are over-written or obliterated by some other method. Even when a file is over-written, an expert in data recovery may be able to extract the original data. Data recovery by a forensic computer analyst is a complicated and expensive process, but a litigation opponent may be able to recover the costs when deleted files can be presented as evidence against the other party.

Not all electronic files need to be completely erased, but certain electronic records must be permanently erased. When sensitive and valuable information must be deleted, it should be completely obliterated. Given today's expensive and risky trend of litigants wanting to examine existing and deleted e-mail messages, it is best to permanently erase those files when the retention program authorizes their destruction.

A number of software applications are available that erase or overwrite data so that retrieval by any means is impossible. When entire contents of a computer disk must be wiped out, some technicians use a powerful magnet. If the hard drive is no longer needed, a sledgehammer works.

THE BAD

Certain characteristics of electronic records and information systems present challenges to systems administrators, users, and records and information management professionals. There are software glitches and hardware failures that corrupt or destroy files. When a single system crashes, vast amounts of information are affected.

Computers, peripherals, and networking capabilities are useless without electrical power and communications capabilities. Power glitches cause unsaved information to disappear or damage hardware. Full blown power outages—planned or unplanned—disrupt business. In 2001, for example, California's energy crisis resulted in blackouts that disrupted daily business operations for weeks.

Technological Obsolescence

Electronic information systems applications today dominate daily operations. Slowly organizations are learning that dependence on electronic information for long-term information storage is not always the best option.

Many businesses and government agencies have already experienced the inability to retrieve electronic data from obsolete systems. Personal computer users have lost valuable records and information or have had to re-key hundreds of pages when they upgrade to a new system.

The rapid pace of change in information technologies forces most organizations to upgrade or replace systems more and more frequently. The livelihood of computer manufacturers and software developers depends on relatively short life cycles of their products. Service lives of hardware and software tend to be from two to ten years. Generally, a computer drive becomes obsolete every five years.

The storage life of electronic records is often shorter than the retention requirement for the records. Even when electronic data are migrated from one CD-ROM to another, the critical question is whether the hardware and software to read the data will be there when Superfund litigation demands production of, say, soil test results from fifteen years ago, or when employees demand an accounting of their retirement plan benefits.

The necessity to copy electronic records to new media or to migrate the data to a newer technology is costly in terms of time and expense. An additional expense is the ongoing preservation of all system components and system documentation required to read and process that data.

Until there are standards for electronic record media permanence and durability similar to those for paper and microform records, an organization assumes known and unknown risks in relying on electronic record storage for extended periods of time.

THE UGLY

Information technologies can also have an ugly side.

As mentioned earlier in this book, employees pose the greatest information security risk because of their knowledge and access. Employee fraud that transfers company funds to a personal bank account and sabotage of information systems are a particularly ugly side of electronic records. The following true story is evidence of how ugly it can be when an employee sabotages a computer system.

At one printing company, computer files were mysteriously garbled and erased, and the entire system occasionally crashed. Files employees were working on disappeared before their eyes, and their backup copies were erased. Invoices had to be entered twenty or thirty times. Payroll and production records disappeared. Frustrated workers quit. One distressed worker was fired for screaming profanities. Customers took their business elsewhere.

The last straw fell when the company lost a new account worth $300,000 in annual revenues because the proposal contained so many errors. On the verge of bankruptcy after six months of chaos, the printer called in the store that sold it the computer and other consultants to find the cause of the problems. One programmer, who suspected sabotage, wrote a program to trap the culprit. The detection program worked, and the employee was eventually sentenced to five years in prison for damaging computer files.

Encryption technologies are used to prevent unauthorized access to sensitive and valuable records and information on laptop computers and on Internet and network communications. Encryption is a useful technology, provided no one cracks the code. The situation turns ugly when the encryption key code is lost, leaving the information owner with no access to the information.

Until organizations gain control over their electronic records, another ugly aspect of electronic information systems is electronic evidence discovery. As discussed in Chapter 5, "A Day in Court," electronic evidence discovery can be devastating. The complexity and expense of electronic evidence discovery are a rude awakening to the organization that is unprepared. The litigation risks can be catastrophic when electronic records cannot be retrieved or when the electronic records found are misinterpreted.

RECORDS AND INFORMATION MANAGEMENT CHALLENGES AND SOLUTIONS

Immediate access to current data and the capability to store vast amounts of information create conditions that beg for management and control. When information technologies are properly managed, they add value to the organization's information assets. When not managed well, they become a liability.

Record Status of Electronic Information

The first step to begin management of information systems is to identify what is and what is not an electronic business record. Although all electronic information is discoverable for court proceedings, not all of it needs to be managed as a corporate record. Among the electronic information created, collected, and maintained are duplicates, superseded drafts, and isolated data elements that are not official records.

Duplicates of official records maintained in other recordkeeping systems can be eliminated for more efficient use of resources. Drafts that are superseded by a more current version should be eliminated to avoid confusion about what version is the most complete and accurate.

Raw, unstructured, unformatted data found in many elements of databases and data warehouses are not considered a record until they are organized or compiled in a meaningful way to represent a particular transaction or decision. As such, it is impossible to apply a retention schedule to something without a definitive classification. Generally, these electronic information resources are preserved for as long as they are useful, or as long as they may be needed to support official records that were created from these sources.

With adequate system planning and design, files identified as official records can be tagged within the information systems to facilitate their ongoing management within the organization's records and information management program. Additional electronic data tags about the records are used to classify, retrieve, and dispose of the records within the records and information management policy and program.

What is more challenging to identify and manage as official records are compound documents that consist of documents from different software applications and media. A decision must be made to retain the output of the compound document and/or to separately retain the individual document components, such as the word-processing document, the spreadsheet, and the graphics. The content and use of the compound document determine how to manage its disposition.

It is not always possible to automate the decision of when electronic information or a word processing document becomes a record. Is the information a work in progress, or a non-record, or a duplicate of an official record maintained elsewhere, or an official record? The record holder needs to do that for desktop computer files, and a team of business experts needs to do that for shared information systems.

The records retention policy and its supporting guidelines may state what is a non-record and therefore is not governed by the retention schedule. Non-records and unofficial record copies should be purged to eliminate costly redundancies and to reduce litigation expense.

(See Appendix IV, "Records and Information Management Best Prac-

tices," for additional common sense guidelines to efficiently manage records and information.)

Systems Planning and Design

Most information systems are designed to meet current information
needs and to store inactive records in less space. Little attention is paid
to longer-term preservation and destruction within retention program
guidelines.

Electronic information systems must offer the functions necessary to
identify, preserve, retrieve, secure, and erase electronic records under a
corporate records and information management program.

Basic records and information management functions must be incorporated into system design as technological capabilities. Thus managers
need to

- develop a systematic method to identify files to be retained as records
- organize official electronic records for retrieval for routine use, litigation, and
  destruction at the end of their approved retention period
- design information systems with utilities that allow easy purging in a systematic manner
- segregate records stored on tapes or disks by destruction dates for easy purging
  in a systematic manner
- train end users to manage electronic information on their desktop computers

Methods to manage and control electronic records need to be as simple
and as painless as possible. Designing recordkeeping practices into systems from the very beginning can accomplish that.

An inventory of information systems already in place is needed for a
number of purposes. Knowledge of what is in an organization's information systems is critical for a timely discovery response in litigation. It
is also useful for routine business operations and for planning integration
of the numerous information systems throughout the organization.

An inventory also helps identify which systems have the greatest business risk because of the absence of minimal recordkeeping practices. All
information necessary to apply records and information management
principles should be collected for each system. Data that are stored separately from their operating systems should be matched with the systems
necessary to access their data.

The following list is a broad overview of what information to collect
about electronic information systems:

- hardware and software
- any interconnectivity between different platforms within and outside the organization
- media storage formats and their characteristics
- related systems and media policies and procedures
- what records are associated with the system
- retention requirements of those records

(See Chapter 8, "Integrating Media Choices for the Ultimate Information System," for more on transforming media systems into information systems that are supported by records and information management principles.)

Individual Users

Individual users have far too much discretion over their use of desktop and laptop computers. There is no automatic method to effectively and permanently preserve, authenticate, and destroy documents created and stored on them.

These computers and the information on them are corporate resources that must be governed by policy and guidelines to minimize security risks and legal liabilities. Users need professional support and guidelines to properly manage their individual information systems. Guidelines established as part of the records retention program help end users make decisions about what is important, how to efficiently manage the important, and how to eliminate the unimportant.

Collaborative Efforts

Electronic information that is a business record must be managed within records and information management guidelines in the way paper records are managed.

Most records and information principles are media neutral. They apply to all record storage media forms because they are applied to the *content* and purpose of a record. Of course, methods to apply records and information management principles to different media must be adapted to different media and technical characteristics.

Decisions about information technologies must not be made in isolation by one department or another. Information systems technicians, records and information management professionals, attorneys, archivists, and end users should contribute to the collaborative effort to overcome challenges of recordkeeping requirements in the electronic records environment. The team effort must develop policy, legal, and technical solutions to challenges of electronic recordkeeping systems.

There is much work to do to recover from past neglect of recordkeeping necessities for electronic records and information. It is essential that records and information management professionals and information services managers work together to define and respond to the records and information management challenges. From this day forward, electronic records and information systems must be developed and managed to satisfy recordkeeping requirements and to add value to the enterprise.

10

The Internet

The Internet originally was created in the 1960s to be a network for educational, defense, and government sites to share information. Today it is a means of information sharing, a communications mode, and a forum for the marketing of goods and services.

The Internet promises new business opportunities, closer relationships with customers and suppliers, and worldwide communications. It enables consumers and businesses to instantly exchange information over great distances. It is a vehicle to advertise and sell products and services, offer customer support, promote a corporate image, and expand markets.

High-speed, broadband communications networks enable users to send large amounts of data to each other, including audio clips and moving images. The Internet offers boundless access to information.

LEGAL STATUS

The Internet presents unique and new legal issues. Court verdicts to date indicate that the courts view the Internet as a new and different form of media not clearly governed by the rules of more traditional media.

Questions remain: Who, for example, is liable for different violations of the law? The Internet service provider? The owner of the web site? The administrator of the bulletin board on which defamatory remarks are made or intellectual properties are posted? Further, what laws govern specific events or transactions? The Internet's reach is global, so what state or country is the jurisdiction under which laws apply to the Internet and e-commerce?

It is understood that contract law applies to business transactions and to users giving consent to specified terms and conditions. For example, when a user clicks on the "Yes, I Agree" button in a privacy policy, the user agrees to the terms and conditions of the web site's privacy policy.

Privacy

International and U.S. laws about privacy of customer and employee private information may be applied to private information that can be accessed through a web site. They may also apply to private information about web site browsers and customers collected through the Internet. The laws vary from one jurisdiction to another, but essentially the organization that collects private information must protect that information from theft, sale, or unauthorized use.

In efforts to avoid wide-sweeping legislation to protect consumer privacy rights on the Internet, several companies offer seal-of-approval programs designed to alert a web site browser that privacy protections are in place. Privacy seals displayed on a web site indicate the web site meets certain standards of trustworthiness established by the privacy seal company. No seal guarantees that a web site will not sell or trade the information, and web sites with the same privacy seal may have widely different privacy policies.

The use of privacy seals is controversial. Because web site owners pay an annual license fee to the privacy seal company, it is a potential conflict of interest. Privacy advocates also charge that the seals are more about protecting the companies from invasion of privacy charges than about protecting customer privacy rights. To earn a privacy seal, a web site must meet the following basic criteria:

- have a privacy policy and make it easily accessible online
- disclose what personal information is collected and how it is used
- provide customers with opportunity to opt out of programs that request personal information
- secure web sites and databases to prevent public exposure of personal information or raids by hackers to gain access to the information

One privacy seal company requires web sites to allow customers to view the information collected about them.

The trust and confidence of Internet consumers must be earned. Customer-focused web site owners post a privacy policy on their sites, and they adhere to that policy.

A related privacy issue concerns monitoring of employee Internet use. The employer must be aware of privacy laws in the different jurisdictions that may affect employee monitoring. (For more on worker rights to privacy and on employer rights to monitor employees, see Chapter 4, "Employer Rights and Responsibilities.")

Intellectual Properties

Intellectual properties laws were not written in contemplation of the types of activities now taking place on the Internet. Courts today are shaping copyright, trademark, and other laws as they apply to the Internet.

Copyright and trademark protections apply to Internet web sites in two ways. Web site owners usually display trademarks, and they often copyright the content of their sites. Web site owners may be liable for posting others' trademarks or copyrighted materials on their site without permission.

Web site owners may also be liable for allowing copyright violations on their bulletin boards. Even if an employee or a site visitor committed the violation, it is best for the web site owner to remove the material from the site when a complaint is made or when the site owner becomes aware of the problem in some other manner.

Copyright infringement also occurs because it is so easy to upload and download copies of copyrighted materials without immediate detection through the Internet. A few enterprising companies are in the business of distributing copyrighted material without permission of the copyright owners—until they are caught. Napster, the site that allowed users to download copyrighted music without paying royalty fees, was shut down in 2001.

Federal registration of a trademark may not be enough protection today in this age of the Internet. For additional trademark protection, an enterprise can register its trademark, as well as variations of the trademark, as Internet domain names to prevent their use by another party. Domain name registration fees are less costly than fighting over the trademark and domain name in court or in arbitration. (For more on trademarks and domain names, see Chapter 2, "Preservation of Legal Rights and Business Assets," and Chapter 3, "Threats to Sensitive and Valuable Records and Information.")

In recent years warrants are sought to learn the identity of individuals responsible for posting trade secrets on the Internet. Trade secret information is sometimes found on Internet bulletin boards or on others' web sites. The perpetrator may or may not have intentionally posted trade secret information. Regardless, the SEC monitors message boards when the agency suspects someone is using the message board to pump up or deflate a company's stock price.

Risky Business on the Internet

Security risks are inherent on the Internet and in e-commerce. The attacks and probes by intruders and malicious software are ongoing. Most intruders succeed by attacking unprotected systems and by exploiting vulnerabilities in software on Internet host servers and computers.

In almost seven weeks in 2001, one worm infected 2.3 million computers. Damages of $1 billion are attributed to the costs to clean the infected systems and to lost productivity.

Denial-of-service attacks affect web sites. A hacker's program floods the server with messages, causing a slow response for site visitors or a complete shutdown of the site.

Sometimes hackers break through system security to deface an organization's web site. They change site content, such as price lists or other text, or they deface the site with offensive graphics and language.

Hackers often break into systems to steal private customer information such as credit card numbers. They use private customer information to commit fraud. If a business is lax in security against computer fraud, it loses customer confidence and business.

Attacks on web sites and computers are prosecutable under a number of federal and state laws, including the federal Computer Fraud and Abuse Act.

EMPLOYEE ACCESS, USE, AND ABUSE

More than two thirds of employees today have access to the Internet at work. More than half of workers with Internet access admit personal use of Internet access for shopping, job hunting, staying current on the news, and other activities.

Many employees claim Internet access for business activities improves their job performance. They also report lost productivity when conducting information searches using Internet search engines. They must scan screen after screen of useless search results, and they may never find what they wanted.

A business has the right to maximize use of its corporate resources. Corporate bandwidth—the electronic communications transmission capacity—is a precious resource. Downloading of music and streaming video for personal use places a strain on the bandwidth available to all users.

A business also has a right to minimize risks associated with Internet access. Inappropriate use of Internet access may result in negative consequences to the company.

Employees increase system security risks when they download information from the Internet. Downloaded software and other files may have malicious programming codes that attack electronic files and systems.

Employees sometimes download copyrighted materials without permission of the copyright owner. If the employer benefits from a worker's copyright infringement, the employer will probably be held liable financially.

Workers who access or download Internet pornography place an employer at risk for sexual harassment claims. Most sexual harassment complaints today are built on evidence from employees' Internet surfing and e-mail messages.

If an employee posts on an Internet bulletin board a message filled with racial epithets, law enforcement may trace the source of the message to the employer. Exposure to liability under a defamation claim is also a risk to employers.

In one case an airline had employees access a bulletin board for flight schedules and assignments. The court said the company could be liable for any defamatory remarks if it is proven that the bulletin board is part of the workplace and the employer did not try to prevent the behavior.

Organizations may be held responsible for the acts of their employees because employers have the right and the ability to oversee their worker's activities. Corporate policy and enforcement of that policy on appropriate Internet use is the first line of defense for the employer.

CORPORATE WEB SITES AND E-COMMERCE

The growth of web sites on the Internet has been explosive in recent years. In 1995 there were 100,000 domain names registered for web site addresses. Five years later, 7.2 million names were registered. Some of that dramatic increase is the result of an increase in the number of personal web sites, but the largest portion of domain names belongs to businesses that want to expand the marketing of their organizations, products, and services.

Corporate web sites are used in a number of ways to build and expand business and markets. They help create demand for products and services. They facilitate communications with customers and suppliers. They offer customer support. And they are a tool to process sales transactions.

A new industry now supports web sites. Web design firms help other businesses build their sites for maximum visual appeal and easy movement within the site. They also organize and index site content for speedy searching by visitors. These and other firms also may help a business write a privacy policy for its web site.

Business web sites are one more point of customer contact for sales of products and services. This electronic exchange of money for goods and services over the Internet is commonly referred to as e-commerce.

RECORDS AND INFORMATION MANAGEMENT FUNCTIONS

Business use of the Internet is a relatively new and growing trend. Many businesses are still searching for business applications that meet long-term objectives, and the body of commercial law will always lag behind the marketplace. There remains much to sort out regarding records and information management support of Internet activities, but some recordkeeping practices must still be applied to certain business activities on the Internet today.

Web Site Content and Business Transactions

A number of records and information management issues must be addressed regarding web site content, protection of private data, and documentation of business transactions.

Corporate web sites often are a large depository of information that must be managed and secured. They display information for the world to see, and they gather information for business use. They also are the doors through which business is conducted.

An organization must determine what information must be documented for regulatory, business, and historical purposes. A web site may show different categories of business records, such as price lists, privacy policy, or technical specifications for a product. Certain information may be needed to defend against charges that false claims were made about a product on the site. Historians and archivists are interested in preservation of an organization's first web site.

The corporate records retention schedule must be applied to each identified business record category in the web site content. After identification of record categories and their retention requirements, a recordkeeping system must be selected to retain the information for the prescribed time period. The records may be retained in electronic form directly from the web files, or they may be retained as the source word-processing document or original artwork. A printed copy may not always be best if metadata may be needed to authenticate the printed copy. If the web site has any links to other internal or external web sites and those linked sites are a critical support document to the official business record, a method to retain the linked site as a business record must be established.

Web sites are often used to collect and forward information to separate databases. For example, most web sites collect data on visitors to the site and they collect customer information and transactions. These databases need a recordkeeping function built in to manage information identified as business records. In addition, they must have built-in security to protect private information that is collected from site visitors and customers.

Customer transactions also transmit through a web site to another information system. The recordkeeping requirements to create and maintain records of business transactions apply to electronic transactions as much as they apply to transactions documented on paper. Consequently, Internet transactions documentation and their supporting data must be preserved.

Internet Security

The global reach and open architecture of the Internet increases security risks. A business has rights and responsibilities regarding protection of intellectual properties and private data, as well as prevention of criminal activity.

The three primary areas of concern for Internet information security are secure data transmissions, prevention of outside intrusions, and preserving the integrity of web site content.

Any and all Internet connections are vulnerable to outside intrusions. Malicious software code can affect servers and desktop computers. Some hackers can take control of a computer to launch attacks on servers and web sites.

Anti-virus software is a corporate necessity as is a firewall, the software that monitors Internet communications and blocks suspicious probing from hackers. Passwords and encryption technologies are used to secure electronic transmissions between computers.

Corporate Policy

An Internet policy defines an organization's rights and responsibilities regarding web site content, Internet communications, and electronic business transactions.

The policy should address a number of issues:

• parameters for what content is allowed on a web site
• procedures to preserve content that is an official record

- appropriate Internet use by employees
- sanctions for policy violation
- employee Internet use monitoring
- identification of records that document business transactions conducted over the Internet
- procedures to preserve electronic records of Internet business transactions
- privacy of customer information and information collected from web site browsers
- security against system intruders

The policy may or may not include e-mail systems. Often organizations have a separate e-mail policy, as addressed in the next chapter.

The policy must be enforced. Employee and systems monitoring and audits help prevent policy violations and they assist in policy enforcement.

Employers have the right to monitor electronic communications for legitimate business related reasons. Software applications are available to monitor web surfing in the workplace. These and other applications can also be set to block access to specified web sites.

11

E-Mail

Electronic mail (e-mail) messaging systems were a revolutionary communications system in the 1980s. Originally, their use was limited to an alternative for informal messages and information announcements. In today's business environment, e-mail is a way of doing business. E-mail systems now are used to transmit legally binding contracts and attached files that are official records.

E-mail systems are valuable communication and productivity tools. As e-mail use grows, so do related business risks. E-mail systems design, along with how e-mail use has evolved in recent years, creates records and information management challenges and certain business risks.

This chapter discusses the recordkeeping challenges and business risks of e-mail messaging systems in business today.

EMPLOYEE USE AND MIS-USE

Most workers depend on their e-mail system to help them do their jobs. Among the many benefits of e-mail systems are

- improved customer service through faster response time
- enhanced productivity and timely decisions through fast transmission of current information
- information easily transmitted worldwide in minutes
- capability to transmit information to multiple recipients for collaborative efforts

• transparent organizational hierarchies and geographical separations
• reduced paper flow and handling

The growing use of e-mail systems began to tax e-mail network resources a few years ago. Increasing business uses and the practice of
attaching large data files to messages contribute to the storage and transmission challenges. Users who download cartoons, photos, and video
clips and those who participate in chain letters also clog servers and
consume worker productivity.

E-mail users can subscribe to a number of services that provide information on a regular basis, such as daily news, jokes, or stock quotes.
Many e-mail mailing list subscriptions offer an inexpensive way to maintain professional contacts. Some subscription e-mail services can be very
valuable because of timely delivery and sharing of useful information.
Others waste time and system resources because of the volume of information coming in or because the subscription services are not related to
the employee's job.

The more one uses e-mail, the larger the volume of messages to manage. And that can become more of a productivity detraction than a benefit. Messages are copied, forwarded, and broadcast, creating a problem
similar to the problem in paper recordkeeping systems when everyone
had to have a copy of every document.

It is easy to accumulate messages in a short period of time. Most e-
mail users keep their messages because they do not want to make a
decision on their disposition, or they do not have guidelines to help them
make those decisions.

Users also have a tendency to keep messages as a tickler file or for
reference about recent decisions and actions. Many workers use the e-
mail system as an electronic filing system. Unfortunately, e-mail systems
were originally designed to be communications systems, so they do not
have electronic document recordkeeping functions.

Expanded uses of e-mail systems also increase information security
risks. Inadequate information security practices may result in information leaks and system attacks from intruders through the infected files
attached to messages.

Quality of Communications

The quality of e-mail communications is under scrutiny as organizations confront strained corporate resources and e-mail discovery in litigation.

E-mail users tend to compose messages using language that is less
formal than what they otherwise would be willing to commit to paper.

There is minimal editing and a mistaken perception that e-mail has a transitory nature because it has no finality of print and ink and because the image disappears from the screen when the send button is selected.

Topics of discussion that once were informal chitchat around the water cooler are now memorialized in e-mail. Some of those never-before-overheard discussions become evidence in discrimination or sexual harassment lawsuits.

This informal approach to e-mail communications also is attributed to employees' mistaken expectations of privacy. Employees perceive that messages are private because they sign on to the system with a password, and their messages are addressed to specific individuals similar to how letters in the postal systems are addressed. But employers have the right to monitor e-mail messages, and outsiders gain access to e-mail messages through litigation and government investigation.

E-mail messages may or may not have value as an official business record within corporate policy, but they are recorded, and that electronic recording is discoverable for court proceedings.

BUSINESS AND LITIGATION RISKS AND STRATEGIES

Today's business and litigation risks of e-mail systems include

- vulnerability to leaks of sensitive and valuable information
- vulnerability to system intruders, such as hackers and viruses
- clogged systems and reduced ability to efficiently retrieve desired information because of the large volume and multiple copies of stored records
- selective destruction by e-mail system end users
- significant discovery expense to preserve and retrieve information relevant to litigation, audit, or investigation
- greater litigation risks because of the informal nature of communications
- liability for employee misdeeds, including defamatory comments, harassment, and illegal activities such as theft of trade secrets or drug dealing

E-mail messages tend to be created, managed, and deleted by each individual user's personal preferences or lack thereof. There is little quality control regarding content of messages, and selective record destruction occurs when the retention policy is not consistently applied to all business records.

The incorrect assumption that "delete" does what it says it will do also contributes to business and litigation risks. There are multiple copies in others' mailboxes, on e-mail servers and backup tapes, and in print on paper. In addition, if deleted messages are not permanently erased, opposing counsel can resurrect the electronic record.

E-mail messages relevant to litigation are treated the same as letters and memos by the courts.

When E-Mail Bites Back

E-mail messages often come back to haunt the innocent, as well as the guilty. News headlines tell of businesses forced to settle a case to avoid the extraordinary burden to produce the e-mail system's contents for the court proceedings, or of businesses that lose a case because of the content of e-mail messages.

Microsoft Corporation became a victim of technology in court as it defended itself against antitrust charges. Because Microsoft had no e-mail policy, millions of messages dating back to the early 1990s were collected as evidence. E-mail and other documents were used against Microsoft in its first antitrust suit, which settled in 1995, in other antitrust litigation brought by other businesses, and in the antitrust investigation tentatively settled in 2001.

Microsoft argued that e-mails between managers are not necessarily company policy. The company uses e-mail to "explore and sometimes shoot down ideas," so one should not look at any single e-mail out of context.

E-mail discovery is a litigation strategy that may have more than one objective. Normally, the objective of discovery is to find direct evidence relevant to the proceeding. Occasionally, the opposing counsel is looking for an e-mail that can easily be taken out of context and misinterpreted because e-mail messages so often are written without concern for accuracy or phrasing. Sometimes e-mail discovery is a strategy to impose a burdensome task on the opposing party.

Whether or not the e-mail messages in litigation discovery are fact or conjecture, the discovery expense, the business risks, and the potential public relations disaster are issues to be seriously considered when designing and managing e-mail systems.

Duty to Preserve

As soon as litigation is imminent or a complaint is filed, the business has a duty to identify and preserve all records and information related to the proceeding. That includes relevant e-mail messages and their attachments.

The original electronic record is usually preferred in e-mail discovery because of the importance of the metadata associated with each message. Metadata is essential for determining the record's reliability and authenticity. E-mail message metadata include a time and date stamp, who sent the message to whom, and other important information.

Every party to litigation should initiate its record destruction hold procedure as soon as possible after a complaint is filed. It should set aside a backup of relevant e-mail files and instruct individual e-mail users to save current and future relevant e-mail for possible production in litigation. All possible locations for relevant e-mail must be searched. That includes preserving backup tapes that routinely are overwritten by information services departments to minimize expense.

In one case in which the defendant had overwritten backup tapes, the judge threatened to issue an instruction to the jury about destruction of evidence by the defendant. Whether the destruction was inadvertent or unintentional does not matter. In this case, the threat of that jury instruction and the great expense to produce the vast amount of preserved messages forced the defendant to settle the case before trial.

The efforts to preserve relevant information should be documented.

Shortly after a complaint is filed, each party must produce a list of relevant records and information to the other party. Often this must be done within a short period of time—in as few as ninety days after litigation commences in federal court. To accomplish this obligation, the business must know what information exists in its e-mail system and how to efficiently retrieve what is relevant to the case.

Many businesses are forced to settle a claim rather than fight it when there is evidence of record destruction after a complaint is filed or when an e-mail shows up that says something similar to "I know it's illegal, but let's do it anyway. We'll toss the records when we're done."

Discovery Expense

The process to retrieve e-mail messages for litigation, audit, and government investigation is complex and expensive. Contributing to that complexity and expense are the large volumes of e-mail messages that are not organized for easy retrieval and that are scattered throughout a number of locations.

E-mail messages can have eternal life beyond the reach of the end user's delete key, but within the reach of a subpoena. Multiple copies often exist in multiple locations:

- The author has a copy of sent messages in the Sent directory and perhaps in the Draft directory of the e-mail system's browser.
- Recipients inside and outside of the business have a copy.
- Recipients reply to and copy or forward messages to others within and outside of the business, or they print messages to paper.

- The e-mail server stores messages, and sometimes another computer is a duplicate of the server available in the event that the active server crashes.
- The e-mail system has backup copies.
- The individual user has backup copies.
- When a message is deleted, it is copied to a Trash folder.
- System users copy messages to other folders in their e-mail browser or to their hard drive.
- System users print messages to paper.
- Internet service providers typically retain messages and backups for a period of time.
- Deleted messages can be recovered when they are not completely obliterated from the system.

The greatest business expense occurs when an organization is not prepared for e-mail discovery.

One company was forced to develop a customized software program to search backup tapes so it could recover e-mail messages requested by the court. The search of 30 million messages was necessary to find the e-mail messages for fifteen employees.

The defendant had to search more than 800 backup tapes at a cost of almost $2 million. The e-mail system used by the company does not allow selective restoration of individual mailboxes from backup tapes, so they had to restore the entire database to retrieve the targeted mailboxes.

If a company is unable to take on an e-mail discovery burden, the judge may order that the opposing counsel will have direct access to the company's e-mail system, thus exposing the company's sensitive information to the other party.

Courts are not sympathetic when a burden to produce relevant information is caused by the organization's own unwieldy recordkeeping systems, be they e-mail, paper, or another information system. In one case, the court held that when a party chooses an electronic storage method for information, the necessity for a method to retrieve the information is an "ordinary and foreseeable risk."

(For more information on e-mail discovery, see Chapter 5, "A Day in Court.")

Litigation Strategy

Information services professionals manage e-mail systems from a technology perspective. When the organization ignores the records management and litigation issues, the e-mail system becomes a large, decentralized, and unmanaged depository of information.

Attorneys, records management professionals, and information services professionals should be involved in e-mail system design and administration. Attorneys, executives, and records managers need to know every place where information could possibly be stored.

To prepare for e-mail discovery, a business can do the following:

Apply the records retention program policy to minimize how long messages are stored and to minimize the number of locations where they exist.

Minimize the number of e-mail backup copies and how long they are retained. (Backups are a matter of security in the event of a disaster, but they become a liability in litigation when retained too long.)

Be prepared to halt destruction of all relevant e-mails as soon as the organization becomes aware of litigation.

Develop litigation response processes that quickly and easily search, identify, and save relevant data at the beginning of the litigation.

The organization should perform an e-mail litigation risk assessment to identify and minimize or eliminate potential and unnecessary risks and expense

RECORDS AND INFORMATION MANAGEMENT STRATEGIES

E-mail systems are not designed to support records and information management functions. They store large volumes of unstructured data that make it difficult to quickly retrieve specific information. In the absence of the records retention function, there is great expense to store and manage unnecessary information.

No single tested and proven approach to management of e-mail as a business record is available as of this writing. E-mail systems do not have the capability to preserve authenticity and reliability, to ensure retrievability for business use and litigation, and to properly dispose of e-mail messages and their attachments when appropriate to do so.

Until e-mail systems can also function as records management systems, an organization must depend on individual end user judgment to determine what is a business record. That judgment must be based on the content, context, and use of the message.

E-mail messages identified as official records by end users must be from the e-mail system to a separate, formal records management system. Official records must be managed by an information system that has the capabilities to identify, retrieve, and dispose of official records. Managing e-mail records in a records management system separate from the e-mail system allows for application of basic recordkeeping practices and the integration of e-mail documents with related records.

Official Records, Duplicates, and Non-Records

Some industry professionals say e-mail is not a business record. Others say e-mail is a business record. Whether or not all e-mail messages are business records, all e-mail messages are discoverable.

Consequently, rules regarding official records, duplicates, and non-records should be applied to e-mail messages and attachments. (Appendix IV, "Records and Information Management Best Practices," includes guidelines to identify and manage official records, duplicates, and non-records.)

A large portion of e-mail messages consists of unofficial records, duplicate copies, and other non-records, such as personal messages unrelated to the business. Redundant and inconsequential messages and personal messages should be eliminated as soon as they have served their purpose.

The remaining messages that are records should be managed efficiently to support and protect the organization in a manner similar to other business records and information. When e-mail messages or attachments contain evidence of business decisions, actions, and transactions, they are subject to the same recordkeeping requirements as any other business record. Indeed, the recognition of digital signatures as having the same validity as a written signature will contribute to an increase in the number of e-mail messages and attachments that are official records.

Because the e-mail system is not a recordkeeping system, significant messages and attachments should be transferred to a formal recordkeeping system where they can be organized for retrieval and disposition.

The segregation of official records from nonessential e-mails offers numerous benefits. It

- reduces expense and time to search and retrieve information for business and litigation purposes
- reduces the need to retain the systems and procedures necessary to retrieve older messages and attachments that are in outdated formats
- reduces amount of storage space required
- improves e-mail system performance
- enables faster system backups
- enables faster retrieval of needed information

A number of tricky issues remain to be addressed. Each organization should do the following in a manner that best meets its unique business and information needs:

Determine what method or methods can capture individual messages into a separate records management system for proper management, retrieval, and retention.

Retain the ability to read attached files for the prescribed life of the record in a manner similar to that used for other electronic records—for example, preserve the word-processing software needed to read a word-processing document.

Determine the method to capture hot-links to other documents or to web sites.

Determine how to preserve encrypted e-mail messages and attachments so they are retrievable for their full retention requirement.

Determine the best methods to permanently erase individual messages from all locations where they exist when it is appropriate to do so.

Establish procedures to suspend deletion of messages related to litigation, audit, or government investigation that are stored in multiple locations.

The records retention schedule is media neutral so it can be applied to the content of all record media forms. The greatest challenge today is that individual e-mail system users are in the best position to know the content and value of each message and what retention category is appropriate for the record.

Unfortunately, end users are unwilling to spend the time and effort necessary to manage their e-mail. Until artificial intelligence capabilities can be applied to e-mail systems, records and information management guidelines used for paper records should be modified and expanded to help end users manage their e-mail consistently throughout the organization and consistent with management of the organization's other records and information systems.

Interim solutions are based on what is currently available to and workable for the organization. A temporary solution may be to transfer messages that are records to the individual user's hard drive or to an electronic document management system. Printing messages to paper has its limitations because the process does not preserve the messages' metadata and any attachments and hyper-links.

These interim solutions remain unsatisfactory because of the dependence on individual end users to identify, classify, and transfer records from the e-mail system and because of the intervention necessary for final record disposition.

Future Records Management Software Solutions

Records and information management capabilities needed in future e-mail management software solutions include the ability to automatically identify messages and attachments that are records. Such messages and attachments should be stored in a standard format. This new technology solution must incorporate methods to

- preserve authenticity and reliability
- generate index of records
- save metadata
- perpetually link messages to attachments
- integrate e-mail records with records in other information systems
- assign retention requirement
- permanently erase records
- document destruction within the corporate records retention program

All software applications to manage e-mail should meet existing and evolving standards for records and information management technologies.

E-MAIL POLICY

An e-mail policy defines an organization's rights and responsibilities regarding employee use of its e-mail systems. More often than not, an e-mail policy stands alone; but some organizations combine it with their Internet policy (covered in the previous chapter).

An excerpt from ForwardThink Corporation's corporate policy statement on e-mail follows:

Employee use of the company's e-mail system is a privilege. The e-mail system is for the transmission of messages dealing with legitimate business activities. Reasonable, responsible, and limited personal use is permitted.

E-mail communications may be intercepted for designated business reasons, such as system maintenance or investigation of possible employee misconduct or compromise of confidential company information.

The e-mail system is a communications system—not a recordkeeping system. Every e-mail user must identify messages that are business records and must manage them according to corporate policy and guidelines that apply to all business records. All other messages must be disposed of within thirty days from their creation or receipt.

Litigation attorneys, information systems administrators, and records management professionals should be involved in e-mail systems design, development of e-mail policy, and employee training.

The e-mail policy and standard practices should address the following issues:

- appropriate use by employees, unacceptable use, and sanctions for policy violation
- employee privacy expectations and e-mail monitoring by employer

- identification of e-mail messages that have a business value and must be retained as official records
- procedures to preserve messages and attachments that are official records in an electronic records management system
- identification of messages and attachments with sensitive and valuable information and their protection according to corporate policy
- security against system intruders

The e-mail policy must be audited and enforced to be effective and to meet business objectives.

Information Security

A number of information security issues must be addressed regarding e-mail systems:

A policy decision is needed to stipulate whether users are allowed to send sensitive and valuable information by e-mail. If they are allowed to do so, the policy must state under what conditions such information can be transmitted, such as using encryption technology or sending a password-protected document.

Monitoring of e-mail traffic and content may be appropriate to prevent or detect information losses, litigation liabilities, and criminal activity.

E-mail networks must have security measures in place to prevent and detect system intrusions. Employees must be educated about the risks of opening message attachments that may be infected with a virus.

Employee Training

Employees are the key to successful management of e-mail. They must be educated about the following:

- application of retention policy to e-mail
- the difference between official business records and nonessential messages
- methods to transfer official record copies of e-mail to a formal recordkeeping system
- practices to protect sensitive and valuable information
- practices to prevent unwanted system intrusions
- guidelines for appropriate and efficient use of e-mail

Periodic reminders of the e-mail policy are appropriate.

Audits and Monitoring

Business may monitor e-mail communications for legitimate business reasons. Courts find that an organization's interest in preventing inappropriate, unprofessional, and criminal behavior outweighs any privacy rights of employees.

One technology company learned about employee theft of proprietary software valued at hundreds of millions of dollars. The discovery was a result of a standard security monitoring process that included sifting through e-mail messages.

There may be a litigation risk if a company chooses to have a policy that e-mail will not be monitored. A court is not bound by the company's e-mail privacy policy, but such a policy may prevent the employer from reading its own e-mail messages to prepare for litigation.

As a courtesy and a deterrent, employees should be notified that e-mail system use may be monitored. Although employee consent to e-mail monitoring is not required, it is helpful to obtain such consent through an employment agreement or a corporate policy statement acknowledgment form.

Software applications are available to help employees monitor their own e-mail communications. They check messages against a large database of words and phrases and present alternative language to the user. The programs look for profanity, racial slurs, sexual content, and anything else the company or the user wants to specify. They can search for a secret project's code name to alert management of potential information security breaches. Securities firms use similar applications to monitor for high-pressure sales tactics and potential insider training.

These programs may have their place in certain situations. However, an opposing counsel would delight in sifting through the database of language added to or deleted from the larger database, and a log of incidents can be used to show a pattern of inappropriate language.

E-mail system monitoring and audits help prevent e-mail policy violations, and they support policy enforcement. Audits of the records and information management program must include the e-mail system. The level of compliance with corporate policies should be assessed in the areas of e-mail content, system use by end users, identification of official records, organization of messages for retrieval and permanent erasure, and more.

12

The Bottom Line

The reasonable and practical approach to records and information management is the recognition that records and information management is a management tool. It is a vehicle to increase the overall productivity and profitability of an organization through systematic application of procedures for the creation, flow, distribution, use, and final disposition of information at the lowest costs possible.

Records and information must also be managed to comply with the law, show compliance with the law, preserve legal rights, protect assets, and avoid undue harm.

A competitive advantage sought by many businesses is manageability at the lowest costs for responsiveness, quality, and service. An enterprise must be able to anticipate, recognize, and quickly respond to changing business opportunities and adversities. In today's competitive, regulated, and litigious environment, a business should take the same care managing its information resources as it does managing its employees and assets because they are valuable data and knowledge for intelligent business decisions, risk management, and compliance.

A business can get by without good recordkeeping practices only if it

- never needs to find a record after it is filed;
- is never sued, investigated, or audited; and
- never has to file a claim for lost or damaged property.

Good records management practices identify and safeguard valuable, useful, and legally required records in all media that are necessary to manage and protect a successful business. They also prevent the unnecessary accumulation of records and the premature destruction of records. The fewer and better records that are retained are organized and stored in ways to ensure prompt availability when needed, at the lowest costs possible.

Along with the benefits associated with recordkeeping are burdens and expenses in terms of human resources, equipment, and facilities. The higher the quality of records management, the lower the costs to create, collect, store, protect, and produce information.

To earn the highest return on the investment, proper management should begin when records are most valuable and most at risk—in their early phase of life. A comprehensive records and information management program provides a higher return on the investment by contributing to a company's profitability through

• reduced risks and expenses
• timely response to changing business conditions
• streamlined internal processes and higher productivity
• enhanced services, products, and effectiveness

This comprehensive records and information management program is described in more detail in Chapter 13, "Organization and Staffing for Records and Information Management."

RISK MANAGEMENT AND RECORDS

A company's records and information, and how well they are managed, will affect certain business risks and legal risks. Worst-case scenarios are those in which records and information management functions are ignored, as in

• loss of revenues, assets, or business
• loss of legal rights
• exposure to losses and penalties in litigation or investigation
• violations of the law

Because the costs of poor recordkeeping generally remain hidden, not many companies have established a comprehensive records management program to limit the associated risks. Eventually the losses show up on the bottom line.

Records and information management is a function of risk management when it is designed to minimize the risks related to information security threats and government or court actions. It enables a proactive approach to potential adversities, rather than a knee-jerk reaction in a crisis. Risk analysis weighs the costs, benefits, and risks of various recordkeeping practices against the relative value of various records groups. Such an analysis identifies those practices that will provide the most flexibility within the legal, ethical, and practical constraints.

There may be risks associated with the existence or the nonexistence of certain records and information. A business will want to ensure that certain records continue to exist in order to protect the organization and its assets and to minimize any risk created by record losses. This does not always translate to keeping everything for all eternity. Because most records lose their value over time, a business has the right to dispose of records no longer required by the government or law in order to meet its own needs of efficiency and profitability.

The relative value of a record depends on its true purpose(s), which may be to

- support business decisions and activities
- analyze and manage business risks
- comply with and show compliance with policy and the law
- preserve rights and protect assets
- document ownership of business assets

The business environment is increasingly more dependant on its records and information systems to remain competitive in this information-based, services economy. Therefore, application of records and information management principles to those information systems is good business sense. The need for conscientious recordkeeping practices is also greater in enterprises at risk for litigation or investigation.

Records and information managers must consider a number of questions when making a risk assessment:

What records truly merit protection because of their content and value?

What are the risks if the information is available, if it is not available, or if it falls into the wrong hands?

What is the likelihood of litigation or investigation, and for how long?

Is there sufficient evidence for a defense or to file a claim?

In response to each business risk identified in the assessment, legal counsel and others should establish criteria to identify which recordkeeping practices are reasonable and which are an exceptional burden.

WHITE COLLAR PRODUCTIVITY

In the modern fast-paced and volatile marketplace, efforts are turning to the improvement of white collar productivity. Efficiencies and better productivity translate into better profitability. Simplification of internal processes allows for more systematic attention to other business fundamentals, such as making decisions and responding to customer needs.

New technologies have already proven capable of helping business work smarter. Management can use the time and effort formerly devoted to the location or production of information for analysis of the information.

Electronic information systems that can be accessed by multiple users offer the capability to redesign internal processes and structures. As critical, current, and accurate information becomes more readily available to more workers, organizations can flatten their structures to gain the flexibility needed to adapt quickly to new opportunities and challenges.

Indeed, management, professionals, and other office workers should be spending more of their time in their areas of expertise instead of looking for information.

If 25 percent of a professional's time is spent tracking down the right information, and that professional's annual salary is $50,000, the annual cost to the company for ineffective use of that professional's time is $12,500. Thus, in a company with 200 professionals, the cost for professionals to hunt for information is $2.5 million each year.

Information Retrieval for Better Productivity

Information is only as good as the ability to put it to work in a timely manner. Timely access to decision support systems may reduce the time it takes to bring a new product or service to market, to enter a new market, or to build market share. If a business does not know it has certain information, or the information cannot be found, it is of no use to the company.

When valueless records are maintained, the human resources necessary to file, sort, retrieve, and maintain those records are wasted. When records are not organized for efficient retrieval, records users have to sort through unrelated information to get to the good information. And when multiple versions of information exist and the end user does not know which version is the most authoritative, misinformation can lead to errors.

Application of records and information management principles at the beginning of a record's life saves time and dollars later, limits liabilities, and ensures consistencies over a longer period of time. The underlying premise is that a business can pay now or pay later.

Over the years records of Metro-Goldwyn-Mayer (MGM) and United Artists were sent to storage with little concern for identification of the contents of the boxes. In 1994 an MGM team was charged with descending into the salt mine storage area to identify records of value to the corporation and records of historical significance. The team reviewed the contents of 12,000 boxes—some labeled only with an executive's name—to find art treasures, scripts, accounting records, and contracts that assigned rights to television shows and other properties.

There are a number of ways to ensure better information retrieval rates and long-term efficiencies at the time a record is created:

- select the most appropriate record form
- keep files and information current and accessible to those authorized for access
- organize and index records so they may be found again once they are stored
- include in or on documents any indexing or other useful information to facilitate proper filing and storage
- include in or on documents any statement necessary about its sensitive and valuable information
- determine where the official copy will be maintained to eliminate the creation and maintenance of unnecessary duplicate copies

A critical aspect of information management is not where one stores the information, but whether the information may be found again. Easy-to-use information retrieval systems are required.

Individual employees and departments, however, tend to develop their own indexing and filing systems in the absence of organization-wide standards. But what happens when the employee resigns or when another department needs the information? Will a record be found again once it is placed in a file cabinet or on film or on a computer disk?

Thinking ahead to the time of information retrieval will determine the appropriate information storage media and the proper design of indexing and filing systems. Information indexing and filing systems that are understood and used by employees will improve retrieval and storage efficiencies.

The House of Good Intentions has an extensive collection of 20,000 slides, 10,000 negatives, 2,500 photographs, and 6,000 video tapes. Until the collection was indexed and cross-referenced, searches for a specific photo or slide were consuming far too much time. Frequently, out of frustration and time constraints, the same photography shots were taken over and over again. After indexing the collection, the firm reported a cost avoidance of $10,000 every month.

Media selection also affects access and retrieval rates. Paper is the most labor-intensive record form to retrieve and store, and misfiles are more likely with paper records than with microfilm or electronic records. The fixed continuity of the files on microfilm reels, cassettes, or microfiche prevents a certain amount of misfiling or the loss of individual records. Electronic information systems also eliminate misfiles and can locate information faster. In addition, reducing filing or data errors eliminates work steps.

Installation of an electronic document imaging system in one business cut the number of work steps from twelve down to three, reduced the number of errors, increased productivity by more than 50 percent, and improved response time to customer requests.

In another example, a major airline installed an electronic document imaging system for information used by its mechanics. By reducing by 75 percent the time it took for mechanics to find necessary information, the airline saw planes returned to service faster and it realized an annual labor savings in excess of $1 million.

In electronic information systems, multiple users can almost instantly access current information on file servers. Efficient information access can also be achieved with proper indexing and files organization practices in place for desktop computers, diskettes, CDs, tapes, and inactive electronic records.

In paper and microfilm filing systems, how records are arranged within filing systems will affect retrieval efficiencies. Filing rules and name authority guidelines are necessary when an alphabetical arrangement is used so that users do not overlook important records in the system. Numeric filing arrangements reduce the chances of filing error, and they work best when the numbers used are less than five digits. Alphanumeric arrangements are the most typical filing method used to organize large volumes of records efficiently and to minimize problems with sequential filing.

Color coding on records containers also improves efficiencies and accuracy similar to color coding on electronic components, electrical wiring, and theater tickets. Manufacturers and users of color-coded labels report from 30 to 50 percent faster and simpler filing and retrieval than possible without color coding. A visual scan of color-coded rows of files, computer tapes, or microfilm cartridges for a break in a color block will easily find a misplaced record.

The design of both visible and digital information systems for speedy and accurate information retrieval begins with an indexing system. Indexing with common terminologies, cross-referencing, and other information search capabilities supports fast information retrieval. Active electronic records and information are accessed from desktop computers and from employee and department files. Inactive records are removed from prime office spaces and file servers to records centers so users do not waste time fumbling through or around inactive records and information to find the needed current information.

Records Management Software Applications

Records management software applications are automated indexing and tracking systems that manage and control records. A wide range of records management applications is available to meet the needs of different organizations.

In the most simplistic form, a records management application is an electronic inventory of records and their locations. A typical program tracks records throughout their life cycles and includes instructions for and documentation of their final disposition.

Prior to installation of a computer indexing system for the records of a casino-hotel, retrieval of records for a grand jury investigation of a hotel guest normally took three people and three days of searching through boxes. After system installation, copies of room and telephone charges and other guest records can be located in a matter of minutes. The records management staff and auditors were especially appreciative of the new system when the casino-hotel was hit with simultaneous internal, outside accountant, and IRS audits.

Records management systems can reduce administrative tasks by generating record container labels, overdue notices, and management reports. The systems support the organization's management functions with data and information about the indexed records. They also create audit trails of records activities and program documentation

Among the records and information management capabilities needed in records management applications are multiparameter indexing, records retention, and records destruction holds. Ideally, all records in all media and in all locations are identified on the system. This enables retrieval of relevant records from a number of information media systems, a capability that is essential for business activities such as product development team projects and litigation support.

The more advanced systems forward records requests to a records center, or they retrieve the electronic document image from a separate but connected information system. Many systems produce instructions for records transfers, vital records, media conversions, valuable and sensitive records, litigation, and records destruction. Systems help identify unnecessary duplication and inefficient layering of information throughout all the information systems covered by the records management software application.

Records and information management software applications have traditionally managed paper files and boxes of records in storage. The best option to apply retention and other recordkeeping capabilities to electronic records and information systems is to link the records management application to those information systems.

Short of that, every single information system in every media must have records management capabilities, and a records management application is needed to unify all paper, microfilm, and electronic information systems into a single system for improved access and retrieval. A media-transparent system supports the consistencies necessary in a records and information management program.

A few records management software applications even organize and index the results of legal research for recordkeeping requirements. Reports generated by these systems expedite attorney review and approval of a records retention schedule. These systems make it easy to update the legal requirements as they change and to document the development of the retention schedule and retention requirements decisions.

Bar code applications are particularly useful methods to process and track records. The paybacks from the use of bar coding are increased speed and accuracy in filing and retrieval, as evident in the next example.

To Your Health, like other insurance companies, is a paper-intensive business. More than 200 files are requested daily by sales, accounting, and marketing personnel. Until recently the files were scattered throughout the facility, and up to 15 percent of the files were misfiled or were not checked out properly. The staff dedicated to finding these missing files spent four hours each day trying to track them down, and the delays in getting back to the customer were sometimes three to four days.

To Your Health installed a bar code system to track its files. Ten temporaries applied bar code labels to file folders over one weekend. When a file is removed, a pen scanner reads the file folder's bar code label and either the department's or the employee's identification card's bar code. These data are downloaded to a personal computer three times a day. The list of missing files was significantly reduced when the new tracking system resulted in a files found rate of 98 percent. The files search staff was reduced by two full-time positions. The investment of $30,000 for the system was paid back in one year by hard dollar (quantifiable) savings. The less-tangible soft dollar savings resulting from improved productivity and customer service is a bonus.

To Your Health plans to install an electronic document imaging system to retain the benefits of the bar code system and to gain the benefits of reduced paper files.

Standards for records management software applications are slowly developing. The Department of Defense's "Design Criteria Standards for

Records Management Applications" is the first technical standard for software that manages records in electronic form. The DoD-STS-5015.2 is used to certify records management applications at the Department of Defense. Records management applications must have specific records management functions built into them, including file identification and indexing, filing of e-mail messages, security, and file destruction.

STANDARDS ADD VALUE

Policies and standards are necessary in any business to help it remain competitive and profitable. Records and information management standards support the records and information management program as it supports the entire enterprise.

Typical areas for records and information management standards include

- information systems design and technical specifications
- information media selection
- records conversions and data migrations
- records retention and destruction
- information security
- vital records protection
- equipment and supplies specifications
- records and information storage facilities
- indexing, organization, and filing methodologies
- procedures and practices
- technical language

Records and information management standards improve cost-effectiveness and productivity. They also ensure compliance with recordkeeping requirements.

Standards for Consistencies and Compliance

Government regulations, industry standards, ISO certifications, rules of evidence, and other pressures are bearing down on businesses to force them to more carefully manage their information resources. Essentially, all these different standards and guidelines can be summarized as promoting the following records and information management principles:

Records shall be legible, identifiable, and traceable to the activity, product, or service involved.

Records shall be organized, stored, and maintained in such a way that they are readily retrievable and protected against damage, deterioration, or loss.

Procedures for identification, collection, indexing, access, storage, maintenance, and disposition of all records, regardless of media, will be established and maintained.

Records retention requirements shall be established and documented.

A comprehensive records management program addresses the requirements of these standards. As national and international standards and best practices are developed and endorsed, organizations should consider adopting them as their own standards. The ISO 9000 standard addresses quality records, and there is the "Australian National Standards for Records Management" (AS 4390).

The first international standard for records management, titled "ISO 15489–1: Information and Documentation–Records Management—Part 1: General," was approved in 2001. This standard sets the parameters within which a records management program should be established. It is supplemented by the more detailed technical report ISO/TR 15489–2: Information and Documentation-Records Management-Part 2: Guidelines.

Standards for Information Media Systems and Information Retrieval

A large body of standards is needed to fully integrate the numerous information systems in every organization. A fully integrated information system crosses all organizational, technological, and information storage media boundaries in such a way that those boundaries are transparent to the end user.

Within this body of standards must be standards for records creation in all media, standards that meet government requirements regarding records media, and standards that satisfy rules of evidence. Organizations also need to consider standards for compatibility of information system components as they find ways to integrate or connect the many information media systems with each other.

Indexing to classify records and information for retrieval must be standardized organization-wide and applied to all information media systems. A standard indexing system superimposed on all company records and information is essential for improved productivity and the integration of media systems. Although much forethought and effort is required to develop a useful indexing system, it will pay off later in long-term benefits.

Standards are also necessary to control records and information in a decentralized environment. In decentralized information systems, the end users have immediate access to high-use records located in their offices and on their desktop computers. This situation typically causes unnecessary duplication of records and information throughout the company. In the absence of indexing standards, the information is usually not accessible by others in the company. End users may not follow information security and records retention rules, resulting in unnecessary expense and exposure to liabilities. In addition, records from incompatible information systems are eventually dumped into a records center, where they continue to be inaccessible if no additional expense is allocated to organize and index them properly.

Centralized information systems offer cost savings, improved access by multiple users, and better control over records conversions, transfers, and destruction. However, centralized filing systems do not meet user needs for immediate access unless they are electronic information systems that are networked to individual work stations.

The concept of controlled decentralized information systems is a compromise between immediate access by end users and the overall business need for standards and controls. Under this concept, departments and individuals maintain their own records and information according to records and information management standards.

Individual users need assistance with their records and information responsibilities in their offices and on their desktop computers. They need education on the benefits of information resources management and controls, as well as knowledge of what recordkeeping practices are endorsed by corporate policy. Standards and guidelines specific to individual user records management challenges must be established.

Standards for Better Productivity

Standards applied to records and information management reduce errors and duplication of effort. They promote efficiencies and improved quality of service.

The following scenario describes what can happen in a company that has no indexing standards or central controls over information in different information systems.

The TechTrack firm's search for all records related to a specific government contract for an upcoming audit is hampered by the lack of a corporate-wide index to records in all media. Further complicating matters is that each record storage media's indexing system is based on different terminologies, so records creators and records users do not talk the same language and do not use common search strategies. The information systems department must check a number of systems for any relevant electronic records. Staff must search every department's paper files and desktop computer. The microfilm collection must be searched box by box. A search request must be transmitted to TechTrack's records storage vendor in hopes of discovering any inactive records related to the government project.

When records management standards are in place throughout the enterprise, the business is better able to implement organizational changes. Training of personnel is easier, and the process of opening, closing, or consolidating office sites is simplified.

The House of Good Intentions has twenty-five offices across the country, all of which have compatible indexing and filing systems. These indexing systems are based on a single subject listing of records, instead of on the organizational structure. When the firm acquired another company to expand its marketing capabilities, the new subject areas were simply added to the records indexing system.

When business conditions in different markets changed, some offices were closed or the operations were consolidated with other offices. Because the records in all facilities were organized and filed in the same manner, they were easily consolidated with the records in their new location. The company wanted to sell the business in certain states to other companies. The gathering of customer records, contracts, and financial information for analysis and determination of a fair sale price was quick and efficient.

Standards for Volume Purchase Savings

Establishment of standards for supplies and equipment may achieve significant dollar savings. Standards provide the opportunity to set up agreements with vendors for volume discounts.

In its first year TechTrack opened twenty-five new offices across the country. Corporate standards were established for its equipment, supplies, vehicles, facilities, signs, and other assets. Among the records-related equipment and supplies to be purchased for each office were file cabinets, a filing supplies starter kit, paper shredders, and desktop computers and printers for the records management application. The ability to purchase these supplies and equipment in volume resulted in a savings of $70,000 that first year.

Most businesses prohibit the use of legal-size paper in order to realize savings in equipment and storage costs. Oversized documents can be reduced to standard letter size by a photocopy machine. Software modifications can replace large computer printouts with standard letter size reports, or the electronic data can be output to microfilm.

COST SAVINGS AND COST AVOIDANCE

Records and information management practices may result in both one-time and ongoing cost savings and cost avoidance. Appropriate records protection methods avoid excessive costs to reconstruct records when they are prematurely destroyed or lost. Records protection also minimizes other liabilities from records and information losses. In addition, good recordkeeping practices reduce the professional fees charged by accountants, attorneys, and other outside professionals who must have access to the organization's records and information.

A records and information management program must be in place before litigation occurs in order to respond to discovery orders within a short time. Excessive and unnecessary expense to search and retrieve the relevant records and information is avoided when records identification and tracking systems are in place. As discussed in Chapter 5, "A Day in Court," serious consequences result when a business is unable to produce information relevant to a proceeding in a timely manner.

Measurement of cost savings and cost avoidance is possible for reduced volumes of records and information storage media choices. How well facilities and equipment are managed to reduce costs can also be measured.

Reduce Volumes of Records

The volume of stored records and information may be reduced by

- avoiding the creation of unnecessary records and duplicates,
- eliminating unnecessary records, and
- converting paper records to microfilm or electronic document images.

Companies with file cabinet flab have high costs for storage, equipment, facilities, retrieval, handling, transportation, and lost data. In a typical organization that has not controlled the growth and volume of its records, anywhere from 30 to 60 percent of its stored records are duplicate, obsolete, or unnecessary records. These valueless records should be eliminated because they are financial and legal liabilities.

When a business has fewer and better records, the unnecessary exposure to liabilities is limited. Efficiencies are improved for storage and handling of the remaining valuable records. Valuable office space is available for the more current records, for people, or for other important business activities.

Computers, photocopiers, and fax machines make a significant contribution to employee productivity. They also contribute to the continuing explosion of paper records and to a proliferation of electronic duplicates and multiple versions. The convenience and minimal expense to produce duplicate copies has resulted in mountains of unnecessary paper records.

Once a record is filed, filmed, or saved by pressing a key, it does not self-destruct—at least, not under normal storage conditions. A planned, deliberate program to physically remove and destroy records on a regular basis controls records growth. Without that, a business will continue to squander its limited resources on records that are no longer useful, valuable, or required.

The House of Good Intentions decided to purge its office of file cabinet flab and unnecessary trash. The records slated for elimination were identified by the newly developed records retention schedule. Out went 45 tons of records and 350 barrels of miscellaneous items, including abandoned shoes, vases, and coffee mugs. Many of the remaining files were microfilmed, and 370 boxes of indexed records were sent to storage. Within the first year not one request came in for the records that had been destroyed, confirming the excellent job done on development of the records retention schedule. Files are now current, and filing and retrieval times have been reduced.

A central filing system and shared electronic information resources help reduce excessive records duplication created by individuals and departments. If a company is able to prevent a duplicate record from being created in the first place, it avoids the expense of its reproduction, filing, and distribution and the time spent reading or handling the record.

The Quick 'n' Dirty Company discovered that a large number of unnecessary duplicate copies had accumulated in files about to be microfilmed. Based on a random sample, it calculated that $450,000 in salaries and benefits and $600,000 in equipment and supplies had been spent on the production of these now unnecessary copies. (Storage and handling costs over the years for these duplicate paper records were not measured.) Because there was no time or staff to search for and remove the duplicate records, the firm went ahead with the filming of the records, creating additional unnecessary expense for processing of the film and its storage.

When employees know which records are official records and which records are duplicate records, it is easier to minimize the proliferation of duplicate copies throughout the organization. (See Appendix IV, "Records and Information Management Best Practices," for more on official records.)

Forms and Reports Management

Forms and reports management are management functions that control the design, production, and distribution of forms and reports. Thousands of dollars, hundreds of hours, and hundreds of square feet of space may be saved by the proper management of reports and forms. Forms and reports have high costs in terms of creation, distribution, storage, and use.

One telecommunications company assembled a financial reporting team made up of the chief financial officer, controllers, and accountants. The team roamed around the company asking employees a simple question, "Do you really need these financial reports?" The team discovered that one employee spends five days each month preparing a twenty-five-page report that no one reads. In the end, the team eliminated 6 million pages of reports—a stack four times taller than the company's high-rise headquarters building.

To manage forms and records well, the management team must consider specific questions about every form and report:

Is it necessary, or could it be consolidated with another form or report?
Can it be redesigned to improve its efficiency and value?
What are the costs to create, copy, and distribute it, and is it worth the costs?
Can the frequency or number of its copies be reduced?
Can it be distributed by the Internet, the corporate intranet, or e-mail?

Most companies now use office technologies to create forms as they are needed, and end users often complete and transmit the form electronically. This reduces printing and storage expenses, as well as saves time for employees.

Media Choices to Reduce Volume

The selection of a record's storage media affects space and equipment requirements and shipping costs. A jukebox, or computer library of optical disks, consumes approximately the same floor space as a photocopy machine, but it holds enough document images to fill 200 four-drawer file cabinets. The costs to ship microfilm are less than the costs to ship paper, and the transfer of electronic data is the cost of a telephone line.

For the best return on the investment, records are created in the medium that best satisfies all business and legal requirements, or they are converted to another media as early as possible in the record's life.

The TechTrack firm replaced almost 9 million pages of paper documents with microfilm. The cost avoidance figure of $280,000 is based on the difference between the production and storage costs for the paper system and the production and storage costs for the microfilm system. Another 120,000 documents were scanned to an electronic document imaging system, reducing space and equipment costs by $200,000. At the same time, the firm implemented a computer output microfilm (COM) application that resulted in an annual cost avoidance of $2 million for space, personnel, and hardware.

(See Chapter 8, "Integrating Media Choices for the Ultimate Information System," for more information on specific record storage media.)

Cost-Effective Facilities and Equipment Management

Office space in corporate America is a significant expense in terms of construction, rent, furniture, equipment, utilities, maintenance, insurance, and other costs. The more efficiently the space is used, the more cost-effective it is. Because business continues to manage paper, microfilm, and electronic records, with paper records the most costly to store, efficient management of records and information is essential to contributing to an organization's efficient use of space and thus its overall cost-effectiveness.

The facilities commitments for records and information may be reduced by:

• reduction of the overall volume of records,
• transfer of records to lower-cost facilities, and
• use of high-density equipment to store records.

Inactive paper, microfilm, and electronic records may be removed to less costly facilities when they are no longer necessary for daily activities. As much as one third of a company's records are inactive and appropriate for off-site storage.

Off-site records centers are one of several less-expensive storage alternatives. A records center stores records and electronic data in uniform-sized containers on shelves much higher than those allowed in an office space, providing the capability to store five times as many records per square foot. Commercial records centers can offer storage cost reductions of 40 to 60 percent. Commercial facilities typically have the security and environmental controls necessary to protect vital, electronic, microfilm, and other records sensitive to adverse environmental conditions.

A business may optimize the volume of active records stored in prime office space through judicious selection of information storage media and filing equipment and supplies. For example, elimination of hanging files used to separate and store file folders may increase the amount of available filing space by 20 to 50 percent, depending on how the hanging files had originally been used.

Vertical file cabinets are adequate for records in small departments and offices, but they become inefficient when the volume of records exceeds four file cabinets. Lateral file cabinets consume more wall space than vertical file cabinets, but they do not require as much valuable open floor space per filing inch. Most lateral cabinets available today may be adapted for storage of various media other than paper files, and they may be converted for installation as a high-density, mobile storage system.

The ForwardThink Corporation is relocating a department to another facility. The department has 5,000 file folders and hanging files in roll-out drawer, vertical file cabinets. The seventeen cabinets now consume 116 square feet of floor space. As new equipment and furnishings are being purchased for the new facility, the company considers the elimination of the hanging files and the use of lateral file cabinets in the new facility. Lateral filing cabinets are chosen for the new space because of the reduced space requirement and the lower cost per cabinet and filing inch. They also will work well in the new open-plan office area. The 5,000 file folders, without the hanging files, will require ten lateral file cabinets and only 34 square feet in the new office space. The old file cabinets will be transferred to other departments where they are needed, or they will be sold as surplus equipment.

Open-shelf records storage units use more vertical space than file cabinets, as they are six or eight shelves high. They also are more efficient because more than one user at a time may access their contents, and no time is lost to the opening and closing of drawers. Like lateral file cabinets, open-shelf storage units may be modified to accommodate a mixture of records storage media by the installation of shelves, bins, tubs, hanging bars, tape racks, drawers, or other accessories.

If a company has a large volume of records to be stored in a small space, high-density shelving is the best alternative. In these mobile storage systems, shelving sections or storage units are supported by carriages on tracks for movement of the rows to create aisles where they are needed. They provide the capability to use 50 to 70 percent less floor space for the same volume of records. High-density systems are not recommended for very active records because of the inability to access all records at once.

Motorized files or carousels are also available for records storage. These systems bring the files to the user. They are much more expensive in terms of cost, installation, and maintenance, and access is limited to a single operator.

Various configurations are possible for high-density systems to fit existing space and to accommodate a variety of information storage media. A leasing arrangement may make a system affordable to certain businesses. Costly facility modifications may be required to support the additional weight of any high-density storage system.

PROTECTION OF REVENUES AND PRESERVATION OF RIGHTS

A comprehensive records and information management program protects business revenues and an organization's legal rights.

When certain revenue-producing intellectual properties are secured against unauthorized access or loss, future income is protected. If a disastrous event occurs, vital records help the business continue or resume operations quickly. Sales contracts and accounting records must be accessible in order to collect revenues.

Sound recordkeeping practices and information security measures contribute to preservation of legal rights to protection under the law, rights to file a claim, and rights to a defense.

When, for instance, an organization routinely identifies sensitive and valuable information, the time and expense to search for and segregate those records during litigation discovery is reduced and rights to protection under the law can be preserved.

One defendant had only ninety days to screen 17 million pages of discoverable material to determine if the attorney-client privilege applied to any of the records and if any of the records contained trade secrets. The company was forced to hire an outside staff of attorneys and clerical help to get the job done on time.

As discussed elsewhere in this book, certain records must be retained and protected to preserve an organization's rights to file a claim against a party that has injured the organization. In addition, certain records must be readily available to build a defense when another party files a claim against the business.

13

Organization and Staffing for Records and Information Management

The visible commitment of senior officials is critical to the success of any organization-wide records and information management program. As executives and the general counsel accept records and information management concepts and their benefits, this commitment must flow down through operations managers to all employees. Only when the support of operations personnel exists can there be program compliance. The decision-makers throughout a business must understand how a records and information management program contributes to the success and livelihood of the business as a whole, as well as to their specific business activities. They must also know that the records and information management function is not an option.

The organization's executives must endorse a company policy on records and information assets and the means to enforce that policy. Senior management further demonstrates its support by the allocation of necessary resources to achieve planned objectives and by transferring authority to the right people.

As a cost of doing business, the records and information management expense is an investment in several long-term benefits:

- protection of information and other corporate assets
- preservation of legal rights
- more effective support to decision-makers
- compliance with regulatory requirements

- litigation support
- improved efficiencies
- reduced expense

Government recordkeeping requirements and those recordkeeping requirements critical to business objectives should be expressed as mandatory in the records and information management policy.

ORGANIZATIONAL STRUCTURE

Where the records and information management function fits in an organizational structure varies from one organization to another. Where it is placed does contribute to its effectiveness throughout the organization.

A single position within the organization, regardless of job title, must have overall responsibility for the records and information management program. The corporate secretary is ultimately responsible for records in corporations, and business owners are ultimately responsible for records in their enterprises.

Executives empower their directors and managers with responsibilities for specific business functions and the appropriate authority to implement company policy. Executives must find the right employee(s) and the right department(s) to most effectively implement a corporate-wide records and information management program.

The size of a business, how it is structured, the nature of its records and information systems, and the records and information management program objectives help determine the best place in the organization for this important business function. Which department is ultimately responsible for records management will vary from one company to another.

In most organizations, records and information management is a staff, or support, function. Although records and information management does not always have its own place on a company's organization chart, its functions do exist in every manager's areas of responsibilities, and it should be a line function in the organization chart. Whether one person or several share records and information management program functions, every employee shares the responsibilities and benefits of records and information management.

A few organizations place the records management function in the finance department because that department holds the bulk of the company's records. Such an approach loses sight of the existence of other important records and fails to recognize that records management involves a wide range of issues beyond departmental records and information needs.

In light of the unique interrelationship of records management and business laws and regulations, some industry experts advocate placing the records and information management function directly in the law department, or they advocate assigning one attorney the responsibility and accountability for records and information management. At the very least, a strong and clearly defined liaison between attorneys and records and information management is necessary to effectively implement policies and procedures that fulfill government, legal, and fiduciary responsibilities.

Records and information management is sometimes linked organizationally to the information systems department. This alternative promotes integration of visible and electronic records and information management systems. As more records and information are created and maintained in electronic form, the link between records and information management and information services must be a strong one in order to achieve a corporate-wide records and information management program.

Most organizations traditionally place records management with administrative services, along with micrographics, reprographics, telecommunications, and the mailroom. Such administrative support systems cross departmental lines to provide necessary services throughout the business. The drawback is that often the organization's overall records and information strategies may be neglected when too much emphasis is placed on the administrative support aspect of records and information management. Records and information management requires corporate-level policies, and so records and information managers need to build strong relationships with those individuals in the organization who can mandate such policies.

Ideally, the records and information management function originates with the start-up of a company. A new organization presents the unique opportunity to start off on the right foot to avoid later facing records and information management challenges that would be a liability to the company.

Small businesses are unlikely to hire a records and information management professional. Records and information tasks in a small organization tend to be lumped with other tasks and assigned to various job positions. One person, usually the office manager, must learn to handle diverse aspects of records and information management. Typically, the office manager lacks sufficient knowledge to do the job well for every aspect of a program. Usually records activities fall to the bottom of the priorities list as other duties become more pressing.

Even if an enterprise lacks a dedicated records and information management professional, it is possible to implement critical elements of a records and information management program.

The TechTrack firm was unable to fund a new job position for a records and information manager. Instead, responsibility for the records and information management program was assigned to the director of administrative services. The office manager became the liaison between this director and the records coordinators identified in every department and branch location. The director of administrative services hired a records management consultant to establish a basic framework for policies and practices that meet the company's needs. The director also contracted with the company's outside legal counsel to develop a records retention schedule.

A task force identified vital records and developed a vital records schedule as part of the firm's business continuity plan. Another cross-departmental committee now regularly works on issues related to information media selection, planning electronic information systems, information security, and other records and information management functions. A commercial records center stores and manages inactive records and backup computer tapes.

Larger businesses need a well-coordinated records and information management staff that includes the following positions:

- records and information manager
- information systems technical experts
- records and information analysts
- litigation support specialists
- records center personnel
- micrographics technicians
- litigation support specialists
- proprietary information coordinator
- privacy officer
- vital records coordinator

In large organizations, the records and information manager and support staff develop corporate policy and standard policies and practices for all office sites.

The ForwardThink Corporation's records and information manager works with corporate executives, information services, and the law department to develop corporate policy on corporate records and information assets. The manager develops standard practices and guidelines that simplify records and information management activities throughout the company. Standard practices, such as guidelines for implementation of the records retention schedule and guidelines for records identification and indexing, reduce employee training expense and improve efficiencies and consistencies of program implementation.

To maintain control over certain records and to relieve field offices of certain recordkeeping burdens, designated records categories are the responsibility of the headquarters departments or records management staff. These records include employee files, financial records, and contracts. Branch offices temporarily rely on duplicate copies when they require information found in these records.

The records and information manager works with the information systems department to establish corporate-wide strategies and policies for electronic records and information systems. The manager also works with the director of corporate security to establish information security policies and practices. The law department maintains a current records retention schedule administered by the records management staff. Litigation support specialists work closely with attorneys and departments on discovery activities.

The records and information management function must be placed within the organizational structure to work effectively with other business functions to develop and implement records and information management strategies for the entire organization. Because business, legal, and technologies environments continually change, the records and information management program must anticipate those changes and respond accordingly.

The Records and Information Management Professional

The records and information management professional is a strategist and advisor to the business. This manager provides controls and support services essential to successful business operations. The manager is directly responsible for a number of records and information management functions:

- program development and management
- retention schedule development, maintenance, and implementation
- identification, classification, and organization of records and information
- vital records program
- program compliance reviews and audits
- development of partnerships with other experts and departments for electronic records and information systems, information security, corporate-level strategies and policies regarding privacy, Internet, and more
- delivery of consulting and support services to end users
- department, facilities, and staff management

Records managers today are well educated and well trained in the disciplines of records management, business administration, library administration, and other fields. Most records managers participate in professional organizations, continuing education, and professional certification programs. A number of professional organizations focus on information security, document preservation, facilities management, and other areas of interest to a records and information manager.

Records and information management has become ever more complex and demanding over the years. New and quickly changing information technologies, records preservation concerns, and other issues are making the job ever more complicated. The records and information manager today needs a wide range of business management skills and a high level of technical expertise in a number of areas.

Given this array of complex skills, there is a shortage today of records and information managers who are qualified to manage a comprehensive records and information program. The ideal records manager must thoroughly understand records and information management principles and all the functions of a comprehensive records and information management program as they apply to various information media. This individual must also have knowledge of information systems technologies, changing regulatory and legal issues and requirements, and evolving information needs of the organization.

General business management skills include risk management, business process design, financial management, staff management, facilities planning and management, purchasing, and more. This professional must have the ability to garner and coordinate corporate support and resources to integrate discrete records and information management program functions into a unified and comprehensive program implemented organization-wide.

Given that traditionally records and information management has not been as well supported as it should be, excellent communications, training, and marketing skills are essential to promote what are often unpopular and poorly understood business practices. The records manager must be proactively involved in business developments and activities that had previously neglected the records and information management functions. The manager should, for example, take affirmative action to participate in merger and acquisition diligence reviews and planning, the determination of records issues related to web sites and e-commerce, and the development of litigation risk management strategies.

The records and information manager must also be proactive in developing supportive, coordinating, and partnership relationships throughout the organization.

Partnerships

Because records and information management involves so many diverse objectives and activities, it may very well be appropriate to assign specific activities to different staff positions and departments. The key to program success then becomes having a single point to coordinate the pieces that constitute a whole program.

A network of interdepartmental relationships is required for close cooperation in the development of an effective information resource management policy and its supporting standards and practices. Such relationships also eliminate redundant activities conducted in several departments and conflicting policies and procedures among the departments.

Functional areas or departments necessary to participate in the development and support of a records and information management program include top management, end users, attorneys, auditors, information systems, security, facility planning, purchasing, risk management, and corporate archives.

The benefits of working with other departments may be realized in co-sponsorship of training programs, effective employee communications, development of corporate-wide policies, procedures, and standards, and more effective information resources management.

In today's business environment, it is critical that records and information management, information systems, and legal staff acquire a basic understanding of each other's areas of expertise. Sharing of knowledge leads to corporate policy and practices that add value to the organization's records and information systems.

Records and information management, information systems, and legal staff need to share their expertise in several areas:

- regulatory and legal requirements related to all information media
- accurate, reliable, and authentic records
- preservation of systems to read electronic records throughout their prescribed life
- records retention
- litigation support
- outsourcing of records and information activities

More than ever before, a close partnership between information services and records and information management is critical to development and implementation of strategies for

- application of the corporate records retention schedule to all information systems
- permanent erasure of useless electronic information
- migration of electronic records and information to newer systems, media, and technologies

- preservation of electronic records and the systems required to read them for as long as they must be retained
- organization and retrieval of important information in a timely and cost-effective manner

These two disciplines must also work together to

- apply the appropriate and necessary records and information management functions to information systems development and to criteria for acquisition of new information systems
- define minimum requirements for outsourcing electronic records and information systems, data, and functions
- establish electronic information systems backup procedures that minimize storage costs and litigation risks

Records and information management professionals need to work with managers from these and other business areas to clarify responsibilities and to determine where to most effectively focus the scarce resources of people and dollars. These relationships not only build a more successful records and information management program but also establish a broad support base for the program.

Teams of experts throughout the organization must work on corporate strategies and policy, legal, and technical solutions to records and information management challenges that cross departmental and information media boundaries. Such challenges include

- information security
- identification and protection of vital records
- content, transactions, and privacy issues related to the Internet, web sites, e-commerce, and intranets
- e-mail systems
- integration of separate information systems through a single user interface

The larger the organization, the more necessary a records and information management advisory group. Responsibilities for certain company-wide issues are distributed to individual subject matter experts and decision-makers. Committee members must

- share technical expertise and advice
- develop corporate-wide policy and standards
- approve retention and vital records schedules
- advise on media selection, information security, and other matters

As the committee chairperson, the records and information manager coordinates the committee's efforts and ensures implementation of corporate policy and committee decisions.

Outsourcing

Certain records and information management activities may be contracted out to a services provider. Commercial records centers store inactive records and provide security for electronic data and vital records. The number of firms dedicated to providing litigation support services continues to grow, especially in the arena of electronic discovery. Micrographics service bureaus manage microfilming projects, and electronic data conversion bureaus convert paper or microfilm documents to electronic document images. Archival document conservation centers restore and preserve paper documents.

A records management consultant may be hired to identify the most critical records and information management issues and propose alternatives for their resolution. A consultant can set up the basic framework of a program for ongoing administration by existing records staff.

Typical records and information management consultant contributions are

- policy and program development and documentation
- employee communications and training
- records management software applications
- planning, development, and implementation of micrographics programs, electronic records and information systems, and records media conversions
- records retention schedule development

The growing reliance on outsourcing and other contract-based support services requires careful considerations to ensure that both the systems and the records involved will be properly maintained, managed, and protected according to corporate policy and practices.

PROGRAM FUNCTIONS

There is no single right way to manage records and information—there is only a smart way that fits the unique organization. The extent and formality of program development and implementation depends on the financial and human resources committed to the effort.

Critical for any successful approach to program development is the expertise available to coordinate all program activities to provide a single information resource that meets the company's present and future needs.

A comprehensive records and information management program integrates business functions to achieve a value greater than the sum of the parts.

A comprehensive records and information management program's basic functions are media neutral and are not limited by department boundaries. Each program function interrelates with other functions to support business goals and information strategies. For example, the creation, retrieval, and retention functions support the organization's litigation and investigation activities, and the preservation function of the program contributes to protection of legal rights and corporate assets.

Briefly described next are the objectives of each records and information management program function.

Records and Information Origination

Records and information generated internally and collected or received from external sources have characteristics of accuracy, reliability, and authenticity. Records required by law or regulation are properly identified and indexed. The information storage media selected for record creation, preservation, and retrieval is appropriate to meet business needs and legal requirements.

Retrieval and Preservation

Records and information systems are organized, indexed, and integrated for timely, cost-efficient retrieval. Records and information storage media and any required systems are protected and preserved for their full retention requirements. Records and information storage facilities and environment are maintained and secured to protect and preserve records and information.

Sensitive and valuable records and information are protected from unauthorized disclosure and loss. Vital records schedules identify records essential to continuation of the business in the event of a disaster and they note how the records are protected.

The various information media systems are integrated through information technologies into a uniform information resource that meets users' requirements for access, processing, and retrieval.

Retention and Destruction

Records and information, regardless of their media, are retained in compliance with regulations and business policy and practices as expressed through the records retention program. Records required for litigation, investigation, or audit are organized and protected. Nonessential records and information are disposed of in a timely manner.

PROGRAM MANAGEMENT

A records and information management program adds value to an organization. When decision-makers are unaware of the benefits of a program, they treat records management as an administrative expense and abdicate responsibility for records and information management to departmental levels where the responsibility tends to be overshadowed by other responsibilities.

Senior management commitment is necessary to provide the authority and to allocate the resources necessary to develop and enforce policy. Organization-wide standards, guidelines, and policies exist to implement, maintain, and continually improve the records and information management program.

To develop a comprehensive records and information management program requires time. Program flexibility is especially important to support constantly changing business environments, legal developments, and technological advances.

Employee Training and Communications

The benefits of a records and information management program must be continually communicated to all employees, from the top down.

Every permanent and temporary employee needs a certain degree of records and information management training because all employees are affected by or are responsible for compliance with records management policies and practices. Training and communications should begin with the first day of employment and continue throughout the term of employment.

An overview of the benefits of an organization-wide records and information management program must be presented to every employee. Employees must understand how the program helps the organization comply with the law, how it protects the business, and how it improves productivity.

Employees must also understand how corporate policy and standard practices affect them, and they must know what their individual responsibilities are regarding e-mail, records retention, and management of the paper and electronic records in their personal work areas.

Guidelines for specific aspects of records and information management, such as identifying records for destruction, are especially useful to help employees make the right decisions with the least effort. (Appendix IV, "Records and Information Management Best Practices," presents suggested guidelines for individual employee use.)

Employee training and communications activities may be developed to target specific records user groups, management levels, and departments. Periodic audits of employee records, management skills, and knowledge will identify areas for improvement and innovation in training activities.

Employee training and communications may be as simple as group meetings or print and e-mail communications, or as elaborate as multimedia presentations and teleconferencing. Increasingly more companies use their corporate intranets for employee access to records and information management policies and practices.

Program Documentation

Records and information management program documentation is useful in program management, training, and communications activities. Program documentation is also necessary to show compliance with regulatory requirements and corporate policy. Documentation of the selection, processing, and management of various information media—specifically microform and electronic—may be a requirement. Program documentation may also be needed in litigation to satisfy any concerns about the trustworthiness of records and to respond to any charges of selective destruction.

Program documentation most often created and maintained includes

- policies and practices
- program changes
- retention and destruction
- information security and privacy
- information systems and technologies
- microphotography

Records and information management program documentation also includes program evaluations and audits.

Program Evaluation for Compliance and Awareness

Program evaluations are conducted to ensure program compliance and to develop appropriate responses to the organization's changing needs.

Records and information management staff conduct their own evaluations for purposes of program development, management, and training activities. Program elements and practices are modified as necessary based on established criteria for program success and on changing opportunities to improve the program and training efforts.

Continuing efforts to be responsive to changing user needs will involve feedback from the records users. Opportunities for such feedback come in the form of on-site visits, customer satisfaction surveys, personal interviews, and program assessments.

An individual outside the records and information management department may annually conduct more formal audits or compliance reviews. Top management commitment to the records and information management program is best demonstrated when enforcement of program compliance is a driving force behind an audit.

Suggested areas for program evaluation include

- conformity with standard practices for indexing, records organization, and so on
- currency of information systems indexes
- compliance with records disposition procedures
- ability to restore vital records in a timely manner
- adequacy of information security measures
- extent of program implementation across all department and information media lines
- records and information user satisfaction

Program evaluation reports and audits are used to submit status reports to top management and to solicit or justify management action. They also become part of the records program documentation.

14

The Challenges Ahead

Information technologies permit us to compress time, improve productivity, and increase profitability. Technologies also affect the way we create, process, communicate, and store records and information. Information-sharing and communications capabilities continue to change the way we do business as they tear down barriers and allow a business to move closer to its customers, suppliers, and competitors.

But our information systems are out of control. We sometimes spend more time chasing information than using it to manage our business well. We must learn how to organize and control vast masses of information as we simultaneously create the mechanisms to gather more information.

Recorded information—whether electronic, microfilm, or paper—is a fact of life. Despite the many resources spent on information technologies, more than 80 percent of business information today remains in sight-readable form—that is, on paper and microform.

Thus one of the greatest challenges facing most businesses today is a game of catch-up regarding their records and information. The evolution from paper-based information systems to multimedia approaches has been a complex process seldom incorporating a strategic plan for records and information management.

LEGAL AND PUBLIC POLICY ISSUES

The law on electronic technologies and the Internet remains unsettled and lags behind business uses of technologies. Related legal and social issues are complex and are changing almost as fast as the technologies.

Applying state, federal, and international laws to an Internet that ignores political and geographic boundaries is problematic. There are conflicting laws and international treaties, as well as uncertainties about jurisdictions. Consider the following facts:

- Import and export policies vary from one country to another.
- A system of taxing Internet sales is yet to be developed.
- No universal standards exist for digital signatures and for the authentication of a web site customer's identity.
- The question remains unanswered as to whether transmission of attorney-client privileged communications through the Internet or an e-mail system constitutes a waiver of the privilege.

There are legal disputes over new uses of intellectual properties through new technologies. These new uses were not addressed in the original contracts and licenses because the technologies for the new uses did not exist then.

The Internet and computer networks present opportunities for criminal activities. Computer viruses destroy data and overload servers. Hackers steal customer private information and company trade secrets. They hijack computers for use in attacks on other computers and networks. Enforcement of the law is not always an easy task when it comes to computer sabotage and other computer-related crimes.

More government intervention is a possibility in a number of areas. Government securities regulators may one day require companies to disclose their computer security and privacy policies as part of their securities filings. The federal government's concerns about Internet security intensified after the terrorist attack on America in 2001, so the pressure is on the computer and Internet industries to improve security.

Privacy

As states aggressively tackle privacy issues, their resulting patchwork of legislation may prove ineffective on the global Internet. Other nations are more aggressive than the United States about protecting the privacy of individuals. Every business must, as a result, understand the laws governing privacy in every jurisdiction in which private information is collected.

U.S. businesses are hiring data protection officers to implement and enforce regulations and policies on stored data and the data flowing in and out of the organization. Unauthorized use of credit card numbers, medical data, and other private information is a significant issue with consumers. Even if a business does not break the law, a public relations disaster could result when complaints of harm caused by information disclosures make the news.

Businesses buy and sell private data for profit. Questions of who really owns the data must be answered. There may also be contractual obligations regarding confidentiality of information, or there may be a reasonable expectation of privacy.

Litigation

One of the most immediate challenges to business is the litigation risk related to electronic records and e-mail systems. Attorneys are becoming more sophisticated in using opponents' electronic records against them. Law schools are developing curricula on electronic discovery, and support organizations for potential plaintiffs are conducting electronic discovery workshops. Litigants who specialize in electronic discovery are recruiting Y2K technicians to be expert witnesses against their former employers because the technicians have valuable knowledge of the information systems.

Businesses are spending more time and money in court or on settlement agreements than they are in preventing future electronic discovery nightmares. Businesses must conduct an electronic discovery risk assessment and take appropriate actions to reduce those risks.

One of the two greatest litigation risks is the large volume of electronic records and information that must be searched for relevant information. Electronic records and information must be adequately identified and organized to enable a thorough search for relevant information and to efficiently retrieve the information.

The other greatest litigation risk is e-mail messages. From Oliver North to Bill Gates, high-profile court rulings demonstrate the potential danger of e-mail systems. How a business manages its e-mail system should be a top priority for any organization that experiences litigation and government investigation.

INFORMATION TECHNOLOGIES

Technological changes are coming too fast for business to know how to use them—or to determine if it should use them at all. The demand that new technologies be installed yesterday leaves little time to properly plan information system design. In the race to adopt new technologies, we are not always careful to use the technologies to automate a more efficient approach to doing business. If internal processes are not improved before tackling the installation of a new technology, an organization is simply automating inefficiencies in an expensive way.

It is easy to create, store, and distribute electronic information for immediate use. There are, however, no standards by which to save electronic data so their authenticity and preservation are guaranteed, thus avoiding the necessity for intervention procedures at a later date.

Top management must insist that decisions about information technologies be rational, appropriate, and cost-effective. Decisions must be made with proper regard for records and information management fundamentals. A risk assessment is needed regarding recordkeeping requirements and electronic records and information.

Toward an Integrated Information System

Business operations, government requirements, and litigation necessitate a focus on record content. Yet our information resources tend to be managed as records and information systems that are independent of each other. Every records and information system must work in concert with other systems to support the organization's information needs and to protect the enterprise.

We must have efficient systems that allow us to work both in the world of visible records and the world of electronic records. Employees need a single point of access from their desktop computers to electronic documents available on different information systems, such as e-mail, employee benefits, and customer services. This unified system should also access a catalog of paper, film, and other records that can be retrieved and delivered upon request.

Compatible and connected systems are necessary for fluidity of information throughout an organization. An enterprise-wide system must be designed so that it is easy to use, easy to manage, and easy to change.

There are tremendous opportunities when paper, microfilm, and computer systems are coordinated for cost-effective information management solutions. Records and information management standards applied within and across the broad spectrum of information systems enhance the effectiveness of those systems, both separately and collectively.

The ForwardThink Corporation has employee records and information in a number of different information systems. Employee benefits, training, and other records are in paper, microfilm, and electronic records storage media. A records management software application knows what employee information exists and where it is located. This application is linked to every electronic information system to communicate when an employee's records should be filmed, sent to storage, or destroyed. Reports are produced with these same instructions for paper and microfilm records. The system also produces reports of employee records that may be relevant to pending litigation.

When an employee leaves the company, the system sends instructions to close the employee's personnel file, worker compensation and medical files, benefits files, training records, employment agreements, and other employee information that is now inactive. The system also sends instructions to cancel the employee's access to e-mail and other information systems and to review and properly dispose of records and information in the employee's work area and on the employee's desktop computer.

Building Partnerships

Increasingly more business records are created, captured, and stored in electronic information systems. The need for records and information management applications is critical. At a minimum, electronic records must be identified and organized for timely retrieval. Information security and records retention policies must be applied to all identified electronic records.

Teams of business experts must work toward an enterprise-wide records and information system. They must develop policy, legal, and technical solutions to records and information challenges related to e-mail, the Internet, and e-commerce. The appropriate mix of experts must collaborate on decisions about information media selection, storage, security, retention, and the use of outside records and information services providers.

In place of unspoken rivalries between information services, records management, and other business functions, there should be a partnership working together to focus on moving toward a comprehensive, company-wide records and information system. Records management professionals know the records and information management fundamentals that must be applied to electronic records. Information services professionals have the technical expertise to design systems with the necessary records and information management functions.

Technological Obsolescence

The mix of hardware, software, and electronic data storage media must be sufficient to preserve the ability to retrieve the information for as long as deemed necessary by the records retention program. Unfortunately, there are significant challenges to overcome in order to preserve electronic information for more than a few years.

When the Census Bureau tackled an electronic media refreshing and data migration program, it faced a challenge regarding 1960 federal census data. Only two computers in the world were capable of reading the magnetic tapes—one in Japan and one in the Smithsonian.

In 1994, Microsoft chairman Bill Gates paid more than $30 million for a notebook of Leonardo da Vinci sketches. The document was created in the sixteenth century. One wonders what software applications and electronic documents will be at auction 100 years from now.

Corporate History

Whether one year old or one hundred years old, every business has records of historical value. Larger and older businesses tend to have formally organized archives for their historical records. A business still in its youth should want to review today's business records that could be tomorrow's valued corporate history.

Years ago, when an organization undertook writing its history, it called upon its employees as important resources for firsthand accounts of organizational changes and events. When corporations began to merge, divest, downsize, and right size in the 1980s, corporate knowledge walked out the door with the employees. The most reliable witnesses to corporate history thus remain in the organization's records.

Preservation of archival records requires professional expertise and appropriate facilities, equipment, and supplies. Archivists have the expertise to determine which records and memorabilia have enduring historical value. In the absence of a corporate archivist, the records manager is the most likely individual to assume responsibilities for corporate history.

Information technologies present a new challenge to preserving corporate history because of technological obsolescence. Businesses must recognize that information technologies are now recording corporate history. Archivists and records management professionals must be involved in the planning and preparations needed to preserve that corporate history, from the company's product packing designs to the contents of its first web site.

A NEW LOOK FOR RECORDS AND INFORMATION MANAGEMENT

Records and information management means different things to different people. Traditional perceptions do not accurately describe the evolving roles of records and information management in an organization's effectiveness and profitability.

Business records and information represent business assets, or they are assets in their own right. They are a strategic corporate resource that should be managed and controlled much like other more visible and

better-understood resources—such as land, labor, and capital property—
are managed.

Recordkeeping requirements do not go away when information is digitized. Ongoing issues related to all records storage media include

- compliance with laws and regulations
- information security
- authenticity and reliability of records
- permanence and durability
- retention and destruction
- information retrieval and storage
- support and services for end users
- costs and efficiencies

Misunderstanding what a comprehensive records and information
management program can do for a business contributes to a gap between
the program's capabilities and its actual applications. Business in general
is not doing as good a job of managing all its records and information
systems as it could or should. Some companies have policies but no
compliance. Others have no policies. Most companies successfully implement individual components of a records and information management program through policy enforcement. Few companies achieve the
advantages of improved organizational efficiencies and effectiveness by
implementing a comprehensive program.

The records and information management business function faces a
difficult task of garnering adequate support amid stiff competition for a
company's limited resources. It is ironic that such a large portion of those
scarce resources is allocated to computer systems when the largest pro-
portion of records continues to exist in paper and microfilm storage media.

Top management, middle management, and end users must understand that records and information management is an operating necessity. Until artificial intelligence capabilities can be built into electronic
information and communications systems, organizations must rely heavily on end users to ensure the organization's compliance with its own
policies. At the very least, end users need to learn to use their systems
to transfer their electronic documents to an electronic records warehouse
and to apply records retention policies to all records and information in
their control.

End users must recognize that recordkeeping challenges and solutions
affect the entire organization. The records and information management
program must cross department lines to be effective. The time is long

overdue for this backroom operation to move into a more visible position in the organization.

Toward a New Chief Information Officer

Proper management of multimedia information systems continues to be more sophisticated and complicated than ever before.

The records and information manager must be involved in corporate planning so all information systems support and add value to the organization. This professional must develop and maintain close working relationships with every department. Empire building is out, and partnerships for developing an effective records and information management program are in.

As businesses continue to adopt new information technologies, there is a need for a new version of the chief information officer (CIO) in the organizational hierarchy. The CIO of the 1990s was a senior executive responsible for establishing corporate information policy, standards, and management control over information resources. Since job incumbents tended to limit their focus to information technologies, perhaps a more appropriate job title would have been chief technology officer.

What is needed is a CIO who does what the job title implies—namely, he or she leads the organization into a future of cost-effective information systems that support and protect the organization. These information systems must not be limited to electronic information systems. The individual with ultimate responsibility for information systems must also be responsible for paper, microfilm, and other records and information resources in the organization.

The new CIO needs to know all the organization's resources and must have the management skills to lead and oversee the organization's strategic plans for managing business records and information. The position should direct records management, information services, archives, and other business functions as appropriate and necessary.

When the CIO position is not appropriate in the smaller organization, the records and information management professional should assume the responsibilities of such a position.

REALIZING CHANGE

From adding new product lines to installing new technologies, business is always in a state of change. A records and information management program provides new capabilities for change. As with a new technology, the program may also necessitate changes in the way a company does business. These changes will cost in terms of financial, human, and other resources.

Corporate change normally originates with commitment from the top. That commitment must be visible enough to get the attention of line managers and end users throughout the entire organization. Continued top management support is necessary for any corporate program to remain viable and responsive to business and user changing needs.

The level of commitment to change is a determining factor for the success of records and information management. Commitment to change depends on specific factors:

• degree of knowledge and understanding of the change
• level of dissatisfaction with the status quo
• desirability of the proposed end state
• practicality and costs of the change

A number of key players will be responsible for redesigning methods and systems required to implement a comprehensive records and information management program. These change agents must identify the roles of records and information in the company's mission and determine how records and information management will support and advance the organization's business strategies.

We need to cast away old habits and exercise the same self-discipline necessary to properly manage a business. It is not a question of if, but a question of when and how we regain control of our business records and information systems.

There is no better time than now to initiate a records and information management program or to dust off an existing one. Records and information systems must be designed and managed to add value to an enterprise. If they do not support and protect a business, they become a liability.

Appendix I: A Vital Records Program

INTRODUCTION

It is critical in today's competitive environment that a company be able to continue operations throughout an emergency situation, and then to be able to resume critical business functions in an orderly and timely manner after a manmade or natural disaster. Action that preserves the ability to continue business operations could prove to be a company's salvation in the event of a disaster.

The ultimate purpose of a business continuity plan is to position an organization so as to assure that operations, employees, and assets effectively survive the impact of a disastrous event. The preservation of vital records is critical to that success, and the vital records program should be a key element of a corporate-wide business continuity plan.

Although it is advisable—and sometimes a government agency requirement—to have a corporate-wide business continuity plan, not all organizations have such a plan. However, it is possible to develop a vital records program in the absence of one.

ELEMENTS OF A VITAL RECORDS PROGRAM

Most business records and information are maintained solely for their business value to a department or for legal, tax, or outside audit purposes. Every business has records that are essential to its operations and to its very existence.

In the event of a disaster, certain business records are essential to

- manage the emergency situation
- substantiate the company's legal and financial status
- continue or reconstruct the company and its operations
- fulfill obligations to shareholders, customers, employees, and others
- substantiate any legal or financial claim for or against the company

Depending upon the industry, typically only 2 to 10 percent of a company's records are vital to the organization's continued operations and must therefore be protected from loss. A well-conceived vital records program can be economical in its development, maintenance, and implementation when it includes the following elements:

- risk analysis
- prevention and protection
- preparedness
- crisis management
- salvage and recovery

Costs involved in a business continuity plan specific to records and information may include expenditures in the following areas:

- planning
- facility modifications for improved environmental and security controls
- support services, equipment, and supplies
- backup systems and record reproduction
- records and information retrieval

Even if a well-structured program does not result in price breaks on insurance, the costs of a program are a simple investment in the company's future. The costs are negligible when compared to potential or real losses in the absence of a program.

The vital records program should be in writing and should be kept current. It must be readily available to the designated disaster team during emergency conditions.

A Team Process

Top management should charter a task force or committee made up of representatives from a number of business areas to develop a vital records program and to coordinate closely with any existing business continuity plan. Information users and subject matter experts should represent many or all of the following business functions:

- accounting and finance
- auditing
- communications
- customer service
- facility management
- human resources
- information systems and services
- legal services
- marketing
- operations and production
- purchasing and inventory
- records and information management
- risk management and insurance
- security
- transportation

Each team representative offers valuable contributions to the tasks of risk analysis and planning for disaster prevention, emergency preparedness, and recovery. The records and information manager, for example, should be responsible for development and administration of the vital records program. This individual chairs the vital records program team and the vital records schedule development team; he or she also coordinates the vital records program with any corporate business continuity plan.

Program development team members complete the following tasks:

- develop criteria, strategies, guidelines, and practices for program planning and implementation activities
- conduct a risk analysis
- identify needed resources (facilities, equipment, supplies, and services)
- determine which individuals will constitute a disaster team to coordinate emergency activities
- determine which individuals will be responsible for salvage and recovery phase tasks

Risk Analysis

Risk analysis is a cost-effective, strategic approach to program development. To determine the scope of the program, the vital records program team assesses the likelihood of various natural and manmade disasters (fire, flood, natural disasters, power losses, etc.), probabilities of loss or damage to documents and data, and consequences of that damage or loss.

The team determines what is most at risk and what truly merits full protection. Time and resources necessary for program development, prevention, protection, and recovery are determined and prioritized. Insurance adjusters may be of assistance in establishing priorities by providing information on repair and recovery costs, time necessary for such repairs and recovery procedures, what documentation is required, and the extent and limits of the coverage currently in effect or available.

Risk analysis balances the costs of re-creation of records versus the costs to protect them. Risk analysis also balances the costs of recovery against the costs of re-creation of lost information or the cost of total information loss.

Prevention and Protection

The practices employed to reduce the probability as well as the consequences of identified risks constitute the prevention and protection component of a vital records program. Prevention and protection procedures are established to ensure appropriate use of records in daily operations and to ensure that records will be readily available during an emergency situation, immediately after the crisis for the recovery phase, and for resumption of normal business operations.

The final determination of prevention and protection methods is based on an analysis of the risks and costs. The costs of prevention and protection must be weighed against the costs of recovery, re-creation, and loss of records and information.

Team recommendations to prevent or reduce damage or loss are prioritized for immediate implementation or later implementation, as funds become available.

A combination of strategies may be used to protect and preserve vital records in various media, as described later in this appendix. The strategies adopted for specific vital records are documented in the Vital Records Schedule, discussed later in this appendix.

Preparedness

Preparedness measures provide for a quick, rational response to emergency conditions. They can also prevent the escalation of damages. The Vital Records Schedule, a document critical to the preparedness aspect of the vital records program, identifies the records to be protected from loss and notes what protection methods are in place.

It is important to plan backup systems for electronic and microform records. The backup systems include the equipment, software, data, hardware, and hot site facilities required to retrieve and process recorded information. Microfilm and electronic records are useless when an emergency destroys the computer facility, computer equipment, and microfilm readers and printers.

The preparedness element of the program also details disaster condition operating and recovery procedures, outlines salvage methods, and lists resources that may be necessary during and after the emergency. Responsibilities of disaster team individuals and their authority are clearly spelled out and available on a moment's notice, along with emergency phone numbers, floor plans, and recovery operations guidelines for each facility.

The list of resources for emergency situations and for salvage and recovery activities must be kept current. Many companies secure agreements with these companies in anticipation of any need. Available resources may include

- owned or leased facilities that would be available for emergency and recovery operations and storage
- owned or leased facilities and equipment for computer operations
- salvage and recovery services, such as computer data disaster centers, film reprocessing centers, vacuum- or freeze-drying facilities, refrigerated trucks and facilities, and transportation companies
- sources for salvage and recovery equipment and supplies (plastic sheeting and trash bags, dehumidifiers, fans, portable pumps and generators, heavy-duty extension cords, plastic crates, forklifts, etc.)
- sources for replacement of damaged or lost equipment and supplies
- technical experts (contractors, exterminators, and data-processing technicians)
- insurance agents

Scheduled and unscheduled audits of the vital records program determine the plan's feasibility and the level of preparedness necessary for effective operations under extraordinary conditions. An audit can also identify any need to modify controls and protection methods to keep pace with changing business needs and changing information systems and technologies.

A common vital records program audit test tells the vital records program team what information needs the company would have after a disaster. The team must demonstrate how the company would re-create or retrieve critical information after an emergency in order to

- continue paying employees and making proper payroll deductions
- notify suppliers of temporary shipping instructions

• prepare an insurance claim for all or part of a facility and its contents
• resume production or services in a specified department

In addition, an audit may test the transfer of records into and out of vital record protection.

Crisis Management

Emergency agencies and personnel to be called immediately when a disaster occurs should be identified in the vital records plan. While the fire department or other emergency services are busy with the crisis situation, the designated emergency team can begin the tasks of damage and loss assessment in preparation for the salvage and recovery phase.

Salvage and Recovery

After the air clears and the water subsides, the disaster team inventories damaged records and refers to the written plan and procedures for follow-up action. Salvage methods and priorities for salvage are determined for an action plan.

Undamaged records may need to be temporarily removed to prevent damage from any facility clean-up activities. Damaged records must be moved to a work area for drying or repair procedures, or they must be prepared for pick up by a disaster recovery service supplier.

Salvage and recovery procedures may differ for preparation and handling of various record and information media—paper, photographs, microforms, magnetic or electronic tapes and disks, and other record forms.

THE VITAL RECORDS SCHEDULE

A vital records schedule is a tool to identify vital records and to document appropriate protection methods and practices. Vital records and information may be in the form of paper, microform, electronic or magnetic data, photographs, or other media.

Records and Information Vital to a Business

The type of industry, regulatory requirements, methods of operation, the nature of products and services, and the marketplace determine which records are vital to a business.

Discriminating selection of vital records limits protection to only those records deemed essential to planned purposes. The determination that a record is vital is based on a number of factors:

- extent to which its loss would delay restoration of operations
- relative difficulty or expense involved in replacement or reconstruction of lost records or information
- extent to which the unavailability of the records would delay recovery of monies for replacement of facilities and equipment
- extent to which destruction of the records and information would jeopardize the general public interest

If legally acceptable copies of any of these records can be obtained from government, commercial, or private sources for a reasonable cost and within a reasonable time, the records need not be considered vital.

In addition to records required for emergency and recovery tasks, records to be protected are those that provide the capability to reconstruct company operations within a reasonable time and at an equitable cost.

Examples of vital records are those that document critical business status, conditions, and transactions, such as the following:

Corporate and Legal: Current list of officers; delegation of authority and succession management; articles of incorporation, bylaws and amendments; corporate seal; meeting minutes of board of directors, shareholders, pension benefits; pending applications, filings and reports to the SEC and other government agencies; current litigation and claims files.

Shareholder Rights: Dividend payment register; current executed shareholder proxies; records of unissued securities; stock certificate register; stock purchase plan; shareholder ledger; shareholder lists; shareholder transfer records.

Financial: Accounts receivable register; current customer billings; bank registers, lists of outstanding checks, and cash books; securities inventories; current capital assets detail and depreciation information; loan records; income tax records for unsettled period(s); financial registers, statements and ledgers; insurance policies and certificates of insurance; mortgages, promissory notes, and commercial paper.

Evidence of Ownership: Deeds; titles; property inventories and values; mineral rights; patent, trademark and service mark documentation.

Employees: Benefit and pension plans and benefits payment summary records; master employee records; recent payroll registers; medical files.

Clients/Customers: Customer agreements; customer lists; critical customer data.

Business Administration: Emergency plans (business continuity, vital records, etc.); records supporting crisis management and salvage and recovery; insurance claim support (claims forms, record of premium payments, proof of ownership, etc.); executive orders and directives of corporate policy; facility drawings and specifications; critical business forms.

Legal Agreements: Major contracts and agreements; real estate leases; easements and right-of-way agreements.

Operations: Operating procedures and practices; manufacturing processes; engineering specifications; research and development projects.

Vital Records Schedule Content

After identification of vital records, the team determines the length of time each should be protected as vital. A record's business function and the frequency of any updates help determine if or how frequently a record is transferred into and out of vital protection.

Some records, such as charters of incorporation, by-laws, and minutes from board of directors meetings, are retained for the life of the corporation and remain vital for that entire time period. Records to be protected for an extended period are those representing legal and financial obligations to employees, shareholders, creditors, and others.

Many vital records are replaced on a scheduled basis as the information is routinely updated. When a list of current shareholders or customers is updated, for example, the superseded list is no longer considered vital. Accounts receivable records are constantly changing, so only the most current records are vital. Vital record rotation frequencies may be annual, quarterly, monthly, weekly, or daily.

Some records need to be retained for periods longer than their vital record status, especially if they are accounting, operations, or other records necessary to meet business and financial needs and retention requirements stated in the corporate records retention schedule.

The Vital Records Schedule should include the following information about each listed vital record:

• media and location of the original record
• reason for protection as a vital record
• proposed protection method
• location(s) of security copies
• priority code for salvage to reduce recovery delays
• appropriate disposition of the record when the record is superseded by an updated version or when the vital retention period expires
• record's normal length of retention
• destruction method to use when the overall retention period expires

The Vital Records Schedule must remain current and complete. An annual review is necessary to make adjustments relative to changes in the business situation and information technologies.

PROTECTION METHODS

Threats to the security of records and information are thoroughly discussed in Chapter 3, "Threats to Sensitive and Valuable Records and

Information." Methods to protect vital records include many of those discussed in Appendix II, "Records and Information Security Program," but additional measures are necessary to prepare for and recover from a disastrous event.

The value of a record as it relates to critical business functions determines the degree to which the record should be protected. Records that can easily be reconstructed from other records designated as vital or from other sources need not be protected as vital. Protection methods may be as simple and inexpensive as returning records to their storage cabinets to reduce or prevent possible water damage. Alternatively, they may be as expensive as creating a microfilm security copy of documents for storage in an off-site vault that has special environmental and security controls.

Record Media

The physical qualities of an information carrier determine its susceptibility to damage or loss caused by adverse environmental conditions, use, and aging. Risks and costs are lowest when protective measures begin at the time the record is created and the record's medium is chosen.

The protection and preservation of paper and microform records will remain significant issues for decades to come for mature corporations and for companies aspiring to grow old. Until electronic signatures are accepted everywhere, certain vital records, such as executed contracts, deeds, and titles, must be maintained in their original paper form or microfilm to retain their value.

Paper and microform are recommended for vital records that need to be retained for more than one year and that must be immediately accessible in an emergency. Electronic information systems should not normally be relied on for long-term storage and security because they are still not proven reliable for long-term information preservation.

If an electronic form is selected for a vital record, it is critical to schedule data and program backups and to identify and make readily available the information system hardware and software required to recover the electronic information.

Security Copying and Dispersal

A common method of protecting a vital record is to physically segregate duplicate copies of the record. In large corporations this activity is often routine. Small businesses are much more vulnerable when they store all records in a single facility.

A vital record may be duplicated in the same or a different information storage medium and sent to another location. Protection is considered adequate when duplicates are dispersed to at least three well-separated facilities. Any equipment necessary to retrieve, read, and reproduce non-paper information must be readily available in the event of a disaster.

Duplicate copy dispersal is the least-expensive preservation method. It is based on the assumption that the same disaster is not likely to strike all locations at the same time. In the built-in (existing) dispersal method, duplicate records are automatically distributed to other departments and locations through normal business activities. These records are retained unaltered at those locations until they are superseded by an updated copy or until their retention period ends and they are destroyed.

A planned dispersal is less risky than a built-in dispersal. In planned dispersal, at the time of record creation a duplicate is made expressly for security purposes. This duplicate is stored at another location for normal use and reference, and the original is sent to a vital records center. If it is not necessary to retain an original record copy, a microform copy for the vital records center will reduce storage space requirements and expense. One copy of the data storage medium should be stored off site, and another copy should be stored in fire- and water-resistant containers and equipment on site.

Caution should be used when relying on duplicate records kept on file by a government agency or by another external organization. The agency or external organization may be hit by the same disaster, or timely retrieval of a duplicate from another source may be unlikely. If a business depends on a creditor to maintain a duplicate record of its liabilities, the business must recognize that the creditor's interests are different from its own. When relying on an accounting or law firm for backup duplicate copies, the company should ensure that the firm retains the records for as long as the company deems necessary.

On-Site Protection

Fire- and water-resistant space, storage equipment, and record containers may accomplish on-site records protection. Records maintained inside closed cabinets that are six inches up from the floor will have less water damage than those stored outside the cabinet or on the floor. To retard the spread of fire, mobile file units should be closed when not in use. Further, to minimize damage from flame and water, use insulated file equipment and polyethylene or metal containers for tapes and electronic media.

Fire-resistant file cabinets are useful for records that would require substantial expenditures of time or money for their reconstruction, but such cabinets are not adequate for full protection of vital records. Vaults on site are best for short-term storage of vital records that are updated or changed frequently, and the copies should regularly be sent off site for even better protection of the information. Vaults are a capital expense and should be treated as such: store only vital records in them—not office supplies—and keep the doors closed.

Like paper records, electronic records are also vulnerable to environmental and human threats. Security backup data and systems must be in place, and unauthorized access to computers must be prevented.

Vital Records Center

A vital records center is designed to meet the objectives of segregation and preservation. As a separate facility dedicated to the preservation of its contents, the vital records center normally houses original records. Duplicate records are generally stored elsewhere for use as a working copy or as backup as needed. More than one security copy of an active record may be needed in additional locations.

A vital records center may be a company's own facility, or it may be a commercial facility. In either case, it must be located away from normal operations, preferably in another city or state.

A vital records center has security and environmental conditions different from those of the standard records center. Proper environmental conditions are especially important for records with a long retention period. Controls must be in place to prevent damage from insects, rodents, ultraviolet light, pollutants, and water and power failures. The condition of records should be periodically checked and storage conditions adjusted as appropriate.

A large number of cities across the country have commercial facilities that provide vital records security and storage, and more and more vendors are specializing in computer data services. For all but the largest businesses, it is most economical to use a commercial facility. These facilities often are in unpopulated areas, and many are located underground or in converted mines to take advantage of previous natural or manmade excavations and natural temperature and humidity controls.

Records may be most vulnerable while in transit to a center, so backup copies should be safeguarded until the records arrive safely at the center.

Usage and Disposition

Vital records must be organized and stored so as to be readily accessible in the event of an emergency. Their use should be restricted to a list of authorized users under certain conditions. A vital record copy should be recalled for use in other than an emergency situation only if all other copies are unavailable. If possible and appropriate, a copy should be made in order to avoid damage or loss in transit or during use. Special procedures to transmit or ship vital records must be established for the occasion when it is necessary to do so for normal operations, during an emergency, and for recovery operations.

In addition, the equipment necessary to retrieve microform and electronic records must be readily available.

Appendix II: Records and Information Security Program

INTRODUCTION

Sensitive and valuable records and information, as defined in Chapter 3, "Threats to Sensitive and Valuable Records and Information," need to be protected from damage, loss, and unauthorized disclosure in order to protect the business and its assets. Every business has detailed procedures to handle cash, operate vehicles, and manage other assets to prevent losses and liabilities. It only makes sense to protect its information assets in a similar manner.

To protect a company's sensitive and valuable records information and to preserve its legal rights, a business must make reasonable efforts to protect its information. In the words of one law enforcement official on the subject of computer hackers:

Cracking a password to get into a system is the same as kicking in a locked door. But when a door is left open, the law may treat the trespasser differently.

What are deemed reasonable security measures, however, depends on the degree of sensitivity and the value of the information, the degree of security risks, and the potential consequences of loss or unauthorized access.

PROTECTION FROM UNAUTHORIZED ACCESS AND LOSS

A risk management approach to program development identifies the security risks and the security efforts needed to offset those risks. A cost-benefit analysis of what security measures prevent what losses helps establish priorities for records and information security.

Because a business cannot reasonably secure all records, truly valuable and sensitive records and information must be identified and appropriately protected for as long as they remain sensitive and valuable. A records and information security program is a combination of loss prevention, preparedness, and recovery measures.

Today's demands and capabilities for easy access to information often exacerbate security efforts. Security measures should be balanced with the need for a smooth flow of information in daily duties, the relative value and sensitivity of the information, and the degree of risk involved. Common sense and good judgment are the keys to making a program manageable.

Clear and consistent policies and practices should minimize or eliminate targeted information security risks. Management commitment is demonstrated through allocation of funds and staff to security measures, a code of business conduct, a drug-free workplace, and policy enforcement. Information security practices are documented in the event that a company needs to show proof of its efforts or to file charges against violators.

Information security policy should focus on the nature of the information. Information to be protected must be located in all its various information storage media and in all its numerous locations to determine how best to protect it.

Adequate records and information security is a combination of measures that affect employees, suppliers, facilities, records and information media, electronic information and communications systems, records disposition, and procedures for information disclosure.

Security for People

Information security measures for people who have or may have access to sensitive and valuable information begin with contractual agreements. Agreements regarding ownership of work products are appropriate for certain employees and contractors. Nondisclosure, or confidentiality, agreements are necessary for employees, suppliers, and business partners.

Nondisclosure agreements bind the recipient of private, proprietary, or classified information to hold that information in confidence. These agreements usually define

- what information is being provided (the information must, in fact, be sensitive or valuable for enforceability of the agreement),
- the intended and appropriate uses of the information,

- the terms and conditions for use of information,
- the restrictions on further disclosure, and
- how to dispose of any records at the end of employment or the contract.

An executed nondisclosure agreement is important both as a deterrent and as a means to enforce any violations. The legal department should retain nondisclosure agreements or at least keep a list of the agreements, if they are stored elsewhere, for reference should a complaint later be filed or in the event of an alleged breach of agreement.

Depending on the nature of a job, a company might consider screening job applicants. Employee background checks to help assess potential security risks are occasionally as extensive as federal government security clearances for classified information.

A nondisclosure agreement is the first formal step toward educating employees on information security. From the point of hire and the orientation period through termination, employees should continuously be made aware of the value of records and information as company assets. Even the best security plan is useless if it is not understood or enforced. By raising information security consciousness, a business reduces the risks of inadvertent information disclosure. Sensitive and valuable information must be clearly and consistently marked, and employees should be trained to recognize such records.

Employee responsibilities regarding the receipt, handling, and use of the company's and others' proprietary information in the course of business-related duties should be clarified in orientation sessions, security briefings, and training sessions targeting specific user groups.

The potential for employee sabotage cannot be completely eliminated, but an organization can implement deterrents and the means to prosecute and recover damages. A confidentiality agreement and company policy may, for example, state that compliance with information security policies and practices is a condition of employment. Any loss, compromise, or suspected compromise of information should be referred to a security, auditing, data-processing, or other appropriate group or individual for investigation and follow-up.

Employee responsibilities for information security do not end when an employee leaves the company. In fact, termination may be the time of greatest risk to information security from an employee. The termination process may include steps to ensure that all records and information in the employee's possession are returned and that future access is denied. An exit interview may reaffirm the employee's continuing obligation to maintain confidentiality of protected information. It may also involve asking the employee to sign a new statement that confirms the return of all proprietary documents, work products, access cards, ID badges, keys, and other assets. Computer system passwords should be deleted or changed immediately.

When an employee leaves to work for a competitor, some businesses have their legal counsel send a letter to the competitor as notification of the employee's obligation not to disclose any confidential information that may have been acquired during employment.

Security for Facilities, Property, and Public Places

A number of security measures can be implemented for the company's facilities and property, as well as for the use of business records and information in other locations. Business travel and the growing trend in working at home add new dimensions to the protection of information developed or used away from a designated work site.

Security efforts will vary according to the degree of risk involved and the nature and value of the records and information. Several practices and security measures are suggested here for consideration:

- Clear off desks at the end of each day and lock sensitive and valuable records in desks, cabinets, safes, or rooms.
- Change locks on file cabinets containing sensitive information so they are different from the standard locks normally provided by the manufacturer.
- Discuss sensitive issues behind closed doors and refrain from using speakerphones.
- Erase boards and remove from meeting rooms documents, drawings, flip charts, and other materials.
- Avoid leaving information in reception areas, rest rooms, and other public areas.
- Lock doors to offices and meeting rooms when not in use, and secure a minimum number of keys.
- Lock telephone system closets, file rooms, and computer rooms.
- Lock exterior doors after hours—or even during business hours if appropriate—and do not prop open locked doors.
- Encourage telecommuters to protect sensitive and valuable information that is needed in their homes and require that all records and work products be returned to the office as soon as possible.
- Prevent theft of computers to minimize data loss and the inability to access and process information.
- Restrict the type of information that can be on a laptop computer or encrypt the information.
- Install satellite-tracking technology on laptops to pinpoint their location if stolen, or install software that transmits an e-mail or fax back to the company

with the phone number and address for the modem connection used by the thief.

- Register and escort visitors and vendors, and restrict casual visitors to designated areas. Question strangers who are not wearing a badge; request their name, address, and identification.

- Restrict the use of cameras and recorders inside the facility.

- In outside facilities, meeting rooms, and public places, avoid leaving unattended any records and information processors, including flip chart sheets, memo pads, handouts, and portable computers. Do your own photocopying, post monitors at meeting rooms to restrict access, and confirm that the public address system serves only the intended room(s).

- Alert employees to information security threats at conventions and trade shows, especially through seemingly innocent conversations.

- Caution employees against inquisitive reporters, especially when asked for "off-the-record" remarks. Reaffirm the importance of information security to sales people, distributors, and subcontractors who may be excited about a new product, and remind them that a press leak would be premature.

- Avoid discussing sensitive information in public places such as lobbies, elevators, restaurants, train stations, and airplanes. If discussion is necessary, consider using code names.

- Inform an advertising agency, printer, or other supplier in possession of valuable and sensitive information of what security measures to follow.

Security for the Information Media

Information security methods may vary according to the medium used, the nature of the information, usage patterns, and the length of the record's retention.

Permanence and durability factors must be considered for high-use records and for those records earmarked for long-term retention, such as financial and legal authority records or evidence of asset ownership. All media are subject to natural disasters, planned or inadvertent actions by people, and adverse environmental conditions and handling. (Chapter 8, "Integrating Media Choices," offers a full discussion of media characteristics that affect permanence and durability.)

The methods of marking sensitive and valuable records and information are based on the record's classification and the information carrier's physical characteristics. It is ideal to include protective markings as an integral part of the information carrier. Paper documents should be marked in a prominent position, and the marking should be visible when the document is folded or rolled. Microforms, audio and video tapes, and software programs may include a protective information marking as part of the film, tape, or program. If unable to mark a record directly, place the record in a clearly marked container. Common restrictive markings are "NOTICE: Not for use or disclosure outside ForwardThink Corporation except under written agreement" or "PRIVATE: This information only for ForwardThink Corporation employees with a need to know."

A cover letter may be needed to advise the user that the records and materials are not to be disclosed to others without first consulting the designated originator. Photocopy control measures may include a policy to reproduce or print records only with authorization of the owner, to remove originals and copies from copy machines, to properly dispose of rejected photocopies, and to use red or a special magenta-colored paper for the original to prevent photocopying. All notes, copies, and rough drafts of sensitive materials should be treated in the same manner as the final record until their proper disposal.

Care should be taken when transmitting sensitive and valuable records. Employees must not remove materials without prior approval when required, except in the regular course of business. Specially marked envelopes and other transmittal containers should be used. Private records should be hand delivered within the company. For outside delivery, they should be sent by registered or certified mail or by a commercial overnight service.

Security for Electronic Information and Communications Systems

Electronic information systems and communications systems should be secured to the degree appropriate to the value of their data contents and business functions. An extensive program of monitoring and security procedures is needed to protect information systems and system products.

Computer tapes and disks consolidate large amounts of key information very compactly, and reconstruction of information could be very costly or impossible. Automated and manual procedures can be implemented to prevent and correct sloppy data input, and audit trails are important for fulfillment of business and government requirements. System documentation, such as user manuals, codes, printouts, and documents, also need protection.

Computer security in organizations has not kept pace as computing power has moved from mainframe computers to desktop and laptop computers scattered throughout the office, in homes, and on the road. Standards for operation of personal computers and networks can address issues of proper use of software applications, memory, and functions.

Certain steps can be taken to prepare for recovery from a computer disaster. Some computer systems can help reconstruct events in the case of inadvertent loss by an employee or by an intruder by creating an audit of information before and after changes, also noting the source and time of changes. If appropriate, a desktop computer's hard disk should be used to hold only programs, not to store data. Backups of data and software should be stored in a remote, safe place.

The computer disaster industry continues to grow. These vendors provide backup data storage and services, and most also provide access to a hot site facility with compatible hardware in the event of damage or destruction to the company's own hardware. When physical transportation of records to a remote records center is a cumbersome, expensive, and not very secure procedure, some vendors have capabilities for electronic transmission of data to the center in such a way that meets a corporation's unique security requirements.

Electrical power problems can adversely affect equipment and thus the information stored and processed on that equipment. In the event of a major power failure, an uninterruptible power system allows computers time for an orderly shut down to enable a soft landing, instead of crash landing. A backup power system allows business to continue as usual, but without the primary power source. Power conditioning is important because the long-term effects of brownouts, power spikes, and line noise have been proven to cause more damage than a major power failure.

Use of communications systems and networks to transmit sensitive information should be avoided whenever possible. Special precautions may be needed for fax, voice, electronic, video, picture phone, and data transmissions, depending upon the sensitivity of the information.

In some situations, different systems and networks are used to separate business functions such as finance, marketing, personnel, and purchasing. System interfaces can be designed to prevent or restrict access to systems, data files, read-write functions, and other applications. An elaborate password system and the assignment of security codes to types of data files and system applications also help restrict access to authorized individuals with a need to know.

For higher levels of security, a business might consider encryption software or hardware, biometrics (the use of finger and voice prints), digital signatures, and eye patterns for system access. Wireless networks typically have a built-in encryption application. Because these encryption standards may be weak, another encryption application may have the complexity level appropriate to the value of the information transmitted.

Gateway safeguards and port protection devices can lock out intruders or limit outside access to preauthorized phone numbers by using a callback program. A virtual private network creates a secure, password-protected access to corporate networks over the Internet.

Hardware and software applications that prevent third-party intrusions, such as anti-virus software and firewalls, are critical for transmission of any electronic information. Computer viruses and other mischief done by hackers may result in the loss of system performance and electronic data.

Threats from intruders can be reduced by following routine computer security procedures and implementing a few specialized procedures:

- Install anti-virus software and a firewall to continuously monitor and filter all files transmitted or received.
- Make sure the most current software patches to prevent security breaches are tested and installed.
- Download only software and files that come from a trusted source.
- Open only those e-mail attachments that come from a known source.
- Partition or segment systems to establish write-protect areas of disks and to help prevent a spread through the system before detection.
- Allow only reputable off-the-shelf software on a system, or quarantine and test new products.
- Regularly check the size of programs to see if they have changed.
- Occasionally reload programs from a pure, original source.

When organizations must expose sensitive and valuable information to a network, they should take necessary and appropriate security measures to protect the information. Networked systems and the security measures designed to protect them need constant testing, monitoring, and surveillance.

In addition, web site contents must be reviewed for appropriate information security. The contents should be screened to eliminate trade secret and other intellectual properties on the web site. Copyright and trademark notices must be posted as appropriate.

Security for Destruction

The creators and users of sensitive or valuable records also frequently have the responsibility for their destruction. A records retention schedule is the formal authority to destroy records according to legal and business requirements. A records retention program will also specify the disposition of outdated and superseded records, drafts, notes, and poor-quality copies.

The proliferation of photocopiers and computers makes it more difficult to ensure that all copies are disposed of at the proper time. The retention schedule must be applied to records in all media: paper, film, electronic, magnetic, optical disk, audio and video cassette, photo, slide, transparency, carbon ribbon, metal offset plates, and so on.

Proper disposition at the end of a sensitive or valuable record's life usually requires obliteration of the contents through mutilation or erasure. This type of destruction is an important substitute for tossing paper and microfilm records into the trash, where they become part of the public domain and accessible to the competition, computer hackers, and others. Erasure is used most frequently for electronic records and data, and for dictation, audio, and video tapes.

A lesson to be learned from Oliver North regarding e-mail and electronic records: When they are deleted or erased, they may in fact continue to exist elsewhere, such as on another computer, on backup tapes, or on paper. A number of electronic file security software applications that really do erase all traces of a file should be used to ensure thorough destruction when appropriate. A sure way to purge data on laptops and desktops permanently is to pull out the hard drive and demolish it.

The shredder equipment and services industry continues to grow. Some companies place shredders at the point of use, or they protect records in security envelopes or locked containers until time for destruction in a central service area.

Shredder equipment comes in all sizes, models, and costs to meet different requirements for capacity, speed, media size and type, shred size, and even baling capabilities. The standard, straight-cut shredder is making way for confetti and disintegrator shredders, which continue to cut paper until it is small enough to fall through a screen. Disintegrators are now required for most Department of Defense records, including those in the possession of government contractors.

Certain shredder models handle more than just paper. Some shredders destroy ring binders, boxes, nylon printer ribbons, computer diskettes, and microfilm and video tape cartridges.

Businesses often turn to vendors for shredding and recycling services. Every commercial service should sign an agreement to protect the records until destruction, and they should be able to provide a certificate of destruction. Most destruction firms post a performance bond to protect their customer in case they fail to perform adequate destruction to prevent information from falling into the wrong hands.

Vendors that offer destruction services from a mobile shredding unit eliminate security risks during transportation of the records to a vendor's facility for destruction. Vendors that destroy or recycle at their facility must have security measures such as securing vehicles when unattended and protection of materials from winds when they are left in open areas.

When an organization prefers recycling for disposal of records and information, certain precautions may be needed. The intent of the recycling process is to destroy documents, but that may not always happen.

One company sent reports of private customer data for recycling. It was later shocked to find on recycled-paper butter cups used in restaurants the legible customer private data.

Obviously, the materials to be recycled should be protected until their content can be obliterated, or they should be shredded before being baled or otherwise sent to the recycling process.

INFORMATION RELEASES TO OTHERS

On occasion it is appropriate or necessary to release valuable or sensitive information to suppliers, customers, other businesses, the courts, the government, and other parties. A business will need to show due care when releasing information for such legitimate purposes.

Handling Requests for Information

After a company's sensitive and valuable records and information have been clearly identified and marked, new considerations come into play in the determination of when disclosure is appropriate and what protective measures need to be taken if the information is released. Clear guidelines are needed for proper information disclosure practices.

Disclosure of valuable and sensitive information is normally accompanied by appropriate restrictions to protect the best interests of the company. Just as a nondisclosure agreement is common for company insiders (employees, temporary workers, and contractors), so it is also used when information is shared with outsiders (government agencies, suppliers, manufacturers, and other parties). When sensitive information is provided orally, a written confirmation to the recipient reaffirms that the information is sensitive and governed by a signed confidentiality agreement.

Very large companies can afford to hire a company proprietary information coordinator to review all proposed information releases. If unable to appoint a single expert, a business could rely on a list of resource people available to review specific types of information releases:

- The marketing or public relations department may handle releases to government agencies and foreign countries.
- An operations manager may review proposed releases of proprietary product information.
- The legal department should handle all disclosures related to legal matters.
- A human resources manager may handle requests for current and former employee information.
- The public relations department may handle press relations, public speaking engagements, and publications.

The individual reviewing an information request should consider the nature of the material, its intended use, and the potential for further distribution. Is there a need to know, and will the information requested in fact meet the stated need?

A decision to release information may rest solely on a court or regulatory requirement to provide the information or to prohibit its disclosure. Generally, information should not be released if an equivalent is available from commercial or public sources, if it will aid someone intent on fraud, or if it will have other adverse effects on the company or others. Consideration must also be given to whether or not the information requested is the property of others and is covered by a nondisclosure agreement, privacy laws, or other protective obligations.

Licensing should be considered for information that was costly to develop or that has intrinsic value. If release of the information would involve a great deal of effort and cost, it might be appropriate to require payment above and beyond printing costs. A prime candidate for licensing or fees is technical information such as software and any related documentation. Additional considerations in the determination of software release might be the technical support required, if any, and plans for an updated version.

Employee Information

A business has an obligation to prevent improper circulation of employee information within its organization and to prevent unauthorized disclosure to outside parties. Under the federal Privacy Act, state statutes, and collective bargaining agreements, employees have a right to know what records are created and maintained about them, who has access to those records, and how the information is used. The employee's right to inspect the information and to submit corrections should be clearly communicated on a regular basis.

Corporate policy usually specifies guidelines for access to an employee's personal information. A current or former employee, as well as a job applicant, usually submits a written request to ensure proper identification of the individual for delivery of the correct information. Other access within an organization is normally restricted to those with a legitimate need to know, such as human resources personnel and the employee's supervisor. Procedures established for routine use of employee information should be documented so that a record of such disclosures may be reconstructed without the necessity for a separate, formal procedure for each disclosure.

Specific regulations or collective bargaining agreements specify the types of records open to access by an employee. These records are those normally used to determine the employee's qualifications for employment, promotion, transfer, termination, compensation, and disciplinary action. Some states allow exclusion from disclosure to an employee certain documents such as letters of reference, medical records, or records of any criminal investigation.

Authorization to release information to an outside party is generally required from current or former employees and from job applicants. Employee information may also be disclosed in the following circumstances:

- in response to requests to verify directory information, such as the fact of employment, dates of employment, job title, and job site location
- to a proper law enforcement authority when the company believes an employee is engaged in illegal activities
- pursuant to a federal, state, or local compulsory reporting statute or regulation
- in response to an administrative summons or judicial order, including search warrant or subpoena
- to a collective bargaining unit pursuant to the contract
- to a company's agent or contractor when the information is necessary to perform its contracted function
- to a physician for the purpose of informing an employee of a medical problem

International and U.S. federal and state privacy requirements must be applied to proper security of employee information.

Customer Information

Customer information is generally sensitive or valuable information that must be protected from unauthorized access and disclosure. Sometimes the information is the customer's own trade secrets. Sometimes the information is private data subject to U.S. federal and state, as well as international, privacy regulations.

A growing concern about private data is fueled by individual customers and privacy and consumer advocates. Increasingly more businesses are selling or sharing customer information as an asset. Certain industries have regulatory restrictions governing how they manage customer information. If the e-commerce industry does not self-regulate regarding protection of private data of others, the FTC may step in to do that.

The greatest risk today regarding customer information is data gathered through the Internet. Breaches of network security result in theft of customer data that leads to criminal actions. A business has a duty to its customers and the general public to prevent crime.

To begin earning the trust of customers and the public, a web site owner should develop an Internet privacy policy and post it on the web site or otherwise make it available to its customers. The policy should state what information is collected, how it is protected and used, and under what circumstances it is shared with a third party. The organization must adhere to its privacy policy or risk breach of contract, invasion of privacy, or other charges.

Toysmart.com Inc. filed for bankruptcy protection and announced plans to sell its customer list of 200,000 as part of the liquidation proceedings. The problem now faced by the company is that the privacy policy posted on its web site promised never to turn over private customer information to third parties.

Suppliers, Outsourcing, and Business Partners

A business typically discloses sensitive or valuable information to another business in a proposal, a request for proposal, or a joint project and when contracting with another party for a product or service. Such information sharing occurs when it is to the mutual benefit of both parties.

When developing a proposal or a request for proposal, consideration should be given to the extent to which it may become necessary to furnish sensitive and valuable information to the other party in order to complete the project. Nondisclosure agreements and other assurances may be needed to ensure that the company retains certain rights to any work products as a result of the contract.

Common today among vendors of hardware, software, and communications are requests for information from other manufacturers or suppliers to assess interface capabilities or feasibility of their own developments. Many of these requests are driven by competitive intentions, but some are not. Occasionally, industry regulations obligate a company to furnish certain information. For example, telecommunications companies must furnish information about voice and data transmission services under certain circumstances. However, a company may apply protective agreements or may take steps to avoid disclosure of information that will aid the competition or make it more difficult for the company to compete. Information requests from potential competitors should be handled with caution, protecting valuable information while remaining in compliance with applicable laws and regulations.

Another growing trend is the outsourcing of business functions. When outsourcing any business processes, it is inevitable that an organization's records are in the hands of the supplier.

When certain business functions are outsourced, the related records created, received, and maintained by the supplier are a product of the services performed by the supplier. Examples of these outsourced business activities include

- payroll processing
- worker compensation claims processing
- medical services
- environmental assessments
- Internet service providers

Other outsourcing relationships purposefully place an organization's records and information in the hands of others. Among these outsourcing groups are

- data conversion service bureaus,
- electronic data storage vendors,
- records centers, and
- application service providers.

In all outsourcing relationships, the contracting organization entrusts another business with its corporate information assets. An organization needs to secure assurances of information security through the service agreement and then should audit for contract compliance. If the records and information are sensitive or valuable, the service provider must employ the same information security measures as those used by the information owner. (Chapter 2, "Preservation of Legal Rights and Business Assets," discusses which recordkeeping issues related to outsourcing should be addressed in the service contracts.)

In the Public Domain

There are a number of situations in which business information is disclosed in such a way that it becomes part of the public domain. A business needs to be aware of what information is provided to such sources —voluntarily or as a legal obligation—and must take the precautions necessary to prevent disclosure of inappropriate information wherever possible. A proprietary information coordinator or other appropriate management personnel should review plans for trade shows, research papers, speeches, books, and other activities proposed by technical people and others. Business and financial news media reporters should be referred to public relations staff.

Government investigations and legal proceedings also put sensitive and valuable information at risk. Congressional hearings on a product, service, or practice are subject to the Freedom of Information Act. The discovery process of legal proceedings can place records directly into the hands of a competitor, and court records are generally a matter of public record. A company may appeal to the court for special consideration in the handling of proprietary information and the sealing of court proceedings and records, but a movement is on today to make that more difficult.

Every business must file records with federal, state, and local governments. A large number of businesses must submit information to state and federal government agencies, such as OSHA and the EPA. Government contractors also have information that is subject to public disclosure requirements, and regulated businesses must file documents with regulatory commissions. Even the attempt to protect one's property through patent and copyright registrations may result in government records that are open to the public.

A business needs to tailor its government filings to minimize release of sensitive information. The Freedom of Information Act, a law requiring public disclosure of federal agencies' records and information, allows certain exceptions for government-classified, trade secret, or private information. Protective agreements should be used when valuable information is provided.

A business may have to defend its desire for confidentiality when one party moves to have the information declared nonproprietary in order to copy it or release it to others. If the business fails to justify the confidentiality of the information, a document will probably need to remain nonproprietary in all other business and legal situations.

POLICY AND PROGRAM DOCUMENTATION

The records and information security policy may be a separate statement, or it may be integrated into other corporate policies such as an information assets and communications systems policy. The policy statement must be supported by guidelines and standard practices for compliance with the policy.

Portions of a model information assets and communications systems policy statement follow:

It is the policy of ForwardThink Corporation to fully protect its information assets. The company will share its knowledge and information with others only when this can be done for the mutual benefit of the sharing parties and without prejudice to the company's interests.

Third parties will be given access to the company's information and communications systems only if they agree to abide by all applicable rules. Exceptions may include law enforcement officials, subpoenas, and government regulators.

ForwardThink Corporation also recognizes the obligations to protect sensitive and valuable information of others that is in our possession for business use, and to comply with the provisions set forth in all licensing agreements entered into by employees on behalf of the company.

Guidelines for employee responsibilities that may or may not be part of the policy statement include the following strictures:

- All employees must treat the company's records and information assets consistent with company policy and guidelines, and protect them from misuse, theft, fraud, loss, and from unauthorized use, disclosure, or disposal.
- Communications of valuable or sensitive information with competitors must be restricted during and after employment.
- Upon retirement or separation from the company, each employee must relinquish all corporate records and information in the employee's possession and may not retain any duplicate copies.

An organization must determine procedures to be followed in the event of security breaches and any sanctions for violation of security procedures. The policy should include a statement of consequences for policy violations. For example,

Failure to comply with corporate policy on records and information security may result in disciplinary action up to and including dismissal.

When a violation occurs, an incident response team may determine what steps are necessary to minimize the damages and to prevent further violations of a similar nature. This team—including an investigator, legal advisor, computer specialist, auditor, and public relations professional—should be familiar with the company's information security policy and basic investigative techniques in order to be able to collect and properly handle evidence that will be necessary to file any charges or claims against the offending party. The team determines the steps necessary to minimize damages and to prevent similar future violations.

Information security policies and practices should be monitored and documented regularly.

Program Documentation

Records and information security program documentation helps preserve rights to protection under the law and the right to prosecute violators by showing that

- the information was in fact in need of protection, and
- reasonable measures were taken to protect the information.

A business must be able to show that it took reasonable precautions to protect trade secrets before a court will extend that protection to its proceedings. Information security program and investigation documentation will be needed to prosecute criminal actions and to attempt to obtain restitution.

Information security policies and procedures help protect an organization from information security crimes and crimes committed as a result of information security breaches. Documentation of information security measures in place to prevent crimes will be needed to prevent possible penalties associated with the Federal Corporate Guidelines for Sentencing.

Records and information security program documentation that may become necessary to prosecute information security policy and law violations includes

- information security policies and practices
- confidentiality agreements with employees, suppliers, business partners, and others
- information security training documentation
- actions taken to stop a known leak and to enforce legal rights
- incident reports, such as firewall logs, and security investigation reports

Periodic security audits to test vulnerability of security systems and practices and to assess compliance with security policies should also be documented.

Appendix III: High-Performance, Low-Maintenance Records Retention

This appendix is a condensation and update of a November 1996 issue of *The Records & Retrieval Report*. Portions of the issue are omitted because they are covered elsewhere in this book. The records retention program methodology presented here supports a program that performs well and that is easy to maintain.

A RECORDS RETENTION PROGRAM

A records retention program is about destruction of valueless records in order to reduce storage costs and improve access to current, more useful information. It also is about standards that ensure the existence of valuable and required records.

The records retention schedule is the foundation of a comprehensive records and information program. A corporatewide records retention schedule provides standards and efficiencies that reduce costs and protect the company. It must strike an appropriate balance between records needed to run the business and the cost of their retention.

THE FUNCTIONAL RECORDS RETENTION SCHEDULE

To achieve consistent and successful records retention program implementation, a records retention schedule and its supporting guidelines must be as easy to implement as possible.

The records retention schedule should be organized, accurate, and current. Supporting guidelines and practices should simplify decision making and tasks to support those who must retain and dispose of records. In addition, the records manager needs to be responsive to the needs of both the organization and end users.

One of two common approaches to development of a records retention schedule is the traditional, detailed schedule. This detailed schedule is a list of record series and record titles, usually organized by departments. Both legal and user retention requirements are assigned directly to the specific record series.

An alternative approach is the functional records retention schedule. Functional retention categories that represent distinct business processes serve as a bridge between retention requirements and the record series and record titles.

Each major functional area listed below includes specific records retention groups that are relatively broad categories of records with similar purposes or business uses. A retention group can represent a single record series, such as I-9 documentation, or it can include a large number of record series, such as bank account statements, check registers, and canceled checks.

Functional Areas and Retention Groups

Functional retention groups are organized into broad areas of similar business processes or functions. Listed here are examples of typical retention groups organized by those broad business functional areas:

Accounting and Finance—(Accounts Payable/Receivable, Payroll, Tax Returns, Bank Transactions, Financial Statements, Investments, and more)

Environment and Safety—(Air Quality Monitoring, Hazardous Waste Disposal, Safety Inspections, and more)

Human Resources—(Benefit Plans, Employee Files, Training Programs, and more)

Operations (Industry-Specific)—(Product Development, Quality Control, Product Distribution, and more)

The functional schedule departs from the more traditional, detailed schedule in a number of ways. The discussion below makes the case for the functional retention schedule as a forward-thinking, more efficient approach to records retention.

Traditional Retention Schedule v. Functional Schedule

Record holders find the traditional schedule useful because relatively little effort is necessary to determine how long to keep specific records.

They need only refer to their department records lists to determine retention requirements of specific records. Although simplicity for the end
user is most assuredly an objective of a records retention program, it is
not the only criteria by which to judge effectiveness. In fact, there are
disadvantages to the traditional approach, explained below, that ultimately lead to end-user frustrations and that increase the risks of inconsistencies and errors in program implementation.

In both the traditional and the functional approaches to retention
scheduling, the lists of record series and record titles need continuous
maintenance as new record series and titles are created or changed, or
as they become obsolete. The difference between the two approaches is
that traditional, detailed retention schedules are only snapshots in time,
whereas the functional schedule is a living document.

As often happens in every organization, records from a dissolved department or
company are discovered in storage, records are found in offices and on desktop
computers of terminated employees, and departments create new record series
and electronic recordkeeping systems. Under a functional schedule, these newly
discovered records are compared with fewer than 150 retention groups to assign
a retention requirement that is already authorized by the retention schedule approval process discussed later. Under a traditional schedule, one would have to
look for similar record titles in a list of hundreds or thousands of record titles
that are organized by department.

The alternative to searching for record titles, under the traditional approach,
is to initiate the legal research, review, and approval process for the records. This
process is time-consuming, but it is more reliable and more consistent than obtaining an ad hoc decision on disposition of the records. Typically, no decision
is made in these situations because of the difficulties in applying the detailed
schedule. Consequently, the records are retained and are one more instance of
inconsistent program implementation.

Under the functional retention schedule approach, retention decisions
are made for fewer, broader categories of records, whereas in the traditional schedule a greater number of retention decisions must be made.
Whether the organization is a college with only hundreds of record series
or a *Fortune* 100 conglomerate with as many as 5,000 record series, the
functional approach organizes those record series into as few as 50 or as
many as 150 broad groups of business functions for retention purposes.

The smaller number of categories through which legal and business
requirements are controlled provides the simplicity and structure necessary for consistent and accurate implementation throughout the organization. In the functional schedule, record series are coded to the
retention groups, linking the record series directly to the business processes to which have been assigned both legal and business retention requirements.

In the traditional approach, the records are not organized by their functions for easy assignment of retention requirements. It is an overwhelming task to link specific legal and business requirements to each of hundreds or thousands of record series scattered throughout a number of departments. (The records inventory of one public utility came up with 3,500 record series, and one brewing company identified 4,300 record series.)

Business process categories also make sense because laws, regulations, and business needs for records retention are based on the purpose(s) and useful life of records and information. The resulting retention requirements for the functional retention groups then apply to all record series and record titles that are coded to those retention groups.

In some situations, there could be as many as several hundred record titles assigned to a single retention group. Consistency and accuracy improve when large numbers of record series and record titles are assigned to specific retention functions with retention requirements that have already been reviewed and approved.

There may be other risks in assigning individual legal requirements to specific record series rather than to the broader functional retention groups. In the absence of grouping similar requirements together and linking them to business processes, it is more likely that a legal consideration, case law, or other area of risk or exposure is overlooked in the detailed schedule.

For example, there are no legal requirements to retain sales contracts, but there are a number of limitations of action for sales contract disputes. In the functional schedule, a single retention group for contracts is used for any and all record series of a contractual nature to be retained for the same time period determined to be sufficient to respond to any litigation. In the traditional schedule, there is no specific legal requirement citation to assign to record series containing contracts, so there is a tendency to make ad hoc retention decisions.

Compounding the problems of inconsistencies and inaccuracies in the traditional schedule are that similar records may appear anywhere throughout the numerous departments in the schedule and that different record titles may be used for the same records. It is difficult to check one retention assignment against similar records that appear in other departments to ensure that the assigned retention periods are consistent.

The functional schedule provides flexibility as new reports, files, and other records are created. More often than not, the records can be coded to an existing retention group in the functional schedule. Occasionally there may be a need to conduct research for a new business process, such as when a company adds a new line of business.

The functional schedule is also more easily maintained than the traditional schedule because there are fewer retention groups to keep current on the legal and business requirements. When a new legal requirement or a changed business need results in a new retention requirement for a retention category, all record series coded to that retention category are automatically updated. In the traditional schedule, every record series in every department must be searched to identify those affected by the new legal requirement or changed business need.

The functional approach is a vehicle for the central control and authority necessary to ensure accuracy and consistency, as well as timely updates. A central authority is necessary for determination of records' functions, assignment of legal requirements and business needs, resolution of the inevitable conflicting perceptions of business value, and the application of standards.

Consistent implementation of the retention schedule mandates its application to all records in all media, including electronic records. When it is time to destroy a record, every form of that record must be destroyed—electronic, paper, microfilm, backup tape, and so on. The broad retention categories of business functions and processes in the functional schedule are easily applied to records in all media because the categories are based on the functions and content of the records.

The functional retention schedule addresses problems found in the traditional, detailed schedule. The functional approach also simplifies the processes of retention program development, implementation, and maintenance.

Following is a summary of the benefits of the functional records retention schedule.

Determination of record retention requirements is relatively straightforward because related laws, regulations, and business needs are based on the use(s) and purpose(s) of individual records.

The frequency of retention schedule updates is reduced because record business functions change less frequently than do business organizational structures.

The use of fewer than 150 broad categories, rather than hundreds or thousands of record series, provides the structure and simplicity necessary for accurate and consistent implementation throughout the company.

The schedule provides flexibility to respond to changing business needs without having to research legal requirements and business needs for every new document, file folder, or record series that is created.

Supporting indexing tools help the end user quickly determine specific retention requirements.

RETENTION SCHEDULE DEVELOPMENT

A number of elements are essential to establish a successful records retention program:

- senior and middle management support,
- a decision-making structure and clearly defined authority levels, and
- a communications structure to interface with work groups and end users.

If the top management and decision-makers of an organization are not committed to the records retention program, implementation will be difficult, if not impossible.

The decision-making structure and communications structure will vary depending on the organizational structure of the company. The decision-making structure is initiated by the chief executive officer, general counsel, or other appropriate senior official who selects a team to develop the policy, retention schedule, and guidelines. The team consists of experienced managers representing the following organizational areas:

- accounting / finance / tax / treasury
- audit
- corporate / administration
- environment / health / safety
- human resources
- information systems
- law
- marketing / sales
- operations

The communications structure revolves around the records manager, who coordinates the efforts of the records management team and communicates policy and guidelines to work groups and end users. In large organizations, each work group appoints a records coordinator as the liaison with records management.

Determining Retention Requirements

The decision to keep records is an easy one. However, it may not be the wise decision. Increasingly, organizations that keep records "just in case" are finding that those records can be used against them when they are sued or investigated.

Before conducting legal research, the organization's lines of business and business processes need to be defined to determine under what jurisdictions the organization is subject to regulation.

A detailed records inventory will also be helpful, but it is not absolutely necessary to have a records inventory in order to begin development of a functional retention schedule. Interviews of key people with knowledge of the business can provide valuable information for initial development of functional records retention groups. The supporting department records lists can be created from the retention groups and other sources of information about the organization and its business processes. The more detailed department lists evolve over time.

Records retention requirements should be determined based on legal requirements and on the business need to have the information available.

Legal requirements are organized into groups of requirements that are related to similar business processes. These groups are referred to as areas of law. For example, OSHA Compliance is one area of law that groups together similar regulations with requirements to maintain records and to report on accidents, illnesses, and other workplace safety matters. Categorizing requirements by areas of law is not only a logical approach for eventual linkage to record series through a retention group, but it also promotes consistency in applying legal requirements and considerations.

For example, a requirement to retain crane equipment safety inspections may be applied to all equipment safety inspections, even if there are no legal requirements to retain the other equipment safety inspections. Retaining all equipment safety inspections for the same time period shows a pattern of compliance with express or implied requirements and a consistent response to the business risk of potential personal injury claims related to the equipment.

Legal requirements are one element of the decision-making process. Determination of business record retention needs reflects not only internal operating needs but also protection of the organization, customer expectations, and industry practice. Every business decision on how long to retain records involves analysis of the costs, benefits, and risks. (See Chapter 7, "Retention and Disposition," for more on legal research and retention decisions.)

Review and Approval Process

During retention schedule development, every attempt is made to reconcile business needs, legal requirements, and the ultimate objectives to reduce the company's expenses and risks. A formal review of the proposed schedule ensures that the most appropriate retention requirements are determined.

Because the retention program should have the force of corporate policy, an approval process similar to that for corporate policy may be considered. It is important to have buy-in and support at the highest levels possible if full compliance is expected. However, involvement of too many people in the approval process presents a concern about the logistics of accomplishing approval in a reasonable period of time.

One alternative for the program authorization process is to identify business contacts and attorneys for the review and approval of retention groups in their areas of expertise. Another alternative is a records management committee of representatives from critical business units, such as accounting, audit, law, operations and tax.

Formal approval by departments is not recommended because the records manager faces the dilemma of having to referee so many conflicting viewpoints and perceptions of business needs. However, as discussed later, it is recommended that there be department reviews of their records inventory lists after the retention schedule is authorized for purposes of fine-tuning the retention schedule and modifying the department records lists.

The authorization process to establish the records retention program should be documented. The final schedule must have written approvals to demonstrate both systematic development of the program and companywide support of the program.

After records management staff code record series from an inventory to the records retention groups, there may be department reviews of their records inventories. Such reviews are useful to confirm the accuracy of the coding of record series to functional retention categories. They also are an opportunity to correct, clarify, and expand record series names and descriptions, to confirm identification of official records, and to train employees and obtain buy-in from departments.

If during this department review any compelling reason warrants a significant change to the retention schedule, it may be appropriate or necessary to request a brief but formal review of the affected retention group(s) by the records management committee or the appropriate subject matter expert(s) and attorney(s).

Supporting Guidelines and Practices

The program shall be in written form and approved by the general counsel or the records management committee. The general counsel and records management are responsible for interpreting the records retention schedule and the guidelines as they may apply to specific situations.

Policy, guidelines, and practices are established as the foundation for program implementation and for subsequent program audits.

A broad policy statement defines the scope and purpose of the records retention program, authorizes its implementation, and identifies the person(s) and their responsibilities for program implementation.

It is the policy of ForwardThink Corporation to retain, manage, and destroy records in accordance with the Corporate Records Retention Schedule and uniform guidelines, practices, and procedures.

Records maintained in electronic form are legally acceptable media and are governed by the same guidelines as are paper, microfilm, and other records. All records and information maintained in individual offices and at any off-site location are subject to these guidelines. No company records may be stored at employee residences or at other personal property.

Records management, under the authority of the general counsel, has the ultimate responsibility for management of the Records and Information Management Program. A number of other individuals and departments share authority and responsibility for program implementation.

The policy statement may then go on to identify those individuals and departments with authority and responsibility, such as the following:

Records Management Committee—Reviews and approves the Corporate Records Retention Schedule, guidelines, and practices for compliance and for meeting business information requirements.

Law Department—Reviews and approves the Corporate Records Retention Schedule, guidelines, and practices for compliance with legal requirements and corporate policy. Notifies departments of the imposition and removal of records destruction holds.

Finance and Accounting—Reviews and approves the Corporate Records Retention Schedule, guidelines, and practices for meeting financial and tax obligations. Notifies departments of the imposition and removal of records destruction holds for tax audits.

Audit—Reviews and approves the Corporate Records Retention Schedule, guidelines, and practices for compliance with corporate policy. Performs regular assessments of program compliance.

Records and Information Management—Manages the Records and Information Management Program, including the governing policies, guidelines, and practices. Provides guidance to employees for program compliance.

Managers—Appoint Records Coordinators, review the Corporate Records Retention Schedule for meeting business information requirements, and authorize program change requests initiated by their areas of responsibility.

Records Coordinators—Administer the Records and Information Management Program in their appointed area of responsibility. Provide guidance and training to other employees for program compliance. Serve as liaison with Records and Information Management.

All Employees—Ensure that records and information are managed, protected, and disposed of in accordance with the Records and Information Management Program.

A procedure to halt records destruction for legitimate reasons is as important as the records retention schedule. This procedure ensures that certain records are not destroyed for as long as they may be needed for litigation, government investigation, or audit—even if they are eligible for destruction according to the schedule.

A destruction hold must be placed immediately on any and all records that may be relevant to the proceeding. A list of relevant documents must be presented to the opposing party. Documents need to be collected, organized, and reviewed by attorneys for relevancy and any sensitive and valuable information in need of protection. Relevant documents must be organized so as not to be an unreasonable burden on the other party.

These activities must be accomplished without delay and with minimal disruption of business.

When the records are no longer needed for litigation, audit, or investigation, record holders are notified that they are released from the destruction hold.

PROGRAM IMPLEMENTATION

After the schedule, guidelines, and practices are finalized, program implementation can begin. Implementation is launched with a directive from the chief executive officer, general counsel, or other appropriate high-level official. The directive should make successful implementation a responsibility of every member of line management and of the heads of all staff functions.

Ongoing formal training programs and informal training activities need to be established. Program promotions may include articles in newsletters and incentive awards to increase program awareness and to encourage program compliance.

Regular, systematic reviews of records for destruction are also an important part of program implementation. What review method or methods are effective may vary from one department or organization to another. Destruction methods also may vary, from pulverizing sensitive records and erasing electronic data through routine trash disposal and recycling of general records.

Records destruction must be documented in a way that can support a claim that the records retention program is systematically implemented in the normal course of business. Companies with a high risk of litigation may also find it necessary to establish a procedure to document premature destruction or loss of records.

Records Indexing and Organization

How well records are indexed and organized will determine how efficiently records disposition is accomplished. When records are organized in a manner consistent with the retention schedule, it is much easier to collect records for inactive storage or destruction. The ability to isolate records with different destruction dates is especially important for computer files, microfilm rolls, and large paper files.

Program implementation may necessitate changes in records identification, marking, and/or filing practices. An exception to this rule of thumb exists when the reorganization of records or changing existing information systems presents an extraordinary administrative burden and expense. An alternative is to begin new processes for compliance from today forward, documenting what records will have a different retention requirement due to the extraordinary burden.

Records management should actively provide assistance to record holders to organize their information systems in ways that simplify purging in the future. One example of such facilitating is guidance on managing records that have a retention period of "Active" plus a specified number of years.

It makes sense to define when "Active" ceases, as in "Active ceases with disposition of the asset," or "Active ceases with expiration or termination of the contract." This definition can be in the retention group or record series description.

Guidelines for closing active files also support record-holder implementation of the retention schedule. Taking it one step farther is a procedure to close active files, such as projects or contracts. These types of records tend to be troublesome for program compliance. However, it is simply a smart business practice to close active files and thus start the ticking of the retention clock.

Guidelines are needed for retention of electronic records and information. One of the greatest challenges related to electronic records is the lack of central control and management of the various electronic information systems. Electronic information is organized differently by each system and user, so not all organizations know what is in their information systems. Implementation of a records retention program is an excellent opportunity for records management to work closely with information systems managers to integrate electronic information resources with other records and to manage them consistent with company policy and guidelines for retention.

Tools for End Users

A number of user-friendly tools can be produced to facilitate program implementation. As support staffs continue to shrink, the simpler the processes, the better. Development of all user-friendly tools is left to the innovative records manager, but this section offers some suggestions.

There may be a number of different documents that represent the corporatewide records retention schedule. The most complete schedule that includes legal requirements and business requirements is part of the retention program documentation that is maintained by records management.

A simpler version of the schedule may be distributed to employees and posted on an intranet. This simpler version has the retention group names and descriptions and their retention requirements. It may also indicate the office of record for each retention category and the retention requirement for unofficial copies. The larger the organization, the more likely that the office of record is best identified at the record series level on department records lists. However the issue of duplicate records is addressed, it is important to provide guidelines for management and control of duplicate records.

Record holders appreciate simpler documents that include only what they need for their applications. Department record lists tend to be the most referenced documents by end users. They typically contain each department's record series titles and brief descriptions; the retention group code and retention period; and any other desirable information such as office of record, active retention, vital record designation, or quality record designation. Other useful tools include an alphabetical list of the organization's record series as well as a one-page or two-page abbreviated list of retention group titles and their retention periods.

End users need to understand that records lists are simply lists of record series that have been coded to the higher authority, the corporatewide records retention schedule, to arrive at a retention requirement for each record series. Therefore, the retention requirement for one record series cannot be changed without reviewing the retention group to which the record series is coded and all other record series coded to that same retention group.

(See Appendix IV, "Records and Information Management Best Practices," for more guidelines to assist record holders in retention program implementation.)

Ensuring Program Acceptance

The functional records retention schedule may require a new way of thinking about a company's records and information. A central authority and high-level controls are necessary for retention requirement approvals and for program policy. In the absence of the force of corporate policy, there is no authority to enforce consistent records retention and destruction throughout the company and in the normal course of business.

Certainly voluntary program compliance is more desirable than mandated compliance. Perhaps a combination of the two will be necessary, especially in the early stages of program implementation. The records and information management department needs to earn credibility and trust to develop the level of comfort necessary for voluntary compliance. Earning that staff acceptance can be a struggle every step of the way, but it will be worth it in the long run.

To ease implementation, records management establishes general and flexible guidelines, allows for reasonable exceptions, and documents both. This includes the anticipation of problem areas and addressing them head on with guidelines.

PROGRAM MAINTENANCE

Records retention decisions are not cast in concrete because record categories, legal requirements, and business processes change. Program compliance can be expected only when the program responds in a timely manner to the organization's changing needs and technologies.

Responsive retention program maintenance includes four basic elements:

- ongoing training that keeps pace with staff turnover
- timely resolution of records retention issues
- program assessments for compliance and improvements
- formal reviews and reauthorizations of the program on a regular basis

As questions and issues arise, timely response not only is good customer service; it also builds trust in the program. The most frequently asked question from end users is how to determine the retention requirement for a specific record. Often the answer is simply a matter of interpretation of the retention schedule, clarification of retention group descriptions, or addition to the department records lists and the records retention schedule alphabetical index of all record series.

Requests for changes in retention requirements and exceptions to policy are subject to the established retention program authorization process. In addition to specific change requests, a formal review of the entire program and the retention schedule should occur regularly.

A form should be available to document specific retention schedule change requests and the response to those requests so that changes can be included in the program documentation. What appears on the change request form depends on what the form is designed to accomplish. At a minimum, any request for a change in a retention requirement should include the justification for the change. ("Just in case we need it" is not a valid reason to change a retention requirement.)

Program Assessments for Compliance

A records retention program assessment, or audit, is a valuable instrument to verify compliance with stated policies and program effectiveness. Regular monitoring of the program's effectiveness is critical to continual program improvements as the program matures and responds to the organization's changing needs.

The assessment process includes a number of defined steps:

- Determine the scope of the assessment.
- Develop the assessment criteria (the policies, practices, guidelines, and regulatory requirements against which collected evidence will be compared.)
- Determine the methods to collect evidence.
- Evaluate the findings to reach conclusions and recommendations.
- Implement follow-up actions.

It is essential that an organization take appropriate action to correct a serious problem uncovered in an assessment. If an issue arises in court about the records retention program, the assessment report and the lack of evidence of corrective action could prove harmful.

Regular monitoring of program compliance results in numerous benefits, enabling the company to

- assess potential business risks
- assess effectiveness of internal management and control systems
- identify areas for improvement, new resources, or commitment
- demonstrate compliance
- uncover compliance problems so they may be remedied in a timely manner
- prevent or detect fraud or other criminal or unethical behavior
- identify areas where employee training is needed
- help prepare for litigation or regulatory inspection
- demonstrate management commitment to the program

CONCLUSION

Organizations must focus on managing their paper, microfilm, and electronic information resources in ways that add value to the organization.

There are compelling reasons to develop a records retention program. A properly designed and implemented records retention program ensures that records are

- retained as long as necessary and in compliance with laws and regulations
- destroyed when they are no longer needed or required
- accessible for conducting business
- preserved if likely to be relevant to judicial or administrative investigations or proceedings

A records retention program is one element of a comprehensive records and information management program that supports compliance with the law and that supports other business objectives. It is the foundation of a records and information management program because it establishes ground rules for a number of recordkeeping practices that also add value to the organization.

Appendix IV: Records and Information Management Best Practices

Much of managing business records and information is common sense. This appendix offers general records and information management practices that support improved productivity and compliance with an organization's records retention program. These best practices are intended for use by individual employees who are responsible for records and information in their offices or cubicles and on their personal computers.

Each subject can be customized to an organization for inclusion in its corporate records and information management program and employee training. Specific recordkeeping guidelines such as these may be posted on the organization's intranet and distributed to employees for periodic office cleanup days.

BEST PRACTICES

The records and information management best practices presented here are applicable to all business records regardless of whether they are paper, microfilm, electronic, or some other information storage media. How they are applied to different information carriers may vary, but the underlying concept of each practice is what is important.

Business Record

A business record is any documentation of a business transaction, activity, process, or condition regardless of the medium on which the information is recorded.

Records Creation

All records created must be complete, objective, factual, accurate, timely, and reflective of concerns for safety, ethics, and compliance with corporate policy, proper business practices, and the law.

Ambiguous language, exaggerations, opinions, subjective comments, and other remarks that can be misinterpreted must be avoided. Corporate policy prohibits communications that contain vulgar, sexually explicit, hateful, or other offensive language.

Remember that every business record is subject to audit and subpoena—including e-mail messages. As a rule of thumb, do not record or transmit anything that you would not want everyone in the company to read or anything that you would not want to repeat on the witness stand.

Records always should include a creation or receipt date. The content and purpose of a record, along with its origination date and last date modified, determine how long it is retained within the guidelines of the record retention program. Refer to the records retention schedule for the proper assignment of records to retention categories to determine the retention and destruction requirement for records.

Documents and Files Management

How well records are organized and indexed determines how efficiently they are managed throughout their useful life. The following brief tips on efficient management of records and information can be applied to electronic records as well as to paper records.

1. Index and organize records for easy retrieval.
   a. Label files with meaningful descriptions rather than general names such as "Executive" or "Project."
   b. Critical information to include in file or document descriptions may include the record's function, such as "Potential Acquisition" or "Paid Invoices," the retention category code and/or retention requirement, and the date(s) of the record.
2. Clearly mark or electronically tag the following for fast and easy disposal:
   a. duplicates, convenience copies, courtesy copies
   b. superseded drafts
   c. reference or subject files
3. Close files when a process, activity, or project is completed.
   a. Remove all extraneous materials (duplicates, general information, drafts, work papers, notes, obsolete information). Retain *only* the most complete and current information.
   b. Identify each file with a label or electronic tag that includes the file description, date(s), and retention requirement.

4. Do not mix the following items:
   a. records with different destruction dates (keep apart, not in the same storage container or on the same information storage medium)
   b. official records and duplicate records
   c. records of different years (e.g., 2001 invoices with 2000 invoices)

Official Record and Office of Record

To more efficiently and responsibly manage large volumes of records, a clear distinction must be made between official records and other information. Common sense and good business practices are applied to determine if information is an official record, a convenience copy (duplicate), or a non-record.

An official record is the most complete record or file of records that document a particular business transaction, activity, process, or condition. This is the record to be preserved for the full retention requirement specified in the retention schedule. The official record may be paper, microfilm, electronic, or another information media.

Official record support materials are records, documents, and information that add important, significant, or critical information to the official record. Generally they are maintained with the official record.

When a record serves more than one distinct purpose, an official record copy is designated for each purpose, and all others are treated as duplicates. For example, payroll and accounting records are official records for tax purposes. A copy of certain payroll and accounting records may be in government contract project files as an official record maintained for the separate business purpose of government contract compliance.

When an electronic information system is the official source of information relied on by users and it is the source used for audits, any paper copies scattered throughout the organization do not need to be retained for the full retention requirement.

The office of record is the organizational group responsible for an official record throughout its full retention requirement and for the record's ultimate disposition. The office of record is the owner of the information and retains decision-making authority over the records. The office of record may not necessarily be the record creator or record holder, as in the following examples:

• One department may generate a report for another department's use.
• A records center is the custodian for a department's inactive records.

• The information services department is responsible for managing electronic data that belongs to another department.

Application of the office of record concept is effective only when employees trust that they can access the official record in a reasonable period of time. Absent that trust, they will be reluctant to discard their duplicate records.

Duplicates / Convenience Copies

To avoid unnecessary storage and retrieval expense, duplicate copies of records must be clearly distinguished from official records. Departments and individuals holding records that are copies of official records are responsible for destroying those duplicates as soon as they are obsolete or not needed. Generally, this is within one year. Note, however, that duplicate records must *not* be retained longer than the official record.

A duplicate record may become an official record in the following exceptional circumstances:

• Significant notations were added to the duplicate copy.
• The official record copy was accidentally lost or destroyed, so the duplicate becomes the official record.

Distribution of copies should be limited to those with a need to know. Copies should be clearly identified and marked as such for efficient and timely destruction.

Drafts

Drafts are destroyed as soon as they are superseded by revisions or by the final document. Documents routed for review and comment are destroyed after they are revised accordingly. Only the final document is retained as the official record. (There may be exceptions, such as drafts of contract negotiations, in which the drafts represent significant business transactions or conditions.)

Diaries, Calendars, and Journals

Diaries, calendars, journals, and similar documents should be retained no longer than one year because they tend to contain informal language that may not be an accurate reflection of the company's position, and they typically contain incomplete information. Any significant information contained in them should be documented in the proper

manner and filed with the related subject matter's record series and retention group.

General Subject Files

Individuals and departments often maintain what are commonly referred to as "General Subject Files." They generally include documents
and publications that are duplicates or are not company records.

Examples include conference, training, and professional development
materials; magazine articles and other publications of interest; and supplier promotional materials.

Because general subject files are typically non-records and duplicate
copies, they are not subject to the corporate records retention schedule.
However, they should be periodically reviewed to purge them of obsolete materials.

Correspondence

Correspondence can be general or substantive, depending on the business value of the correspondence.

General correspondence has relatively little value beyond its initial
use, or it has short-term value. Such correspondence includes routine
letters and notes that require no follow-up, completed cycles of correspondence, telephone messages, FYI documents, reminders, announcements, bulletins, notices, routing slips, and other general matters.
Typically such documents are discarded as soon as they are obsolete, or
within one year.

Substantive correspondence, in contrast, is correspondence that documents important business transactions, conditions, and processes. It
must be maintained with similar subject matter records for the same
retention requirement.

The differences in business value of correspondence are evident in the
following example:

The cover memo that states, "The enclosed is for your information," is general
correspondence, whereas a cover memo that states, "Pay close attention to par-
agraph 4 on page 2 for its pricing implications. Advise Marketing to postpone
the proposed advertising campaign pending review by the Executive Board" is
substantive correspondence. In both cases the attached document is a record or
duplicate and should be maintained accordingly.

Electronic Mail (E-Mail)

Electronic messaging (e-mail) systems are designed for convenient and
efficient communications. They are *not* electronic filing systems. Individ-

uals must delete e-mail messages as soon as they are no longer useful, and no later than the time period stated in the corporate policy. Individuals are responsible for transferring any substantive e-mail messages and attachments from the e-mail system to another recordkeeping system for retention according to the e-mail's subject matter's retention requirements.

Chronological Files

Chronological files, sometimes called "reading files," are convenience copies of official records. (The official record is maintained with the appropriate subject file.) Reading files are maintained in chronological order as reference and backup by authors or recipients. Because they are duplicates, and because they are difficult to search to retrieve information by subject matter, they should be retained for no longer than one year.

Vital Records

A small percentage of an organization's records are considered vital to the company's continued operations and thus should be protected from loss. The records management department has guidelines to identify vital records and what methods are recommended to protect them.

Historical Records

Corporate historical records are records or memorabilia that have enduring value because they document the people, events, business developments, and achievements of the company. They also document the company's involvement in the community. They may include photographs, videos, product samples, publications, and more.

Historical records may be duplicates of official records, such as company publications and annual reports. They also may be official records that are eventually reclassified from their original retention category to the corporate history retention category, such as photographs that are no longer needed for routine business activities but that document a significant event. These records are generally selected by the company archivist and are periodically reviewed for continued historical value.

Non-Records and Reference Material

Similar to the general subject files described earlier, often information and publications in the public domain are maintained for reference purposes. Individuals and departments tend to collect unsolicited supplier products and services brochures, magazine articles, and other reference materials.

Non-records may include the following:

- industry or professional association meeting proceedings and publications
- competitor publications
- unsolicited supplier products and services publications and price lists
- government regulations
- commercially published books, magazines, catalogs

Generally, non-records are not addressed in a records retention schedule because they are not business records. However, they should be reviewed periodically to purge them of obsolete materials.

Glossary

Active record. A record referenced on a regular basis during the normal course of business, such as current invoices, personnel records, correspondence, or reports on current projects.

Admissibility. A characteristic of evidence that enables it to be introduced in a court proceeding.

Adverse inference. A finding by a court through a reasoning process that information in records that were inappropriately destroyed by a party is unfavorable to that party, even though the information was not available to the court.

Anti-virus program. A software application that seeks out computer viruses, quarantines the viruses, and eliminates them.

Application service provider (ASP). A company that offers hardware and software required to host electronic information systems. The service often is used by small- and medium-size businesses when the cost of buying hardware and software is prohibitive.

Archival record. A record that is to be preserved for an extended period of time, such as a historical record.

Attachment. A document, such as a word-processing document, that is associated with another document. Most often used when describing electronic documents appended to or embedded in an e-mail message for transmission through an e-mail communications network.

Attorney-client privilege. The right of a client or an attorney to refuse to disclose and to prevent any other person from disclosing confidential communications between the client and the attorney.

Audit hold. The procedure to halt destruction of records when it is determined that an audit is foreseeable or pending.

Authentication. The determination of the genuineness, reliability, or trustworthiness of a record as evidence.

Authenticity. Refers to the fact that a record is what it purports to be and has not been tampered with or otherwise corrupted since its creation.

Backup. The process that creates a copy of records and information for security purposes. Most often used to protect vital records and to be prepared for a computer disaster that destroys computer software and data.

Browser. A software application used to navigate on the Internet's world wide web and to retrieve information from web sites.

Business continuity plan. A plan intended to position an organization so that employees, operations, and assets survive the impact of a disastrous event. Includes procedures and information necessary to prepare for and to manage the catastrophe and to resume or continue business operations.

Business records organization chart. A method of classifying records by functional and subject categories for indexing, organizing, filing, and retrieval of records, as well as assignment of record retention periods. More commonly referred to as a file structure.

Chief Information Officer (CIO). An executive-level position responsible for establishment of corporate information policy and standards, and for management control over information resources.

Civil case. A court proceeding to determine and enforce rights between parties, to prevent future rights violations, and to provide appropriate damages or compensation.

Compact disk (CD). An optical disk that stores electronic information. May be in rewritable or write once, read many formats.

Compact disk, read-only memory (CD-ROM). An optical disk that is written to once and the stored information only can be read.

Compact disk, recordable (CD-R). An optical disk that can be written to using a CD-R drive. Information can be written to the disk in multiple sessions, but it cannot be erased.

Compound document. A document that contains information in several forms, such as text, graphics, and image, and that is assembled from several information sources. Most often used to describe electronic documents assembled from a number of different software applications.

Computer-assisted retrieval (CAR) system. A records system that films and encodes documents for indexing by computer.

Computer output microfilm (COM). An original record produced directly from computer data onto microfilm.

Confidential record. A record or information that is shared only on a need-to-know basis and that its owner or subject does not want freely disclosed or used by others without prior permission. Confidential information encompasses various types of private, technical, financial, business, and customer information. The term *confidential* is sometimes used to describe proprietary information.

Conservation. Processes and actions to retard or control the deterioration of a record form or information carrier.

Contract or agreement. A mutual agreement between two or more parties that creates, modifies, or dissolves a legal relationship between the parties.

Copyright. The legal right granted to an author, composer, playwright, publisher, or distributor to exclusive publication, production, sale, or distribution of a literary, musical, dramatic, or artistic work, including computer software.

Custodial capacity. A relationship in which one party has the responsibility to protect property in its possession that is owned by another.

Cyber squatter. An individual who registers an Internet domain name that is identical to or similar to the name or trademark of a well-known company or its products to turn an easy profit by later selling the domain name registration to the owner of the name or trademark.

Data. A general term used to denote any or all facts, numbers, letters, and symbols that refer to or describe an object, transaction, event, condition, and so on. Most frequently used in reference to electronic information.

Data migration. The periodic transfer of data from one hardware or software platform to another, or from one generation of information technology to a subsequent technology generation. Migration is a necessary action to preserve electronic information.

Data warehouse. A central depository for all or significant parts of the electronic data that an enterprise's various business systems collect. Data from various electronic transaction processing applications are selectively extracted and organized on the data warehouse database for use by analytical software applications and user queries.

Database management system. A software system used to access, process, and retrieve electronic data stored in a database.

Defendant. The individual or organization that must defend itself against a complaint filed in a civil or criminal action.

Designated record copy. An original or duplicate record that is the official record to be retained and protected according to a record retention schedule.

Destruction. The process of obliterating information on a record by making the information unreadable or unusable.

Destruction hold. The procedure to suspend routine and other destruction of records when it is determined that those records may be relevant to foreseeable or pending litigation, government investigation, or audit.

Digital signature. An electronic signature that is used to authenticate the identity of the sender of a message or document, to authenticate the signer of a document, or to ensure that the original content of the message or document that is sent is unchanged. A digital certificate contains the digital signature of the certificate-issuing authority so that anyone can verify that the certificate is valid.

Digitize. The process to convert printed information into electronic signals for reading by a computer.

Directory. The organizational structure of electronic records into logical groups.

Discovery. The legal process that allows parties involved in a legal proceeding to obtain records and information relevant to the proceeding that are in the possession of another party.

Dispersal. The process of placing copies of vital records in locations other than those housing the originals.

Disposition. An action taken on a record, such as transfer, conversion to another medium, or destruction.

Document production. The process of retrieving and producing a record for review by opposing counsel in a government investigation or a legal proceeding.

Documentation. The creation of records to describe an event or act, and to show compliance with a policy, procedure, or process.

Domain name. The address that Internet browsers use to access a particular web site.

Duplicate record. A reproduction of an original record by means of photography, mechanical or electronic rerecording, chemical reproduction, or other techniques that accurately reproduce the original.

E-commerce. The electronic exchange of money for goods and services between two or more parties.

Electronic bulletin board. A system that users with computers and modems can access through network connections. Users can post messages and send electronic files to the bulletin board and receive messages and files on their own computers.

Electronic data transmission and storage. A technique used to transmit backup computer files periodically to remote sites for added security and data protection.

Electronic document management system. A software application that indexes, profiles, and controls electronic documents on desktop computers.

Electronic imaging system. A computer-based technology that scans a document image and stores it in electronic form for retrieval.

Electronic record. Any record that, in the ordinary course of business, is used and set aside or stored in digital form, regardless of whether it was made or received in such form.

E-mail. A document created or received using an electronic mail communications system and network. May include brief notes, formal documents, and attachments transmitted with the message.

Fiduciary capacity. A relationship in which one party is responsible for the management of the financial matters and records of another party.

File management. A management function that provides for the analysis of filing equipment to determine the most efficient type for a given operation at the most economical price and to establish a method of indexing and arranging records.

File server. A storage device that can be accessed by other computers through a network. Also a computer dedicated to processing and storing data and for sharing software in a computer network environment.

File structure. A method of classifying records by functional and subject categories for indexing, organizing, filing, and retrieval of records, as well as assignment of record retention periods.

Filing system. A method of organizing and storing physical records and information for easy retrieval.

Firewall. Software or hardware that monitors a computer's Internet traffic going into and out of the network and that blocks suspicious probing from outside intruders.

Foreseeable. The reasonable anticipation that an activity or event, such as litigation, investigation, or audit, will occur in the future.

Freedom of Information Act (FOIA). A federal law that requires public disclosure of the records, opinions, findings, policies, and procedures of federal agencies, with the exception of information that is privileged, confidential, or classified.

Hot-link. A hypertext link that is embedded in an e-mail message that allows the user to go directly from an e-mail application or web site to another web site.

Hypertext markup language (HTML). A standard language for an electronic data format that is readable by every computer with the browser installed. HTML is primary format for web site contents today.

Inactive record. A record that is not referenced in the course of normal business activities, but is retained because it contains information of real or potential use or value.

Indexing system. A method of categorizing and encoding records for efficient organization, storage, retrieval, and processing.

Information carrier. A general term to describe a record storage medium or record form.

Information disclosure. The act of providing a record or information to another party.

Information processor. A mechanical or electronic means to transmit, convert, or manipulate data, information, or records.

Information resources. Records, publications, electronic information databases, and other sources of data and information.

Information security program. A component of a records and information program that establishes methods and procedures to protect sensitive and valuable records from loss, damage, or unauthorized disclosure.

Information security threat. A condition, event, or action that may lead to damage, loss, or unauthorized disclosure of records and information.

Intellectual property. The protected expressions of scientific, artistic, or other creative and/or commercial endeavors; a special type of intangible personal property arising from the creative endeavors of the human mind and research, including patents, copyrights, trademarks, trade names, or service marks.

Intelligent agent. A software application that follows instructions given by its creators and that learns independently about information it is programmed to gather. Sometimes called smart assistant.

Internet. The worldwide interconnection of computers and computer networks that allows access to web sites and electronic communications.

Internet service provider (ISP). A company that offers access to the Internet and e-mail communications and also hosts web sites.

Intranet. A network and communications system based on Internet technology for use within an organization's environment.

Jukebox. An automated device that stores and retrieves multiple optical disks for use on one or more read-write drives.

Legal considerations. Various laws, regulations, rules of evidence, and case law (and their interpretations) that affect rights and responsibilities regarding recordkeeping.

Legal hold. The procedure to halt destruction of records related to foreseeable or pending litigation or government investigation.

Life cycle. The time period from the creation of a record and its active use through its ultimate disposition, whether archiving or destruction.

Limitation of action. *See* Statute of limitations.

Limitation of assessment. The period of time after a tax return is filed or the tax becomes due during which the taxing agency can determine or modify the amount of taxes owed.

Machine-sensible record. A term used by the Internal Revenue Service to indicate computer-readable data or a record that is not visible but that is accessible with appropriate equipment.

Mainframe computer. A large, centralized computer used for data processing and storage.

Maintain (maintenance). The actions necessary to retain and preserve a record.

Media management and integration program. A component of a records and information management program that controls the forms or storage media of records and that provides a system or methodology to index and organize all existing record forms into a uniform records and information system that is media-transparent and that treats all record forms alike for purposes of records retrieval, retention, and disposition.

Media stability. *See* Permanence and durability.

Medium (Media). The material or substance on which data or information is recorded, such as paper, optical disk, magnetic tape, microfilm, or photograph. Also referred to as a record form or an information carrier.

Metadata. Bits of electronic data attached to an electronic file, such as an e-mail message or word-processing file, which provides information about the document. Data structure, interrelationships, time and date stamps, and other characteristics of stored and transmitted electronic data and records are metadata.

Microform. The generic name for any of the various forms in which the use of microphotography reproduces a record. A microform may be microfilm rolls or cartridges, microfiche, film jackets, aperture cards, and so on.

Name authority. A standardized method of formatting personal, government, and corporate names to facilitate data manipulation, filing, and retrieval of information. The use of name authority ensures that information on the same person or entity is indexed under a single name instead of under a number of variations representing a single person or organization.

Need to know. A requirement for access to, knowledge of, or possession of confidential information in order to perform tasks or services essential to the fulfillment of job responsibilities.

Nondisclosure agreement. A written contract between two parties wherein one or both parties agree not to disclose certain information to other parties.

Non-record. Materials that lack evidence of an organization's business activities or that lack information of any value to the organization. Most often refers to records and information available in the public domain.

Obstruction of justice. A deliberate act to interfere with a government investigation or judicial proceeding. Intentional destruction of evidence is one example of obstruction of justice.

Office of record. The group, department, or office responsible for maintaining a designated official record copy.

Optical disk. A record storage form, or information carrier, on which data is recorded using laser optic technology.

Original record. A newly created document, recording, or record intended to be the same as an original under rules of evidence, including a printout or other sight-readable output of computer data that can be shown to accurately reflect the data or information.

Outsourcing. The process of contracting with another organization to perform a specified business function or activity.

Patent. A grant made by the federal government to an inventor that assures the exclusive right to make, use, license, and sell a new and useful design, process, machine, manufactured item, or other composition, or any new and useful improvement on it. The concrete expression of a novel and useful idea or design is protected for a limited period of time prescribed by statute.

Permanence and durability. The characteristics of an information carrier, or record medium, that determine its ability to withstand use, abuse, adverse environmental conditions, and aging.

Personal record. A record belonging to an individual that has no content relevant to the business, was not produced using resources of the business, and has no place in the business environment.

Plaintiff. The individual or organization that files a complaint in a civil action.

Preservation (preserve). The process and actions to maintain and protect a record for as long as it is needed, including efforts to retard or control deterioration of the information carrier and to prevent loss of the record.

Privacy. The claims of individuals, groups, or institutions to determine when, how, and to what extent information about them is communicated to others.

Private record. A record or information about an individual or organization that must not be disclosed without proper authorization. Frequently referred to as a confidential record. Private information includes, but is not limited to, employee or customer records and attorney-client privileged records.

Proprietary information. Information, knowledge, data, and know-how owned by a company. Proprietary information includes a company's technical, financial, or commercial information, as well as intellectual properties protected under the law, such as patent applications, trade secrets, and copyrights.

Read-only memory (ROM). A term describing an electronic record that may be read, but may not be added to, modified, or deleted.

Record. Any form of recorded information that is created or maintained for use at a later time, including but not limited to paper, photographs, negatives, microfilm, maps, drawings, charts, cards, digitized data, magnetic tapes, software, motion pictures, videos, optical disks, and microfiches.

Record conversion. The process of changing a record from one medium or form to another.

Record form. *See* Medium (Media) and Information carrier.

Record series. A group of similar or related records that normally are used or filed as a unit. The group or category is the product of an official function or activity and permits the evaluation of records as a unit for retention scheduling, control, storage, and other purposes.

Recordkeeping. Actions and processes related to the creation, maintenance, information carrier(s), protection, and disposition of records.

Recordkeeping requirements. Policies, laws, regulations, and practices related to the recordkeeping functions that are based on business needs, government requirements, and other legal considerations.

Records and information management. A management function that systematically controls the life cycle of records and information from creation or receipt through processing, distribution, maintenance, protection, and re-trieval, to their ultimate disposition. This management function ensures that adequate records are created to document business activities and conditions and to meet administrative, legal, and other operational needs. Records and information are retained and disposed of based on their business functions and value.

Records and information manager. A knowledgeable individual designated to control the records and information management program.

Records center. A room or building devoted to the proper storage and protection of records.

Records management application. A software application used by an organization to apply records management principles to records and information in all records storage media. Its primary management functions are to categorize, locate, and identify and protect records and information for disposition and to document their disposition.

Reliability. Refers to the ability of a record to stand for the facts it contains. Reliability depends on the degree of completeness of the record's form and the degree of control exercised over its creation.

Retention period. The period of time during which records must be maintained in a certain location or media form because they are needed for operational, legal, fiscal, historical, or other purposes. A retention period may be stated in terms of months or years and sometimes is expressed as contingent upon the occurrence of an event.

Retention program. A component of a records and information management program that controls the creation, maintenance, and ultimate disposition of records at the appropriate time.

Retention schedule. A document prepared as part of a records retention program that lists the periods of time needed to maintain records in active status in a certain form, location, and so on, up to final disposition of records archiving or destruction.

Rewritable optical disk. An optical disk on which data can be recorded, deleted, and re-recorded.

Risk management. A business management function or process that analyzes the costs, risks, and benefits of alternatives in order to determine the most desirable alternative.

Security copying. The process of duplicating a record as a method of ensuring the continued existence of the record and information.

Semi-active record. A record referenced occasionally in the course of conducting normal business.

Sensitive records and information. Records that must not be disclosed indiscriminately to others because of the nature of the information.

Software. Statements or logic in any form, medium, or language, intended as instructions for machine processing. Includes codes, related documentation, user manuals, and other descriptive material related to programming procedures, techniques, or principles.

Software application. Software used to automate a specific business function or process.

Statute of limitations. A statute prescribing limitations to the right of action on certain described causes of action or criminal prosecutions; the time period after an event or from which a right begins, during which a legal action or lawsuit may be initiated. Also referred to as limitation of actions.

Subpoena. A court order requiring a witness to appear in court, to produce relevant records in his or her possession or control, or to provide testimony.

System. An organized collection of hardware, software, supplies, people, maintenance, training, and policies to accomplish a set of specific functions.

Tax hold. The procedure to halt destruction of records related to a foreseeable or pending tax agency review of returns and tax records.

Trade name. A distinctive name that may serve as a trademark or service mark but is used to designate the business entity itself.

Trade secret. Any formula, process, method of operation, pattern, device, know-how, or compilation of technical, financial, or business information that provides a distinct advantage over a competitor who does not know or use it, and its secrecy is protected by reasonable measures. Trade secret laws prohibit others from wrongfully breaching such secrecy through the commission of a tort or the violation of an express or implied contract.

Trademark. A distinctive symbol, word, letter, number, picture, or combination thereof adopted and used by a merchant or manufacturer to distinguish and identify its goods. May be registered under state and federal laws. A trademark seeks to guarantee a product's quality and creates and sustains a demand for the product.

Trustworthiness. The degree to which evidence may be relied on as being what it claims to be.

Uniform laws. Laws prepared by the National Conference of Commissioners on Uniform State Laws in an effort to establish consistencies among the states. Uniform laws that affect recordkeeping in business include the Uniform Business Records as Evidence Act, Uniform Preservation of Private Business Records Act, Uniform Photographic Copies of Business and Public Records as Evidence Act, Uniform Rules of Evidence, Uniform Electronic Transactions Act, and more.

Valuable records and information. Records that represent a tangible or intangible asset or that affect the income, losses, or profits of a business.

Virus. A software program designed with the intention to alter the way a computer operates, usually to cause damage to hardware, software, and files. Examples of computer viruses include stealth viruses, worms, trojans, and bombs.

Visible record. A form of record for which the image is visible directly by sight or with the assistance of magnification.

Vital record. A record essential to the preservation, continuation, and protection of a company, its rights, employees, customers, shareholders, and business in general. A vital record is necessary for resumption and/or continuation of operations; for the re-creation of the legal and financial status of the company; for the fulfillment of obligations to stockholders, employees, and/or outside interests.

Vital records center. A facility devoted to the storage and protection of vital records.

Vital records program. A component of a records and information management program that manages the protection of vital records from damage or loss. Also is a component of a business continuity plan.

Vital records schedule. A document prepared as part of the vital records program that lists vital records and how they are to be protected.

Web site. A collection of interrelated web pages, or documents, and a host page that reside on the same Internet network location.

Write once, read many (WORM). A term describing an electronic information carrier as "write once, read many times," indicating that the record may be created once and can be read many times, but it may not be added to, modified, or deleted.

Resources

ARMA International, the Association of Records Managers and Administrators, (13725 W. 109th St., Suite 101, Lenexa, KS, 66215, 1–800–422–2762) offers a number of publications for the records management professional, including a professional journal, books, reports, videos, and slides on topics such as industry standards, disaster prevention and recovery, microform and electronic records, records retention, and much more.

ARMA International Standards Committee E-Mail Task Force. Guidelines for Managing E-Mail. Prairie Village, KS: ARMA International, 2000.

Branscomb, Anne Wells. *Who Owns Information? From Privacy to Public Access.* New York: Basic Books, 1995.

Business Laws, Inc. *Guide to Records Retention.* Chesterfield, OH: Business Laws, updated annually.

DiGilio, John J., J.D. "Electronic Mail: From Computer to Courtroom." *Information Management Journal* (April 2001).

Duff, Wendy M., Ph.D., Wally Smielianskas, Ph.D., CPA, CFE, and Holly Yoos. "Protecting Privacy." *Information Management Journal* (April 2001).

Hill, Lisa B., and Dr. J. Michael Pemberton. "Information Security: An Overview and Resource Guide for Information Managers." *Records Management Quarterly* (January 1995).

Jones, Virginia A., CRM, and Kris E. Keyes. *Emergency Management for Records and Information Programs.* Prairie Village, KS: ARMA International, 2001.

Jones, Willie M. "Trial by Tornado." *InfoPro* (March 2000).

Lewis, Steven. *Disaster Recovery Yellow Pages.* Systems Audit Group. 10th edition, 2001.

Leyzorek, Michael, Ph.D. "A Missing Feature in Some Records Management Systems." *Records Management Quarterly* (October 1998).

Miller, Bruce. "Surfing the Issues of Corporate Intranets." *InfoPro* (December 1999).

Montaña, John C., J.D. "Copyright Law and the Internet." *Information Management Journal* (January 1999).

———. "Retention of Merger and Acquisition Records and Information." *Information Management Journal* (April 2001).

Sampson, Karen L. "High-Performance, Low-Maintenance Records Retention." *The Records & Retrieval Report* 12.9 (November 1996).

Skupsky, Donald S., J.D., CRM, FAI. "Applying Records Retention to Electronic Records." *Information Management Journal* (July 1999).

———. *Legal Requirements for Business Records: Federal Requirements and State Requirements*. Denver: Information Requirements Clearinghouse, updated annually.

———. *Recordkeeping Requirements*. Denver: Information Requirements Clearinghouse, 1994.

———. *Records Retention Procedures*. Denver: Information Requirements Clearinghouse, 1995.

———. *Retention Manager®*. Denver: Information Requirements Clearinghouse, updated regularly.

Skupsky, Donald S., J.D., CRM, FAI, and John C. Montaña, J.D. *Law, Records and Information Management: The Court Cases*. Denver: Information Requirements Clearinghouse, 1994.

Smith, Dr. H. Jefferson. "How Much Privacy Do We Owe Customers?" *Beyond Computing* (January/February 1998).

Stephens, David O., CRM, CMC. "Managing Records and Information in Web Environments: Policies for Multinational Companies." *Information Management Journal* (April 2001).

Stephens, David O., CRM, CMC, and Roderick C. Wallace, CRM. *Electronic Records Retention: An Introduction*. Prairie Village, KS: ARMA International, 1997. (Second edition planned for 2002.)

Stremple, Rosalie, and Michael F. Martone. "Disasters Come in All Sizes." *InfoPro* (March 2000).

Terenna, Barry J., CRM. "Risky Business: Proactive Strategies Help Reduce Records-Related Risks." *InfoPro* (March 2001).

Index

About the Author

KAREN L. SAMPSON heads Scenarios by Sampson, a consulting firm in Parker, Colorado. Formerly Manager of records and administration for a major airline and earlier a consultant associated with other firms, she holds advanced degrees in library administration and secondary education. She has published widely on business practices, including records and information management.